FROM THE MARVEL VAULT

...ern with **Joe Edkin** (plot assist)
...tes
...Colors: **Lee Loughridge**
...Art: **Mario Albert...**
...ennan

...: **Derec Aucoin**

...bino

& **Ellie Pyle**

...hire

Breakdown...
Script & Finishes: **Karl Kes...**
Colors: **Val Staples** • Letters: **Jared K. Fletcher**
Cover Art: **Mark Bagley, Danny Miki** & **Paul Mounts**
Associate Editor: **Lauren Sankovitch**
Editors: **Tom DeFalco** & **Tom Brevoort**

"Mind Slam"
Plot: **Fabian Nicieza** • Script: **Kurt Busiek**
Pencils: **Mark Bagley**
Inks: **Andrew Hennessy** • Colors: **Chris Sotomayor**
Letters: **Chris Eliopoulos**
Cover Art: **Mark Bagley, Andrew Hennessy**
& **Chris Sotomayor**
Editors: **Tom Brevoort** & **Rachel Pinnelas**

Gambit
Writer: **Scott Lobdell** • Art: **George Tuska**
Color Art: **Nick Filardi** • Letters: **Dave Sharpe**
Cover Art: **David Yardin**
Assistant Editor: **John Denning**
Editors: **Mike Marts** & **Ralph Macchio**

Collection Editor & Design: **Cory Levine**
Editorial Assistants: **James Emmett** & **Joe Hochstein**
Assistant Editors: **Alex Starbuck** & **Nelson Ribeiro**
Editors, Special Projects: **Jennifer Grünwald**
& **Mark D. Beazley**
Senior Editor, Special Projects: **Jeff Youngquist**
Senior Vice President of Sales: **David Gabriel**
SVP of Brand Planning & Communications: **Michael Pasciullo**

Editor In Chief: **Axel Alonso**
Chief Creative Officer: **Joe Quesada**
Publisher: **Dan Buckley**
Executive Producer: **Alan Fine**

FROM THE MARVEL VAULT. Contains material originally published in magazine form as DOCTO... STRANGE: FROM THE MARVEL VAULT, INCREDIBLE HULK AND HUMAN TORCH: FROM THE MARVE... VAULT, THUNDERBOLTS: FROM THE MARVEL VAULT, DEFENDERS: FROM THE MARVEL VAULT an... GAMBIT: FROM THE MARVEL VAULT. First printing 2011. ISBN# 978-0-7851-5784-7. Publishe... by MARVEL WORLDWIDE, INC., a subsidiary of MARVEL ENTERTAINMENT, LLC. OFFICE O... PUBLICATION: 135 West 50th Street, New York, NY 10020. Copyright © 2011 Marvel Characters... Inc. All rights reserved. $14.99 per copy in the U.S. and $16.99 in Canada (GST #R127032852... Canadian Agreement #40668537. All characters featured in this issue and the distinctive name... and likenesses thereof, and all related indicia are trademarks of Marvel Characters, Inc. No similarit... between any of the names, characters, persons, and/or institutions in this magazine with those o... any living or dead person or institution is intended, and any such similarity which may exist is purel... coincidental. **Printed in the U.S.A.** ALAN FINE, EVP - Office of the President, Marvel Worldwide, Inc... and EVP & CMO Marvel Characters B.V.; DAN BUCKLEY, Publisher & President - Print, Animation &... Digital Divisions; JOE QUESADA, Chief Creative Officer; JIM SOKOLOWSKI, Chief Operating Officer... DAVID BOGART, SVP of Business Affairs & Talent Management; TOM BREVOORT, SVP of Publishing... C.B. CEBULSKI, SVP of Creator & Content Development; DAVID GABRIEL, SVP of Publishing Sales &... Circulation; MICHAEL PASCIULLO, SVP of Brand Planning & Communications; JIM O'KEEFE, VP o... Operations & Logistics; DAN CARR, Executive Director of Publishing Technology; SUSAN CRESP... Editorial Operations Manager; ALEX MORALES, Publishing Operations Manager; STAN LEE, Chairma... Emeritus. For information regarding advertising in Marvel Comics or on Marvel.com, please contac... John Dokes, SVP Integrated Sales and Marketing, at jdokes@marvel.com. For Marvel subscriptio... inquiries, please call 800-217-9158. **Manufactured between 9/22/2011 and 10/11/2011 b... QUAD/GRAPHICS, DUBUQUE, IA, USA.**

10 9 8 7 6 5 4 3 2 1

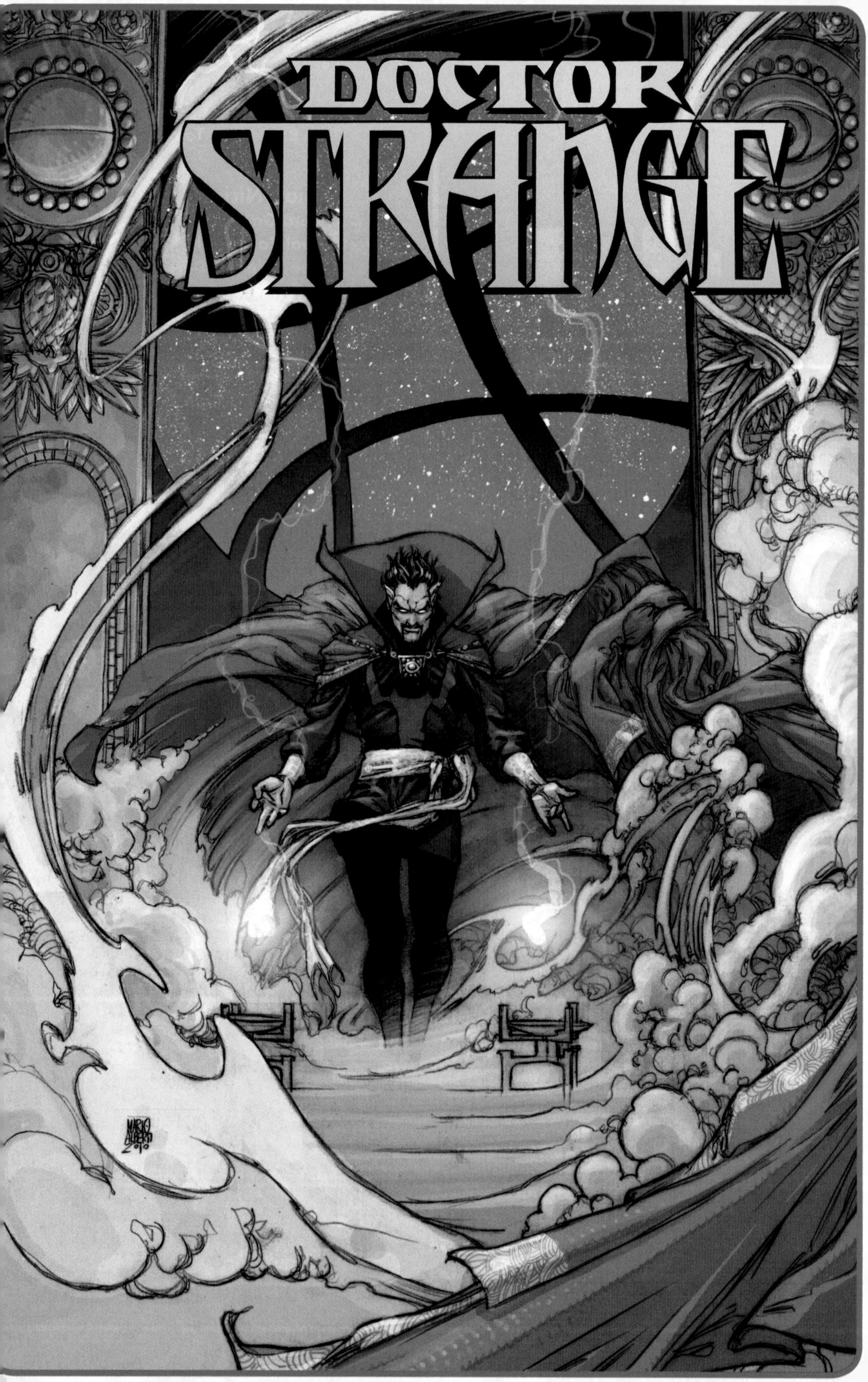

DOCTOR
STRANGE

SECRETS OF THE VAULT!

Way back in 1998, I was writing a series entitled MARVEL UNIVERSE. It was planned as an ongoing monthly series that would explore the farthest corners of Marvel's vast realities. Unfortunately, the series didn't find its audience and was canceled after just seven issues ...even as we were working on this Doctor Strange story.

I had plotted the story - with a welcome assist from fellow scribe Joe Edkin. Said story was penciled by Neil Vokes and subsequently inked by Jay Geldhof, the gents who had produced the art for UNTOLD TALES OF SPIDER-MAN: STRANGE ENCOUNTERS (also scripted by Yours Truly). And I had just started to rough out the script when I received word that the MARVEL UNIVERSE book would be no more.

It's always disappointing when a series is canceled out from under you. Doubly so, when a series had given you an opportunity to write about some of your favorite characters in collaboration with such talented folks. But it happens. You dust yourself off and move on.

And sometimes, there are second chances in the world of comics. As when Tom Brennan recently called and said that Marvel wanted to print our orphan Doctor Strange story.

The two or three pages of script that I had roughed out, all those years ago, had been lost a couple of computers ago. But I still had a hard copy of the plot in my files, along with photocopies of Neil's artwork. So, I was able to dust off my old print-outs, and script the story ...over twelve years after it was originally plotted.

And now, at long last, the story can be told!

We hope you enjoy it.

- Roger Stern

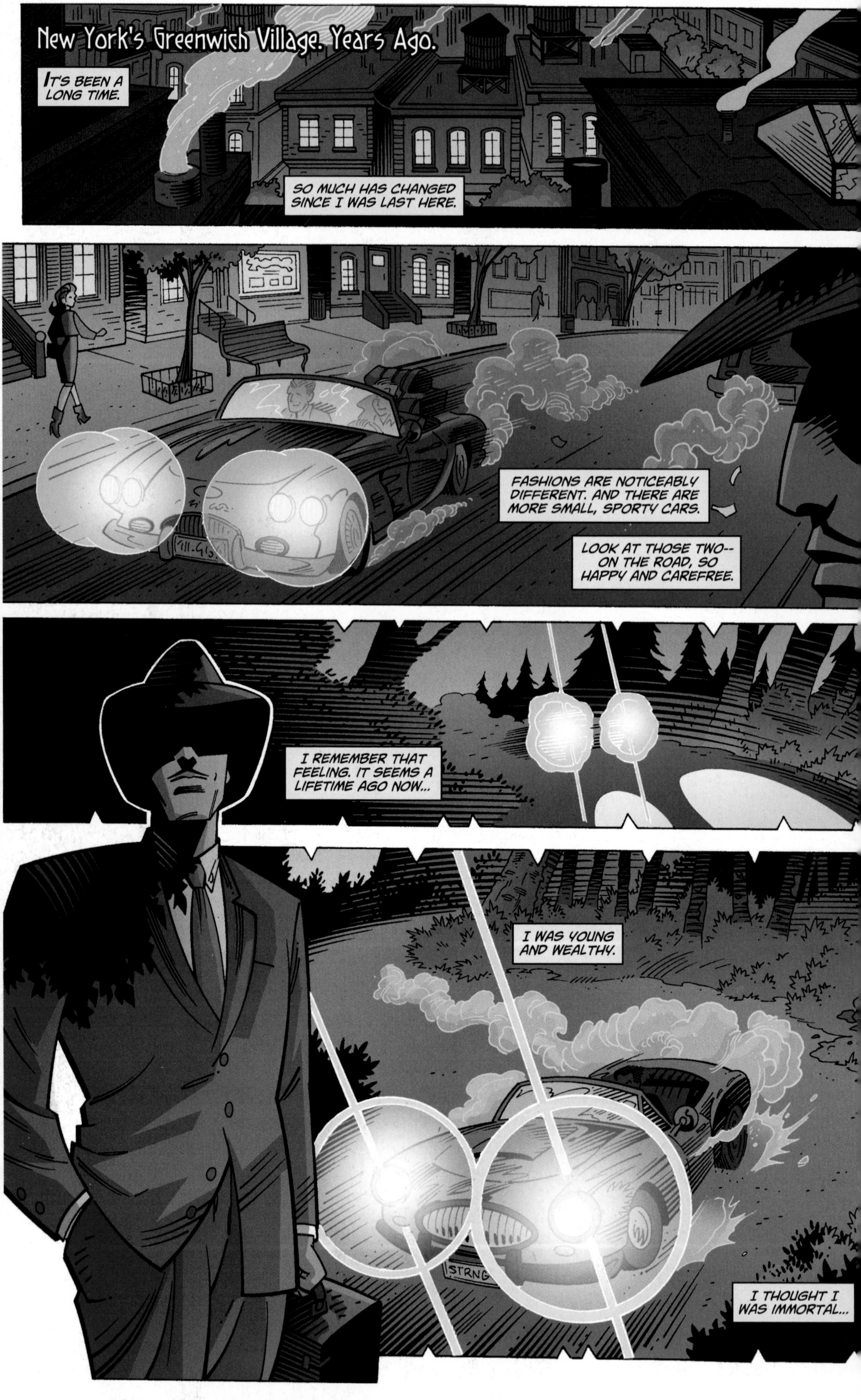
New York's Greenwich Village. Years Ago.
It's been a long time.
So much has changed since I was last here.
Fashions are noticeably different. And there are more small, sporty cars.
Look at those two-- on the road, so happy and carefree.
I remember that feeling. It seems a lifetime ago now...
I was young and wealthy.
STRNG
I thought I was immortal...

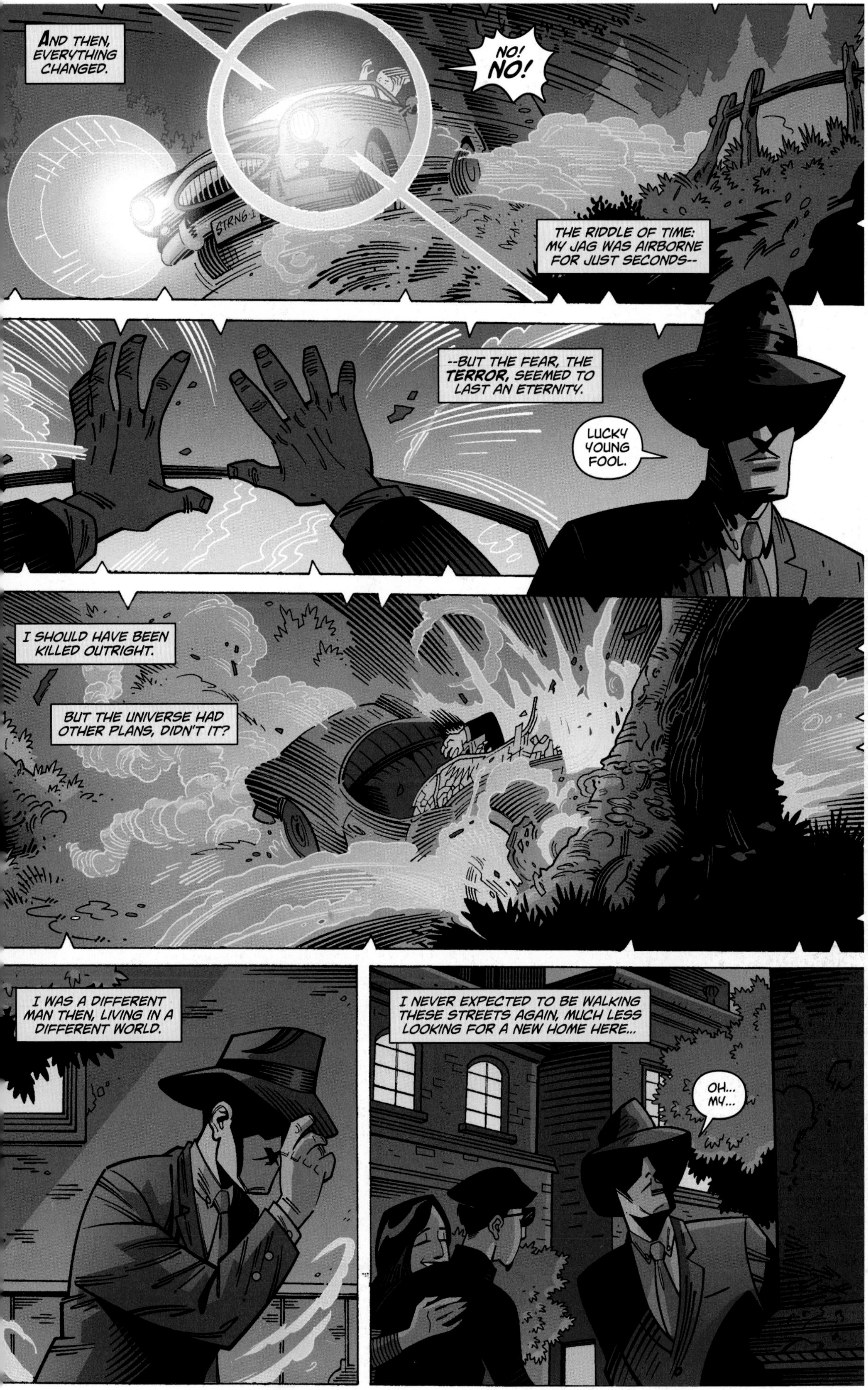
AND THEN, EVERYTHING CHANGED.
NO! NO!
STRNG-1
THE RIDDLE OF TIME: MY JAG WAS AIRBORNE FOR JUST SECONDS--
--BUT THE FEAR, THE TERROR, SEEMED TO LAST AN ETERNITY.
LUCKY YOUNG FOOL.
I SHOULD HAVE BEEN KILLED OUTRIGHT.
BUT THE UNIVERSE HAD OTHER PLANS, DIDN'T IT?
I WAS A DIFFERENT MAN THEN, LIVING IN A DIFFERENT WORLD.
I NEVER EXPECTED TO BE WALKING THESE STREETS AGAIN, MUCH LESS LOOKING FOR A NEW HOME HERE...
OH... MY...

This OLD HOUSE

ROGER STERN writer (with thanks to JOE EDKIN for the plot assist)
NEIL VOKES penciler JAY GELDHOF inker LEE LOUGHRIDGE colorist
JARED K. FLETCHER letterer TOM BREVOORT & TOM BRENNAN editors across
JOE QUESADA editor-in-chief DAN BUCKLEY publisher ALAN FINE executive pro

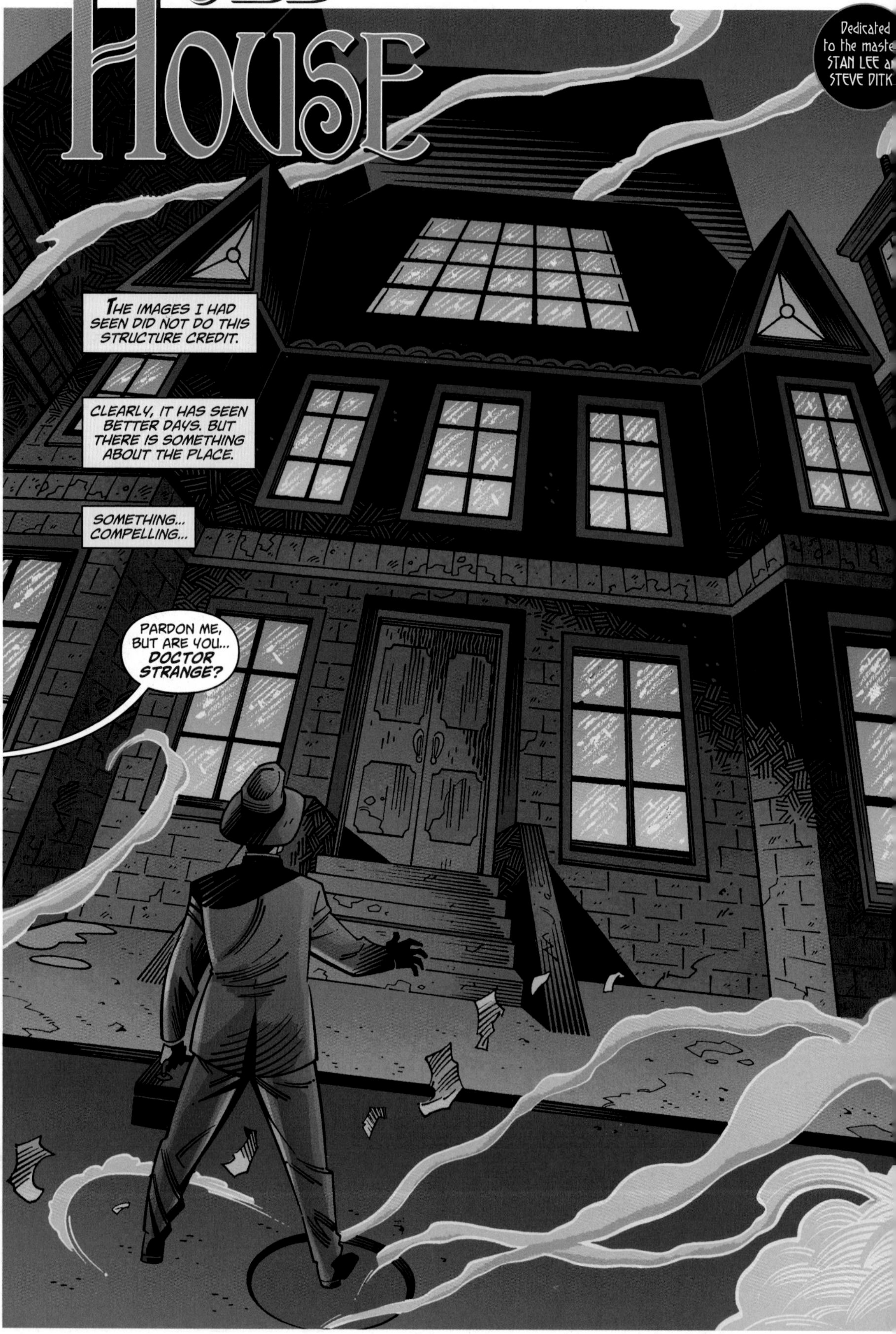

Dedicated to the maste STAN LEE a STEVE DITK
THE IMAGES I HAD SEEN DID NOT DO THIS STRUCTURE CREDIT.
CLEARLY, IT HAS SEEN BETTER DAYS. BUT THERE IS SOMETHING ABOUT THE PLACE.
SOMETHING... COMPELLING...
PARDON ME, BUT ARE YOU... DOCTOR STRANGE?

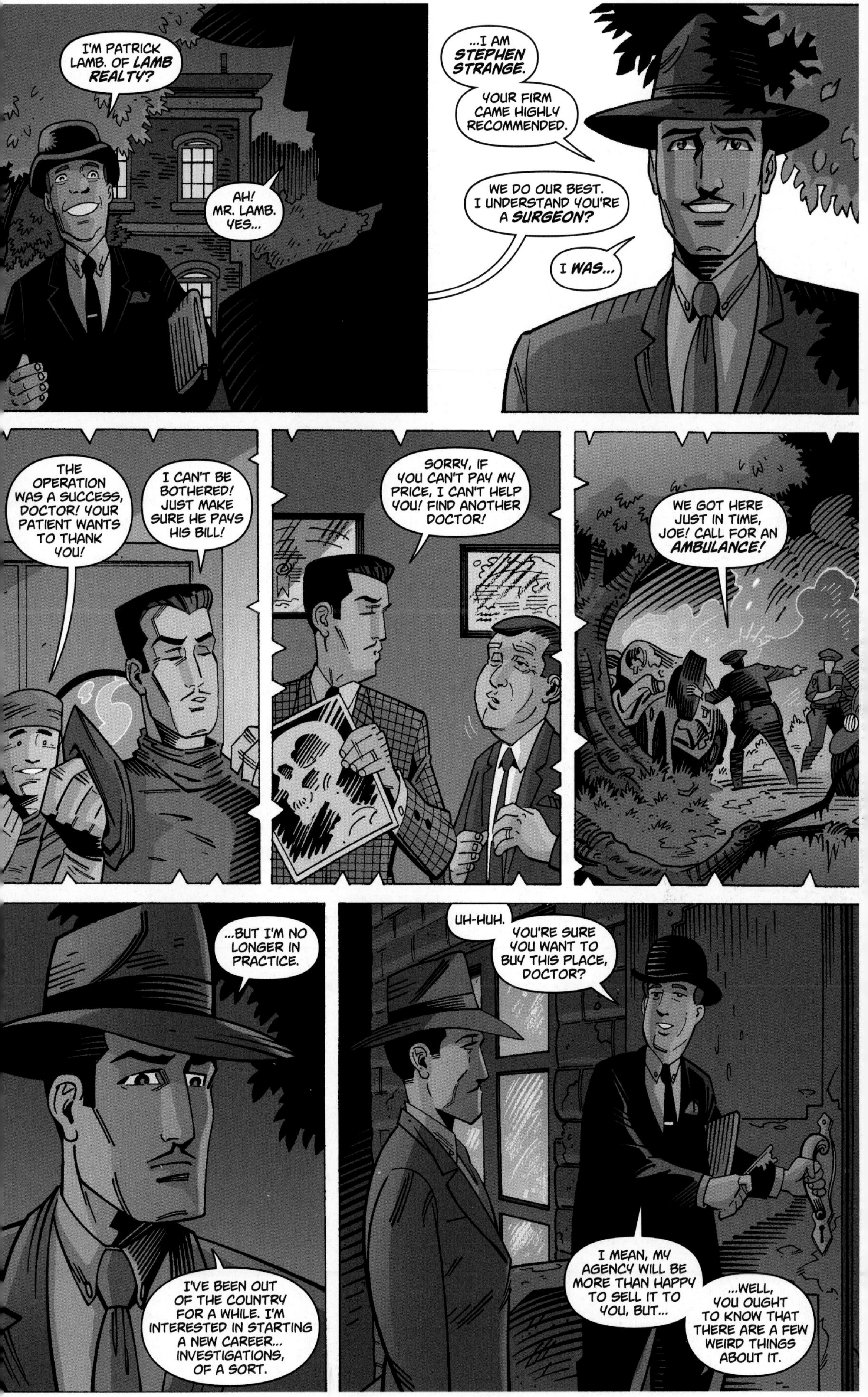

I'M PATRICK LAMB. OF LAMB REALTY?
AH! MR. LAMB. YES...
...I AM STEPHEN STRANGE.
YOUR FIRM CAME HIGHLY RECOMMENDED.
WE DO OUR BEST. I UNDERSTAND YOU'RE A SURGEON?
I WAS...
THE OPERATION WAS A SUCCESS, DOCTOR! YOUR PATIENT WANTS TO THANK YOU!
I CAN'T BE BOTHERED! JUST MAKE SURE HE PAYS HIS BILL!
SORRY, IF YOU CAN'T PAY MY PRICE, I CAN'T HELP YOU! FIND ANOTHER DOCTOR!
WE GOT HERE JUST IN TIME, JOE! CALL FOR AN AMBULANCE!
...BUT I'M NO LONGER IN PRACTICE.
I'VE BEEN OUT OF THE COUNTRY FOR A WHILE. I'M INTERESTED IN STARTING A NEW CAREER... INVESTIGATIONS, OF A SORT.
UH-HUH.
YOU'RE SURE YOU WANT TO BUY THIS PLACE, DOCTOR?
I MEAN, MY AGENCY WILL BE MORE THAN HAPPY TO SELL IT TO YOU, BUT...
...WELL, YOU OUGHT TO KNOW THAT THERE ARE A FEW WEIRD THINGS ABOUT IT.

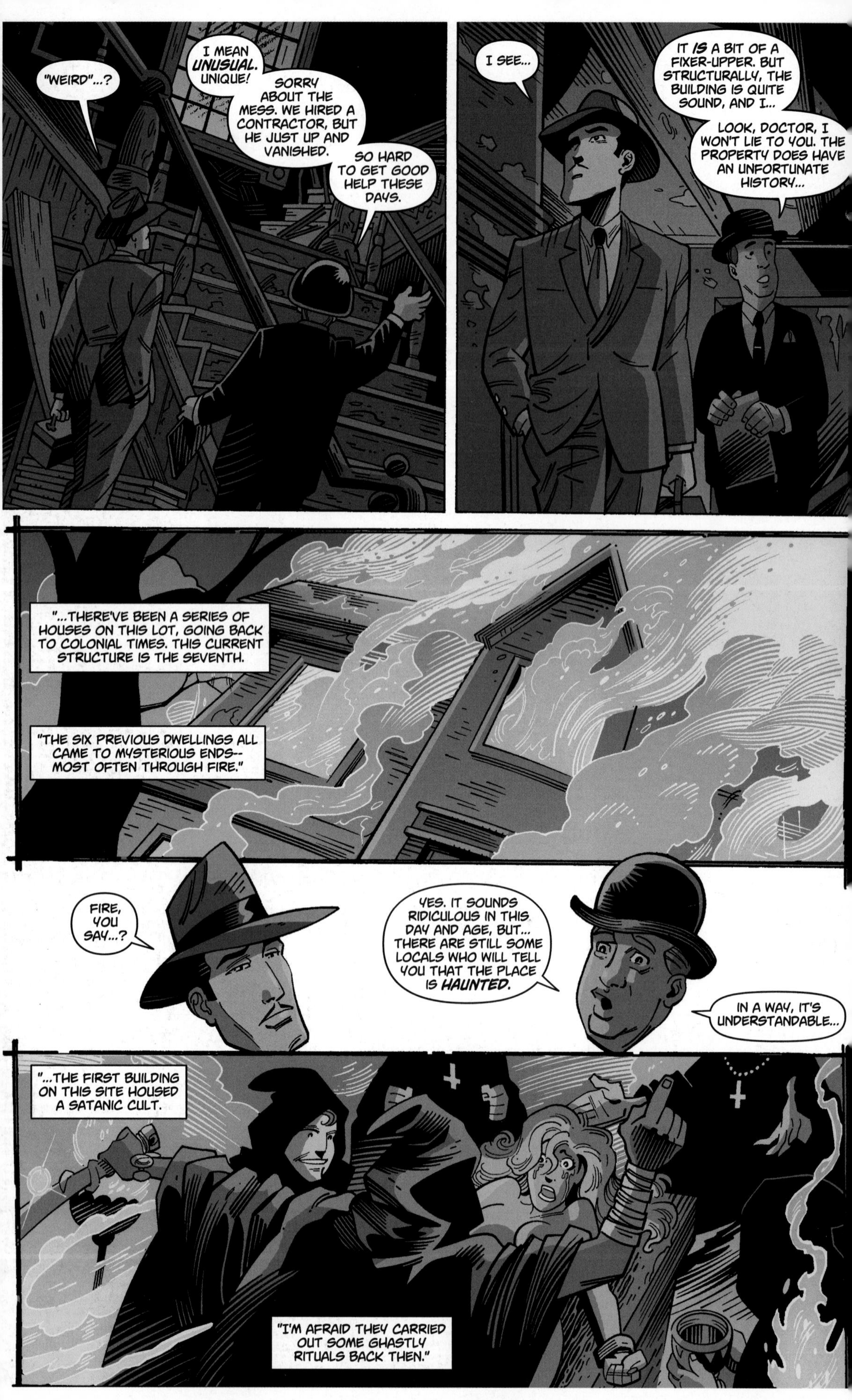
"WEIRD"...?
I MEAN UNUSUAL. UNIQUE!
SORRY ABOUT THE MESS. WE HIRED A CONTRACTOR, BUT HE JUST UP AND VANISHED.
SO HARD TO GET GOOD HELP THESE DAYS.
I SEE...
IT IS A BIT OF A FIXER-UPPER. BUT STRUCTURALLY, THE BUILDING IS QUITE SOUND, AND I...
LOOK, DOCTOR, I WON'T LIE TO YOU. THE PROPERTY DOES HAVE AN UNFORTUNATE HISTORY...
"...THERE'VE BEEN A SERIES OF HOUSES ON THIS LOT, GOING BACK TO COLONIAL TIMES. THIS CURRENT STRUCTURE IS THE SEVENTH.
"THE SIX PREVIOUS DWELLINGS ALL CAME TO MYSTERIOUS ENDS-- MOST OFTEN THROUGH FIRE."
FIRE, YOU SAY...?
YES. IT SOUNDS RIDICULOUS IN THIS DAY AND AGE, BUT... THERE ARE STILL SOME LOCALS WHO WILL TELL YOU THAT THE PLACE IS HAUNTED.
IN A WAY, IT'S UNDERSTANDABLE...
"...THE FIRST BUILDING ON THIS SITE HOUSED A SATANIC CULT.
"I'M AFRAID THEY CARRIED OUT SOME GHASTLY RITUALS BACK THEN."

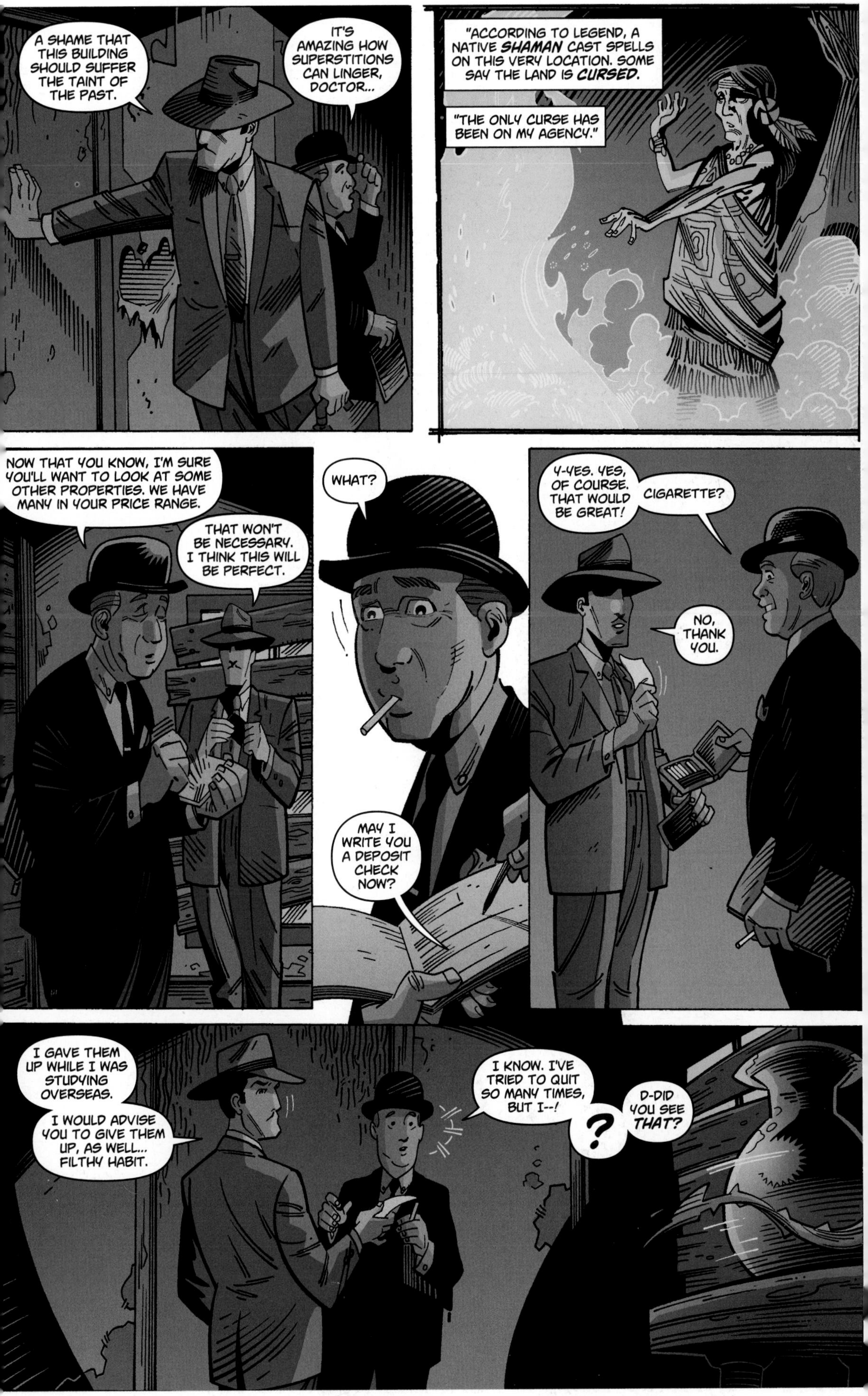
A SHAME THAT THIS BUILDING SHOULD SUFFER THE TAINT OF THE PAST.
IT'S AMAZING HOW SUPERSTITIONS CAN LINGER, DOCTOR...
"ACCORDING TO LEGEND, A NATIVE SHAMAN CAST SPELLS ON THIS VERY LOCATION. SOME SAY THE LAND IS CURSED.
"THE ONLY CURSE HAS BEEN ON MY AGENCY."
NOW THAT YOU KNOW, I'M SURE YOU'LL WANT TO LOOK AT SOME OTHER PROPERTIES. WE HAVE MANY IN YOUR PRICE RANGE.
THAT WON'T BE NECESSARY. I THINK THIS WILL BE PERFECT.
WHAT?
MAY I WRITE YOU A DEPOSIT CHECK NOW?
Y-YES. YES, OF COURSE. THAT WOULD BE GREAT!
CIGARETTE?
NO, THANK YOU.
I GAVE THEM UP WHILE I WAS STUDYING OVERSEAS.
I WOULD ADVISE YOU TO GIVE THEM UP, AS WELL... FILTHY HABIT.
I KNOW. I'VE TRIED TO QUIT SO MANY TIMES, BUT I--!
?
D-DID YOU SEE THAT?

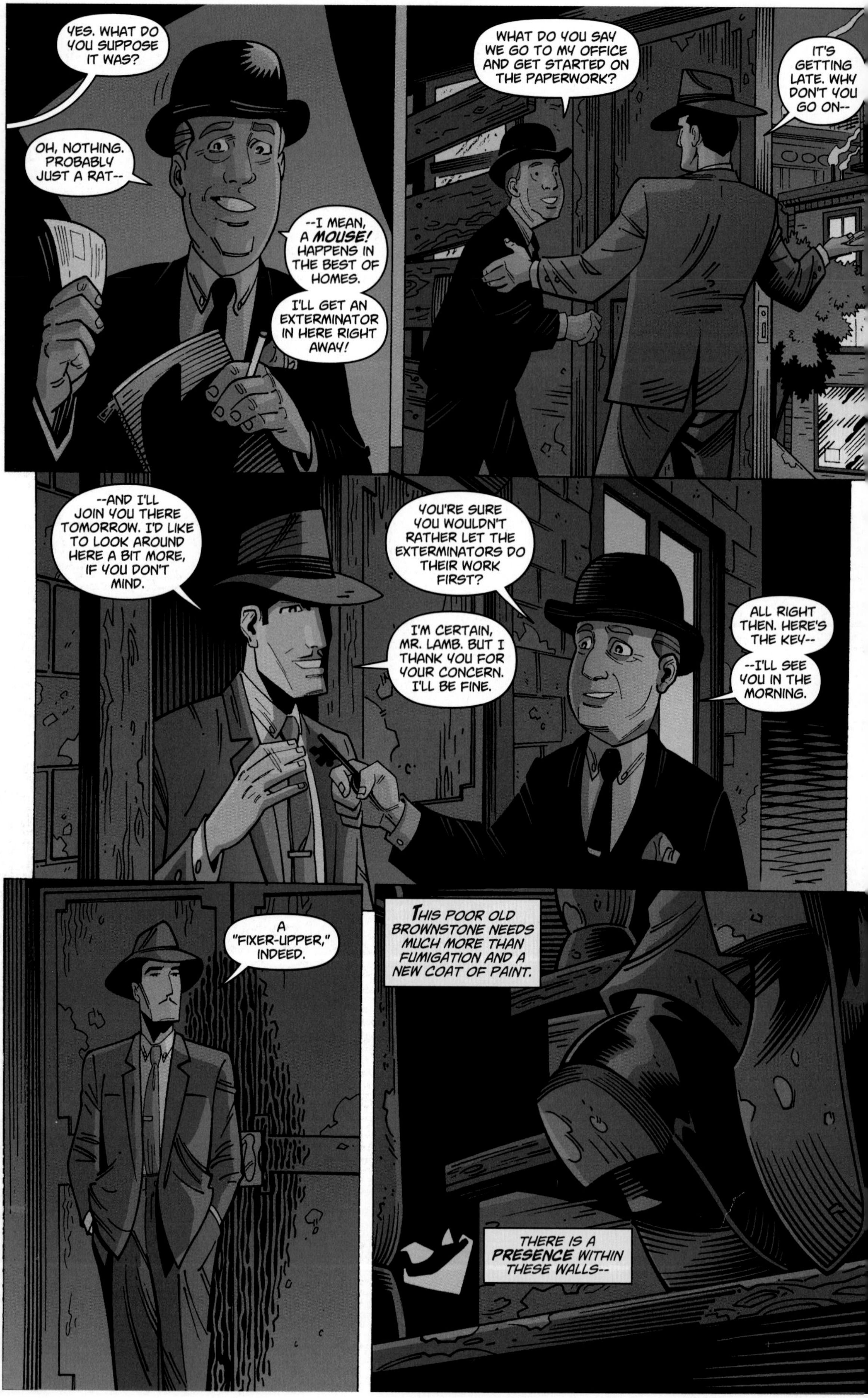

YES. WHAT DO YOU SUPPOSE IT WAS?
OH, NOTHING. PROBABLY JUST A RAT--
--I MEAN, A *MOUSE!* HAPPENS IN THE BEST OF HOMES.
I'LL GET AN EXTERMINATOR IN HERE RIGHT AWAY!
WHAT DO YOU SAY WE GO TO MY OFFICE AND GET STARTED ON THE PAPERWORK?
IT'S GETTING LATE. WHY DON'T YOU GO ON--
--AND I'LL JOIN YOU THERE TOMORROW. I'D LIKE TO LOOK AROUND HERE A BIT MORE, IF YOU DON'T MIND.
YOU'RE SURE YOU WOULDN'T RATHER LET THE EXTERMINATORS DO THEIR WORK FIRST?
I'M CERTAIN, MR. LAMB. BUT I THANK YOU FOR YOUR CONCERN. I'LL BE FINE.
ALL RIGHT THEN. HERE'S THE KEY--
--I'LL SEE YOU IN THE MORNING.
A "FIXER-UPPER," INDEED.
THIS POOR OLD BROWNSTONE NEEDS MUCH MORE THAN FUMIGATION AND A NEW COAT OF PAINT.
THERE IS A *PRESENCE* WITHIN THESE WALLS--

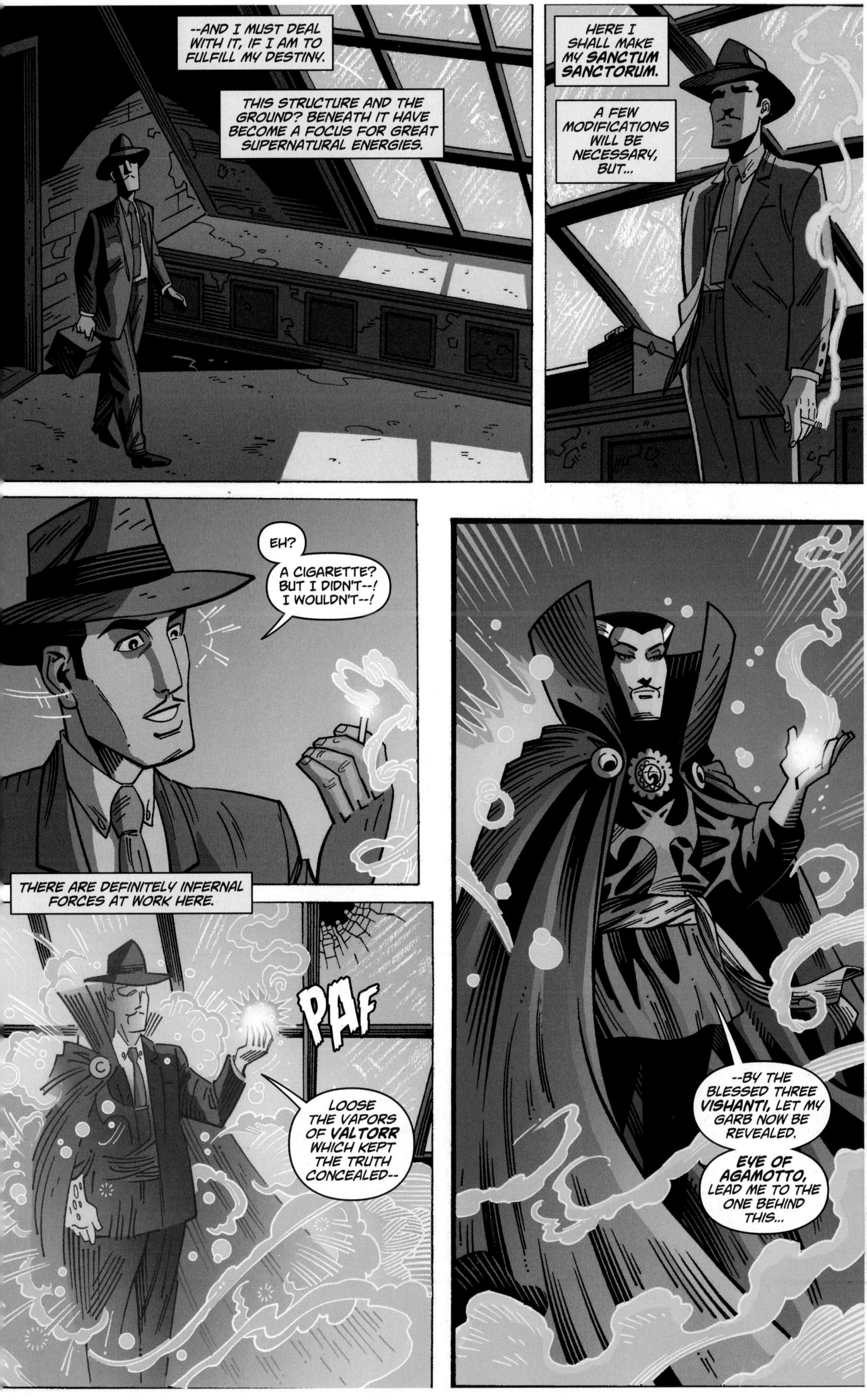
--AND I MUST DEAL WITH IT, IF I AM TO FULFILL MY DESTINY.
THIS STRUCTURE AND THE GROUND? BENEATH IT HAVE BECOME A FOCUS FOR GREAT SUPERNATURAL ENERGIES.
HERE I SHALL MAKE MY SANCTUM SANCTORUM.
A FEW MODIFICATIONS WILL BE NECESSARY, BUT...
EH?
A CIGARETTE? BUT I DIDN'T--! I WOULDN'T--!
THERE ARE DEFINITELY INFERNAL FORCES AT WORK HERE.
PAF
LOOSE THE VAPORS OF VALTORR WHICH KEPT THE TRUTH CONCEALED--
--BY THE BLESSED THREE VISHANTI, LET MY GARB NOW BE REVEALED.
EYE OF AGAMOTTO, LEAD ME TO THE ONE BEHIND THIS...

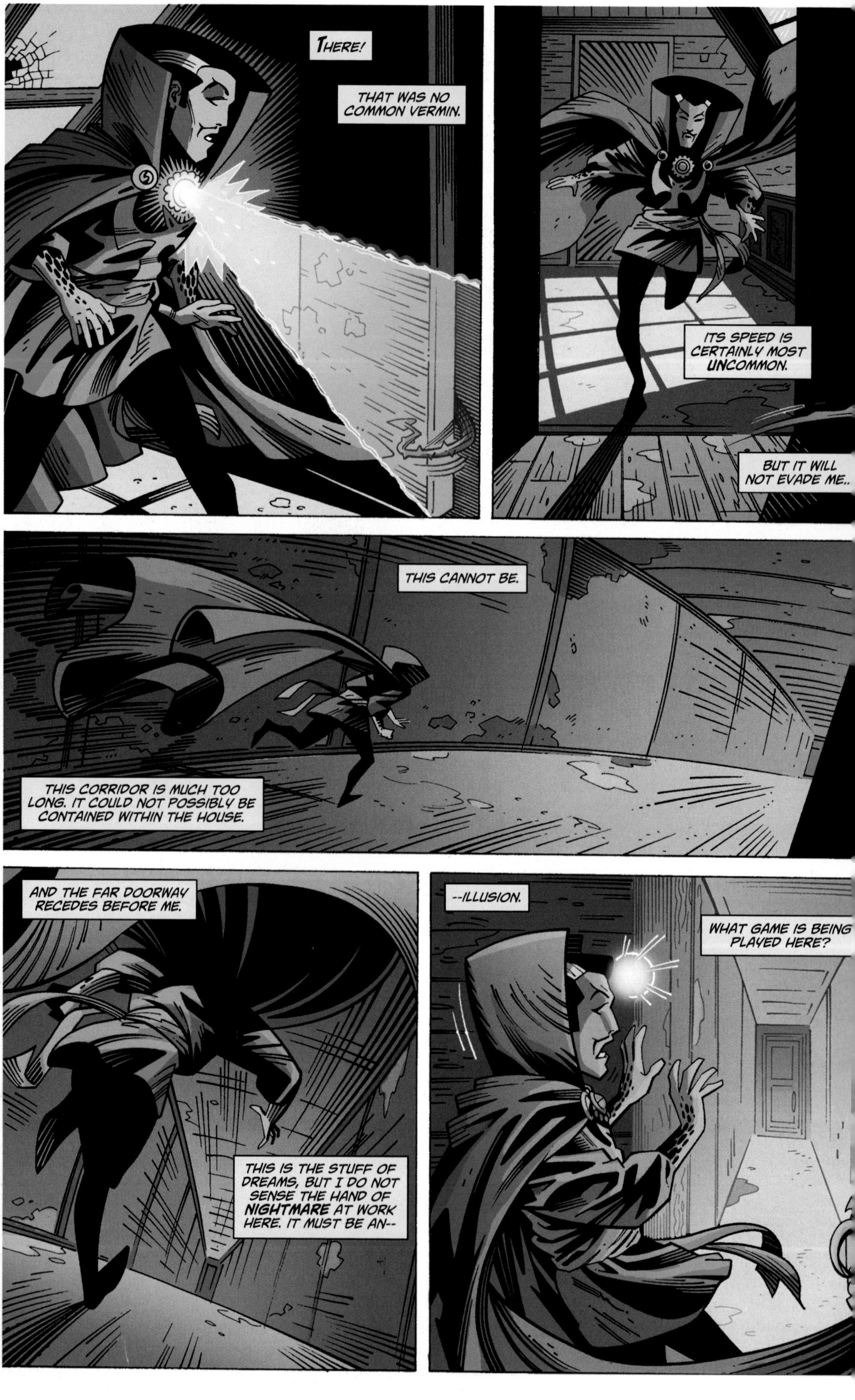
THERE!
THAT WAS NO COMMON VERMIN.
ITS SPEED IS CERTAINLY MOST UNCOMMON.
BUT IT WILL NOT EVADE ME..
THIS CANNOT BE.
THIS CORRIDOR IS MUCH TOO LONG. IT COULD NOT POSSIBLY BE CONTAINED WITHIN THE HOUSE.
AND THE FAR DOORWAY RECEDES BEFORE ME.
THIS IS THE STUFF OF DREAMS, BUT I DO NOT SENSE THE HAND OF NIGHTMARE AT WORK HERE. IT MUST BE AN--
--ILLUSION.
WHAT GAME IS BEING PLAYED HERE?

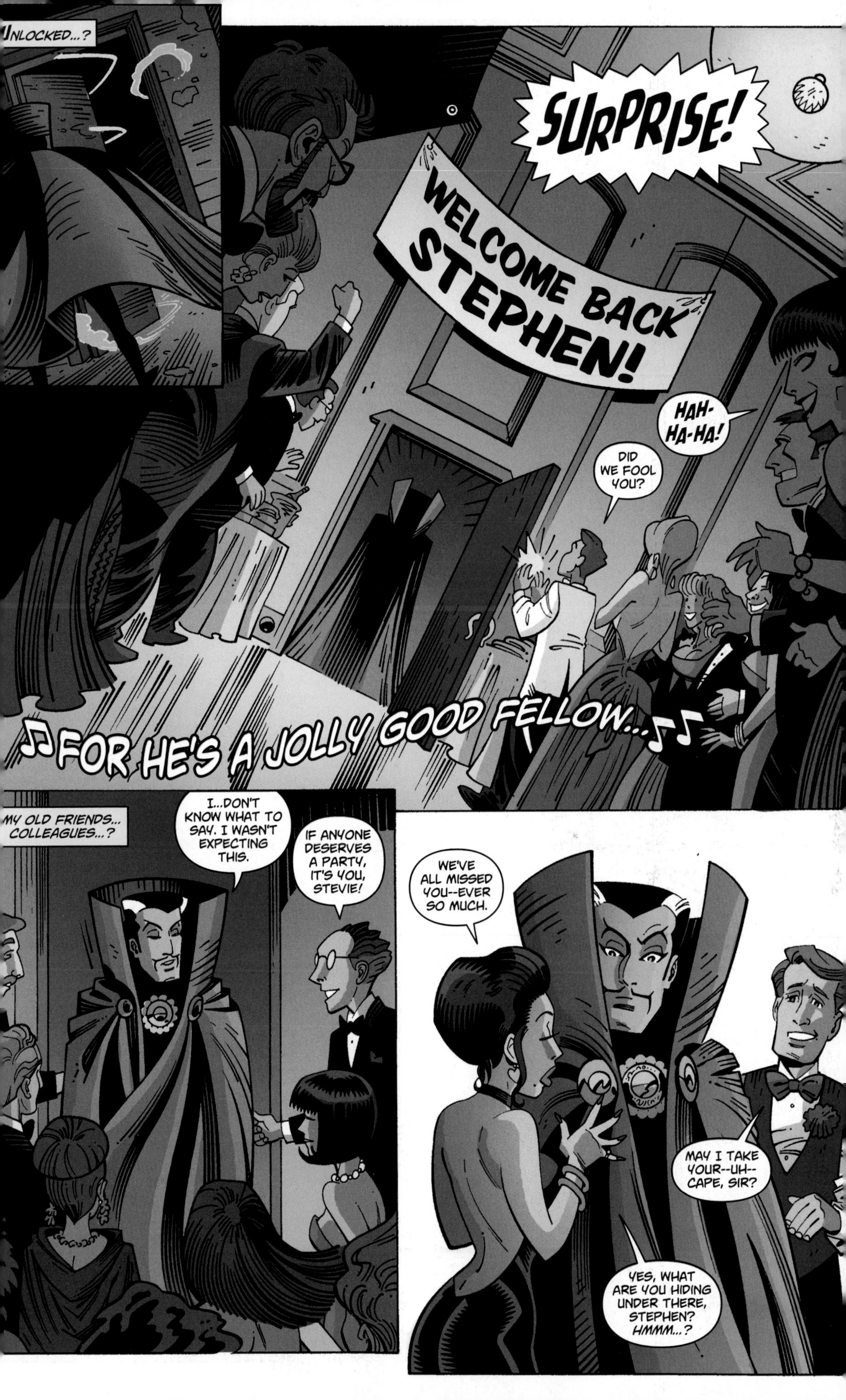
UNLOCKED...?
SURPRISE!
WELCOME BACK STEPHEN!
HAH-HA-HA!
DID WE FOOL YOU?
FOR HE'S A JOLLY GOOD FELLOW...
MY OLD FRIENDS... COLLEAGUES...?
I...DON'T KNOW WHAT TO SAY. I WASN'T EXPECTING THIS.
IF ANYONE DESERVES A PARTY, IT'S YOU, STEVIE!
WE'VE ALL MISSED YOU--EVER SO MUCH.
MAY I TAKE YOUR--UH--CAPE, SIR?
YES, WHAT ARE YOU HIDING UNDER THERE, STEPHEN? HMMM...?

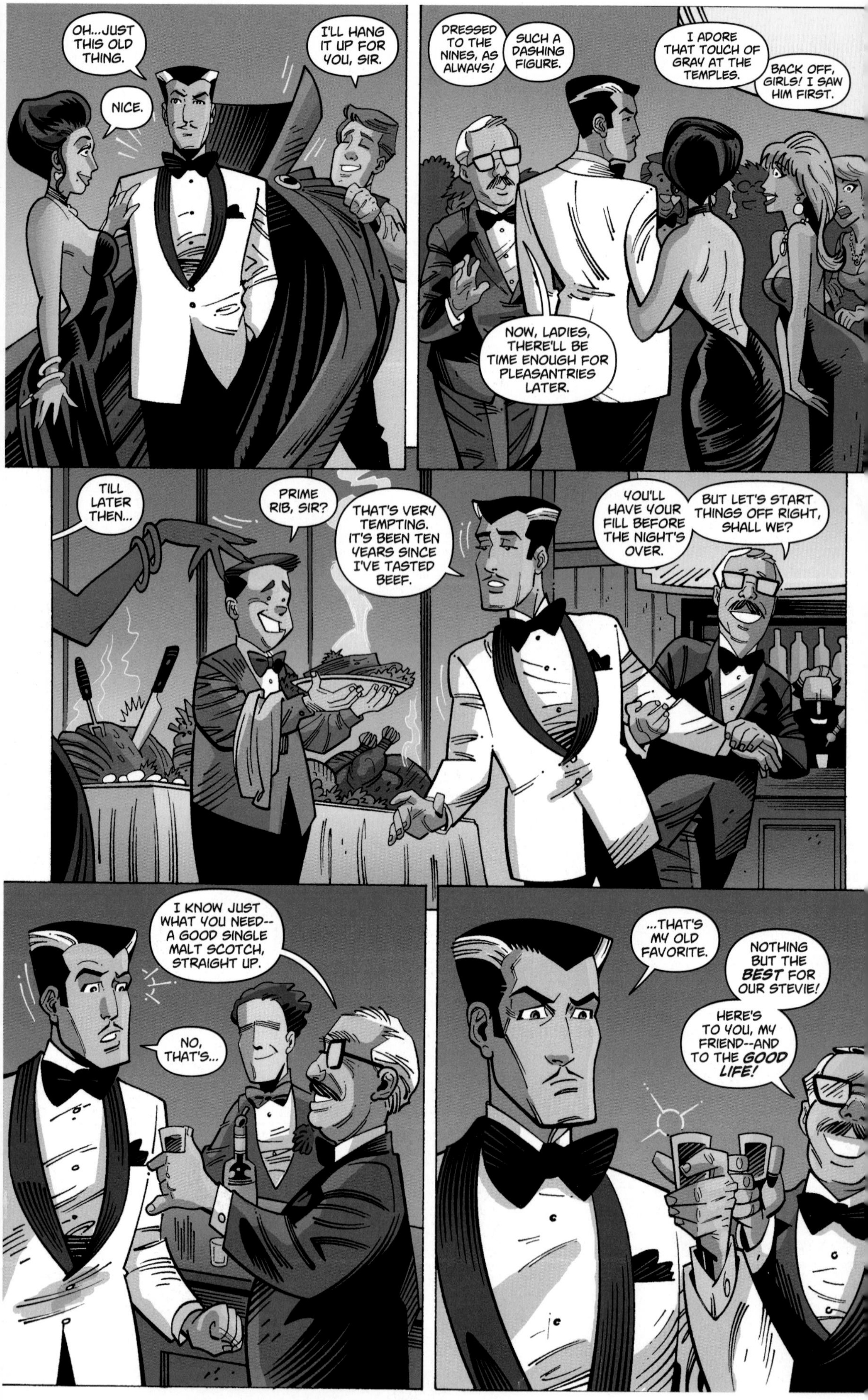

OH...JUST THIS OLD THING.
NICE.
I'LL HANG IT UP FOR YOU, SIR.
DRESSED TO THE NINES, AS ALWAYS!
SUCH A DASHING FIGURE.
I ADORE THAT TOUCH OF GRAY AT THE TEMPLES.
BACK OFF, GIRLS! I SAW HIM FIRST.
NOW, LADIES, THERE'LL BE TIME ENOUGH FOR PLEASANTRIES LATER.
TILL LATER THEN...
PRIME RIB, SIR?
THAT'S VERY TEMPTING. IT'S BEEN TEN YEARS SINCE I'VE TASTED BEEF.
YOU'LL HAVE YOUR FILL BEFORE THE NIGHT'S OVER.
BUT LET'S START THINGS OFF RIGHT, SHALL WE?
I KNOW JUST WHAT YOU NEED-- A GOOD SINGLE MALT SCOTCH, STRAIGHT UP.
NO, THAT'S...
...THAT'S MY OLD FAVORITE.
NOTHING BUT THE BEST FOR OUR STEVIE!
HERE'S TO YOU, MY FRIEND--AND TO THE GOOD LIFE!

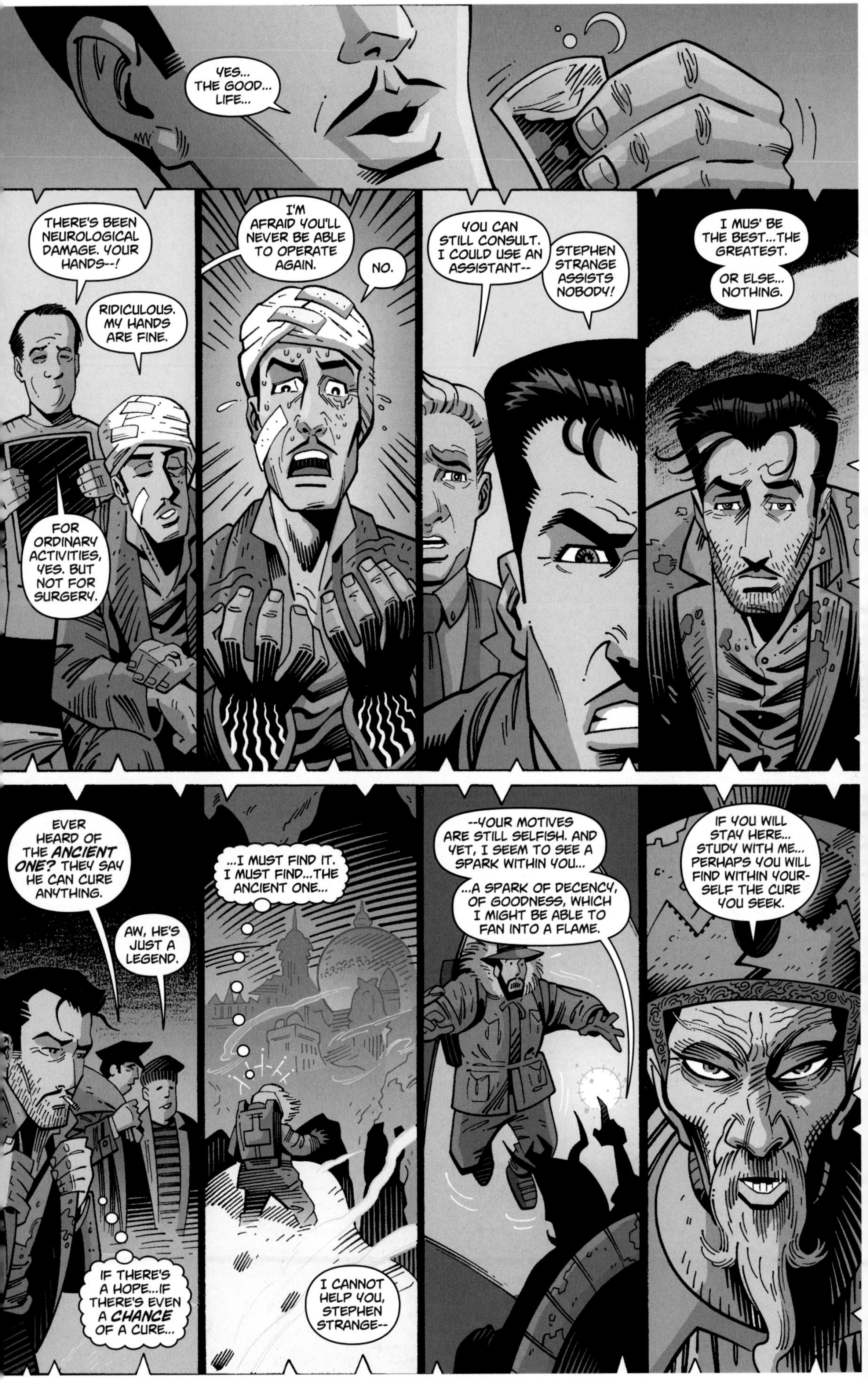
YES... THE GOOD... LIFE...
THERE'S BEEN NEUROLOGICAL DAMAGE. YOUR HANDS--!
RIDICULOUS. MY HANDS ARE FINE.
FOR ORDINARY ACTIVITIES, YES. BUT NOT FOR SURGERY.
I'M AFRAID YOU'LL NEVER BE ABLE TO OPERATE AGAIN.
NO.
YOU CAN STILL CONSULT. I COULD USE AN ASSISTANT--
STEPHEN STRANGE ASSISTS NOBODY!
I MUS' BE THE BEST...THE GREATEST.
OR ELSE... NOTHING.
EVER HEARD OF THE ***ANCIENT ONE?*** THEY SAY HE CAN CURE ANYTHING.
AW, HE'S JUST A LEGEND.
IF THERE'S A HOPE...IF THERE'S EVEN A ***CHANCE*** OF A CURE...
...I MUST FIND IT. I MUST FIND...THE ANCIENT ONE...
I CANNOT HELP YOU, STEPHEN STRANGE--
--YOUR MOTIVES ARE STILL SELFISH. AND YET, I SEEM TO SEE A SPARK WITHIN YOU...
...A SPARK OF DECENCY, OF GOODNESS, WHICH I MIGHT BE ABLE TO FAN INTO A FLAME.
IF YOU WILL STAY HERE... STUDY WITH ME... PERHAPS YOU WILL FIND WITHIN YOURSELF THE CURE YOU SEEK.

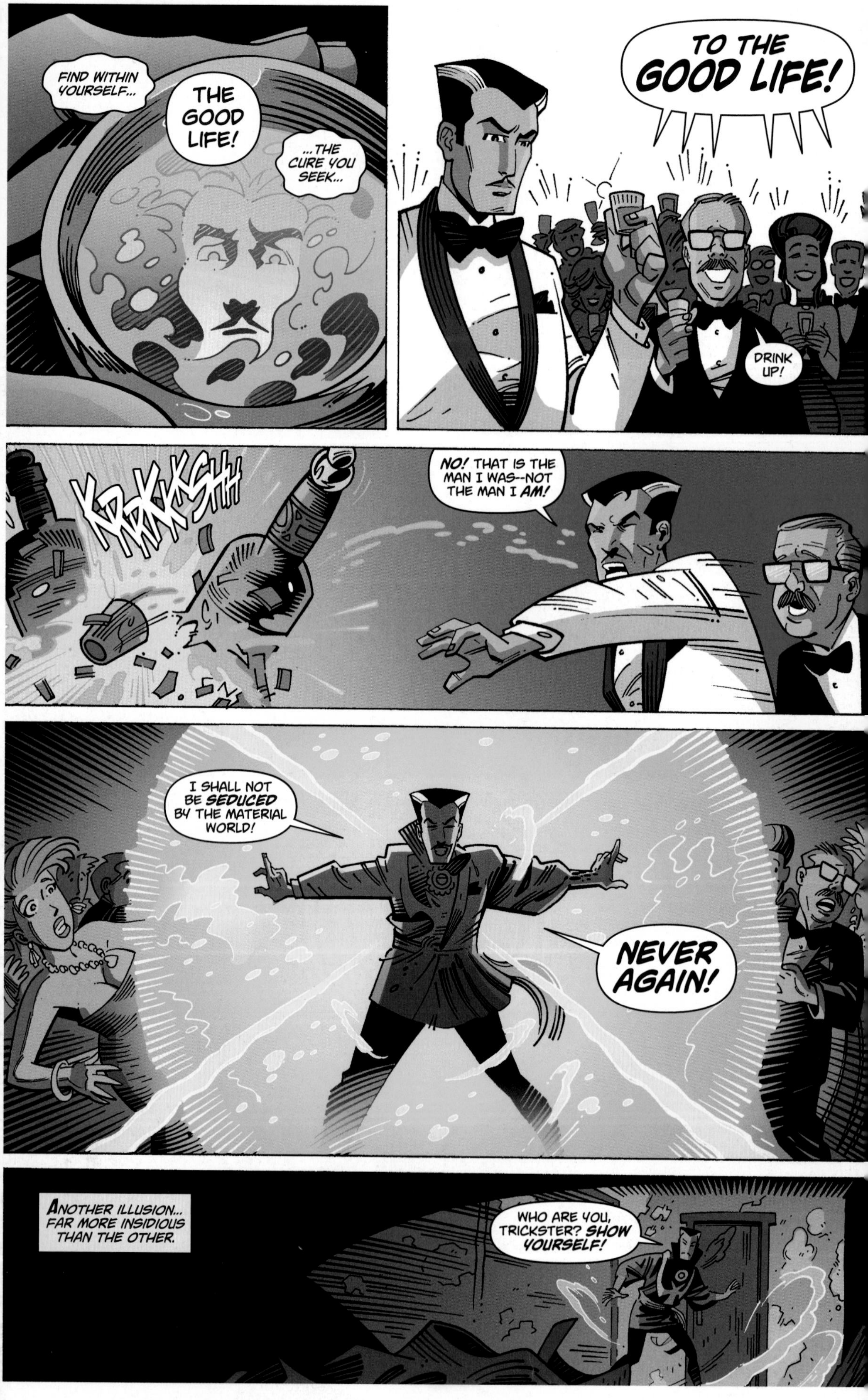
FIND WITHIN YOURSELF...
THE GOOD LIFE!
...THE CURE YOU SEEK...
TO THE GOOD LIFE!
DRINK UP!
KRRKKKSHH
NO! THAT IS THE MAN I WAS--NOT THE MAN I AM!
I SHALL NOT BE SEDUCED BY THE MATERIAL WORLD!
NEVER AGAIN!
ANOTHER ILLUSION... FAR MORE INSIDIOUS THAN THE OTHER.
WHO ARE YOU, TRICKSTER? SHOW YOURSELF!

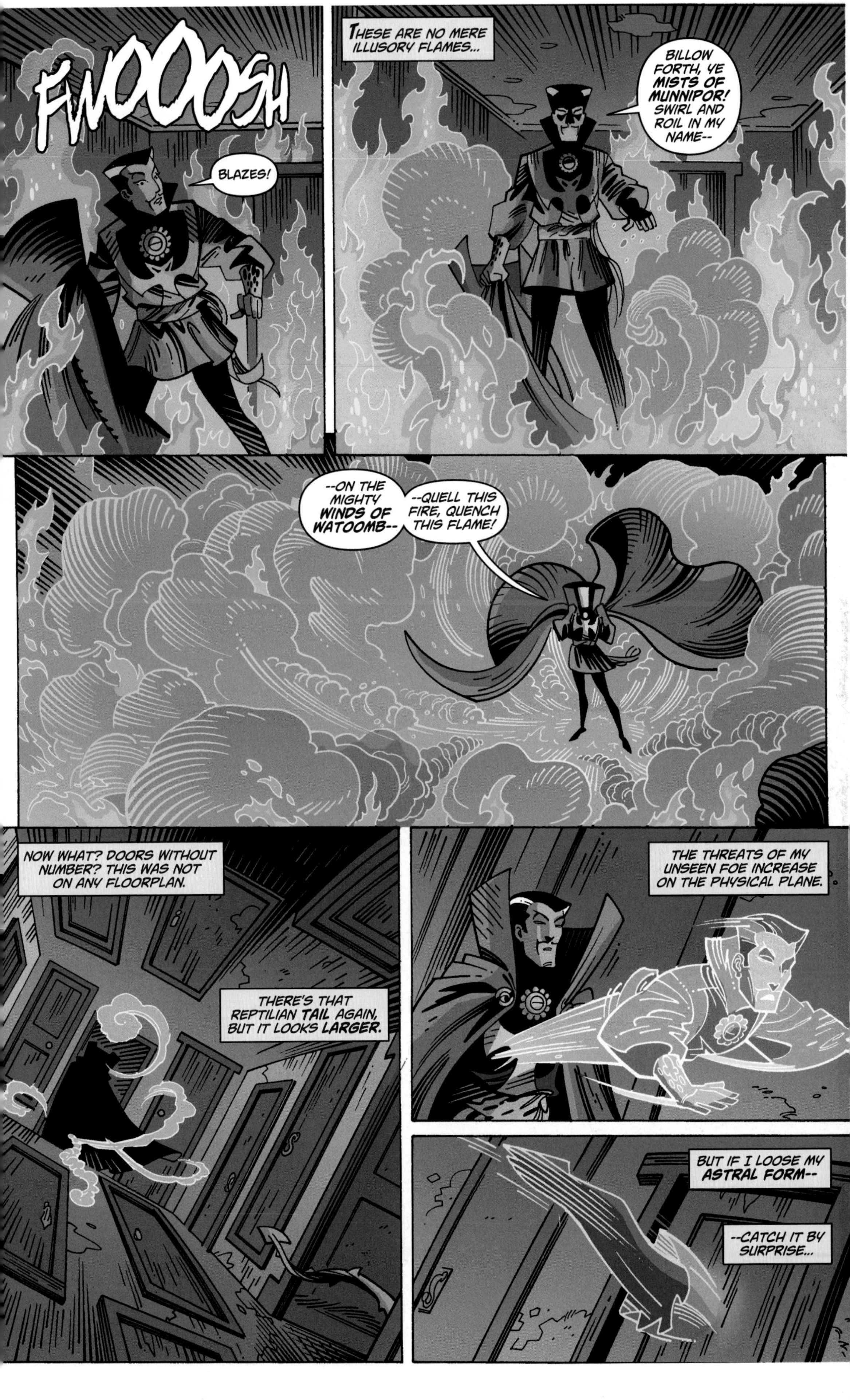
FWOOOSH
BLAZES!
THESE ARE NO MERE ILLUSORY FLAMES...
BILLOW FORTH, YE MISTS OF MUNNIPOR! SWIRL AND ROIL IN MY NAME--
--ON THE MIGHTY WINDS OF WATOOMB--
--QUELL THIS FIRE, QUENCH THIS FLAME!
NOW WHAT? DOORS WITHOUT NUMBER? THIS WAS NOT ON ANY FLOORPLAN.
THERE'S THAT REPTILIAN TAIL AGAIN, BUT IT LOOKS LARGER.
THE THREATS OF MY UNSEEN FOE INCREASE ON THE PHYSICAL PLANE.
BUT IF I LOOSE MY ASTRAL FORM--
--CATCH IT BY SURPRISE...

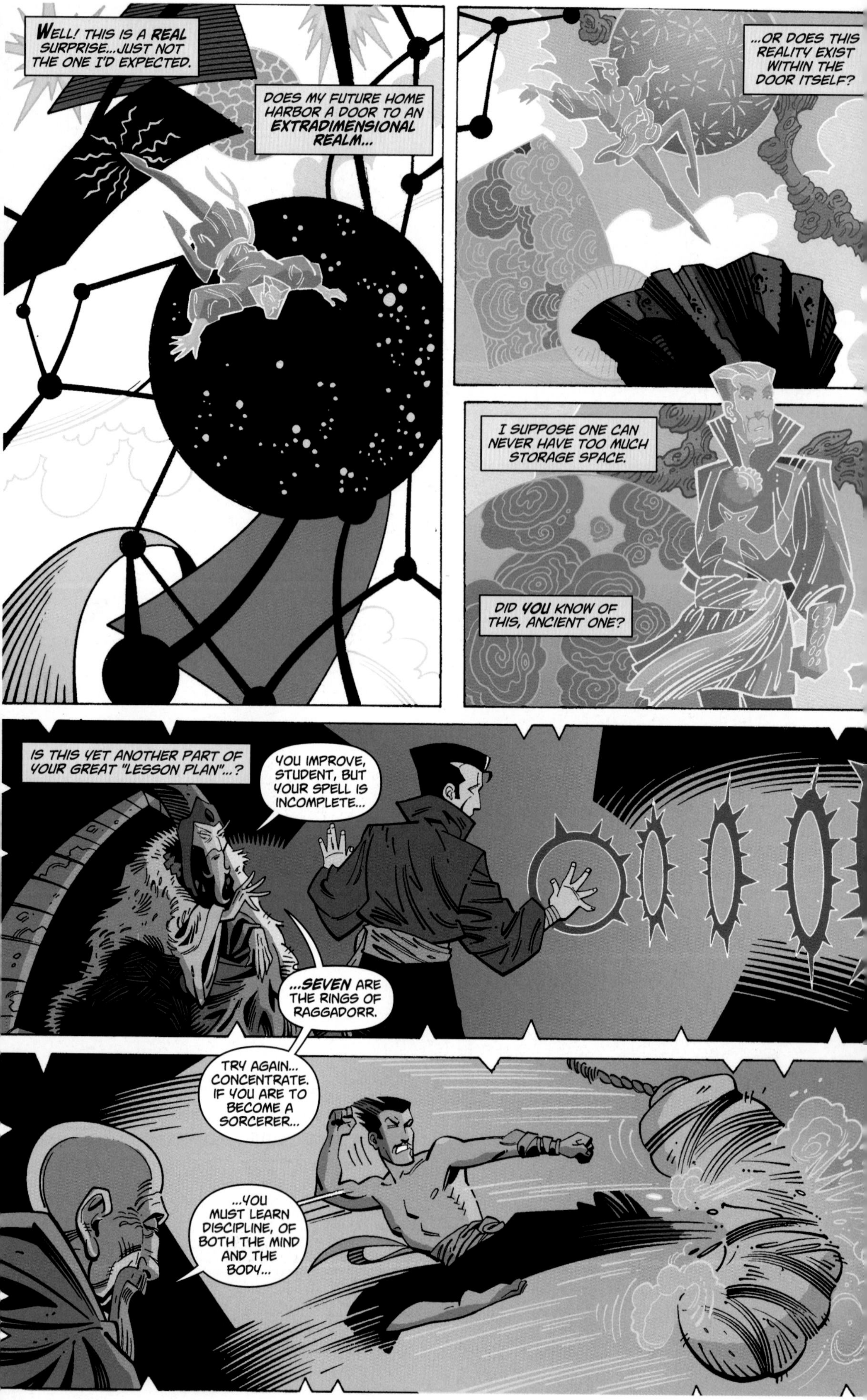
WELL! THIS IS A REAL SURPRISE...JUST NOT THE ONE I'D EXPECTED.
DOES MY FUTURE HOME HARBOR A DOOR TO AN EXTRADIMENSIONAL REALM...
...OR DOES THIS REALITY EXIST WITHIN THE DOOR ITSELF?
I SUPPOSE ONE CAN NEVER HAVE TOO MUCH STORAGE SPACE.
DID YOU KNOW OF THIS, ANCIENT ONE?
IS THIS YET ANOTHER PART OF YOUR GREAT "LESSON PLAN"...?
YOU IMPROVE, STUDENT, BUT YOUR SPELL IS INCOMPLETE...
...SEVEN ARE THE RINGS OF RAGGADORR.
TRY AGAIN... CONCENTRATE. IF YOU ARE TO BECOME A SORCERER...
...YOU MUST LEARN DISCIPLINE, OF BOTH THE MIND AND THE BODY...

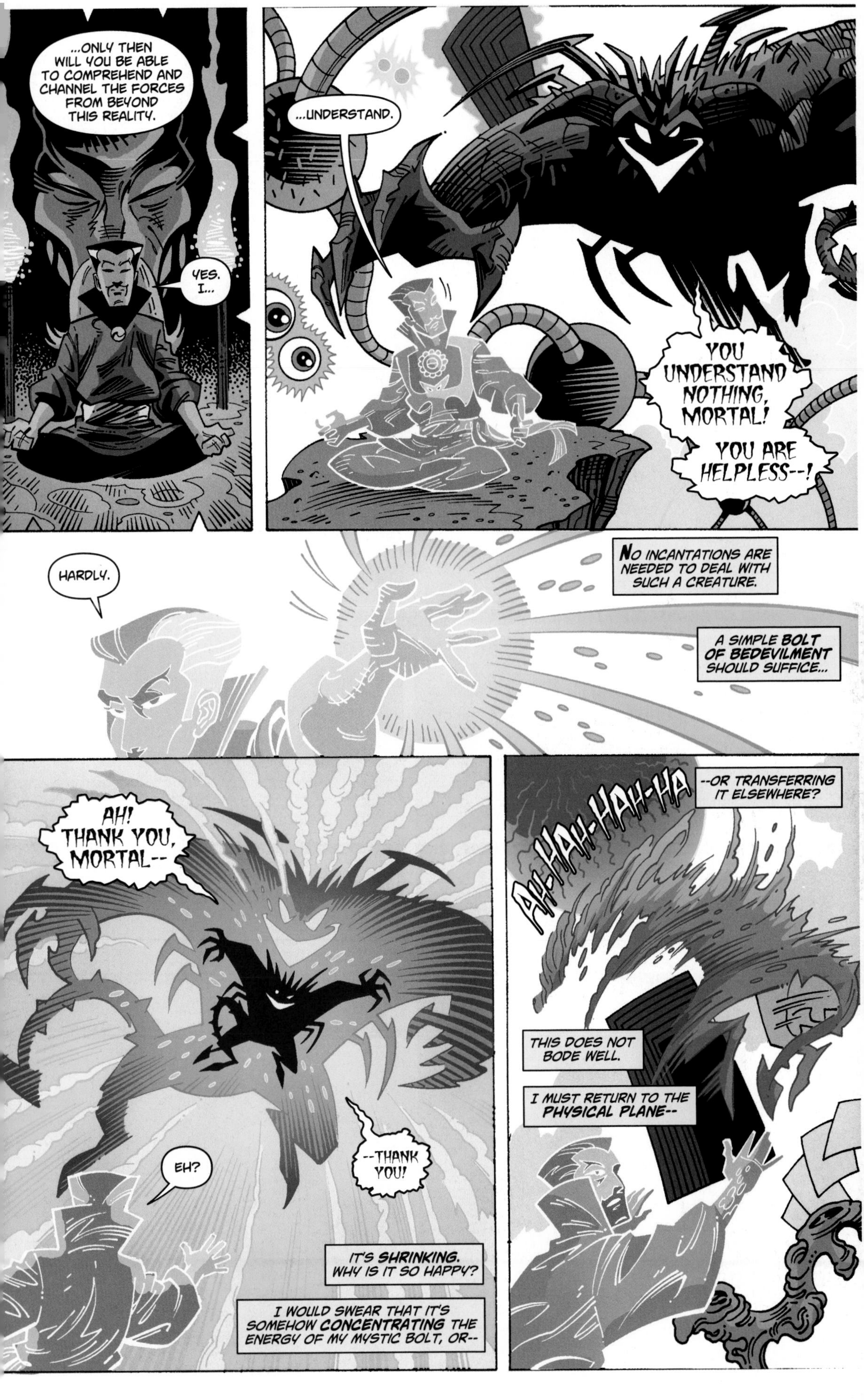
...ONLY THEN WILL YOU BE ABLE TO COMPREHEND AND CHANNEL THE FORCES FROM BEYOND THIS REALITY.
YES. I...
...UNDERSTAND.
YOU UNDERSTAND NOTHING, MORTAL!
YOU ARE HELPLESS--!
HARDLY.
NO INCANTATIONS ARE NEEDED TO DEAL WITH SUCH A CREATURE.
A SIMPLE BOLT OF BEDEVILMENT SHOULD SUFFICE...
AH! THANK YOU, MORTAL--
EH?
--THANK YOU!
IT'S SHRINKING. WHY IS IT SO HAPPY?
I WOULD SWEAR THAT IT'S SOMEHOW CONCENTRATING THE ENERGY OF MY MYSTIC BOLT, OR--
--OR TRANSFERRING IT ELSEWHERE?
AH-HAH-HAH-HA
THIS DOES NOT BODE WELL.
I MUST RETURN TO THE PHYSICAL PLANE--

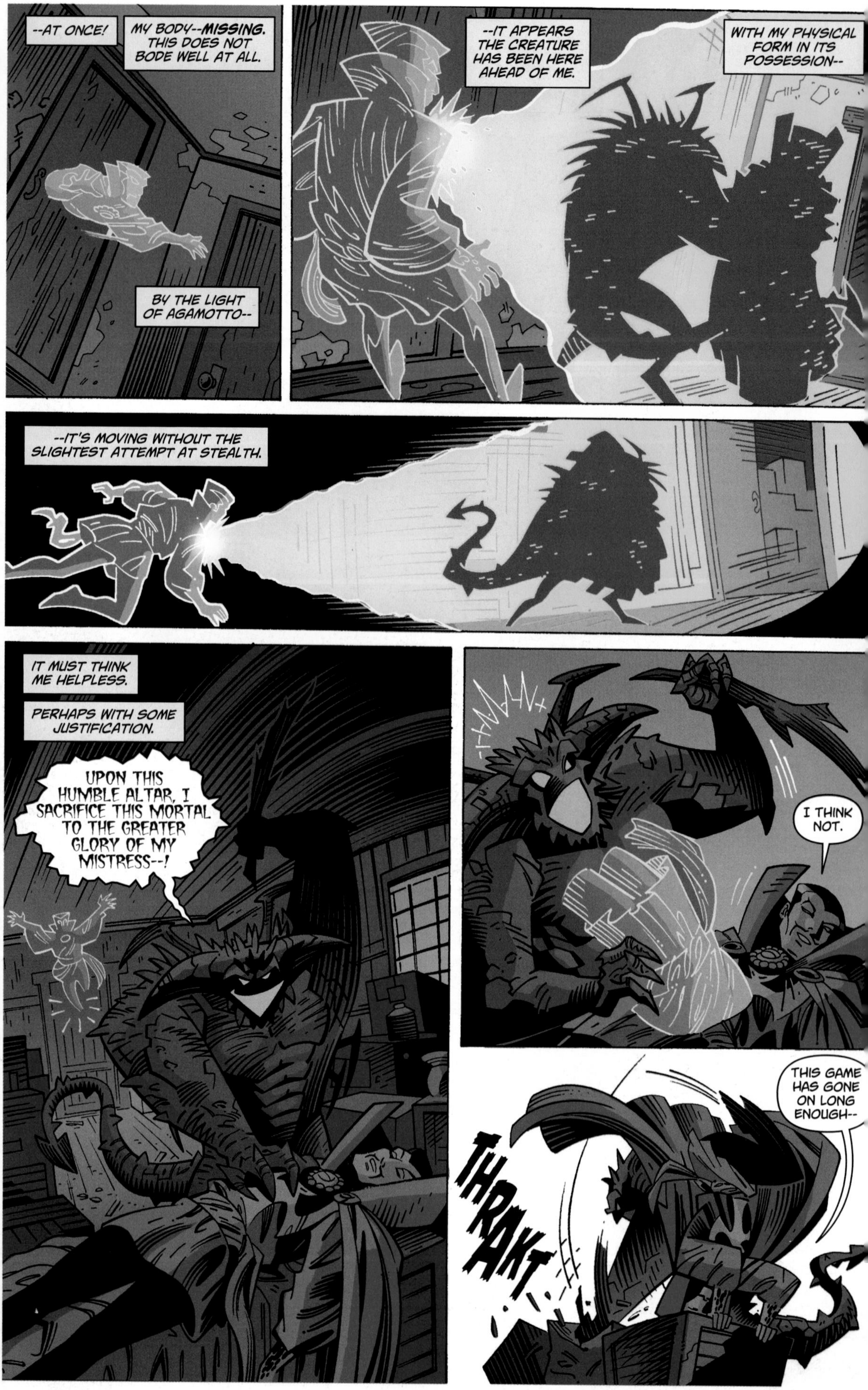
--AT ONCE!
MY BODY--MISSING. THIS DOES NOT BODE WELL AT ALL.
BY THE LIGHT OF AGAMOTTO--
--IT APPEARS THE CREATURE HAS BEEN HERE AHEAD OF ME.
WITH MY PHYSICAL FORM IN ITS POSSESSION--
--IT'S MOVING WITHOUT THE SLIGHTEST ATTEMPT AT STEALTH.
IT MUST THINK ME HELPLESS.
PERHAPS WITH SOME JUSTIFICATION.
UPON THIS HUMBLE ALTAR, I SACRIFICE THIS MORTAL TO THE GREATER GLORY OF MY MISTRESS--!
I THINK NOT.
THIS GAME HAS GONE ON LONG ENOUGH--
THRAKT

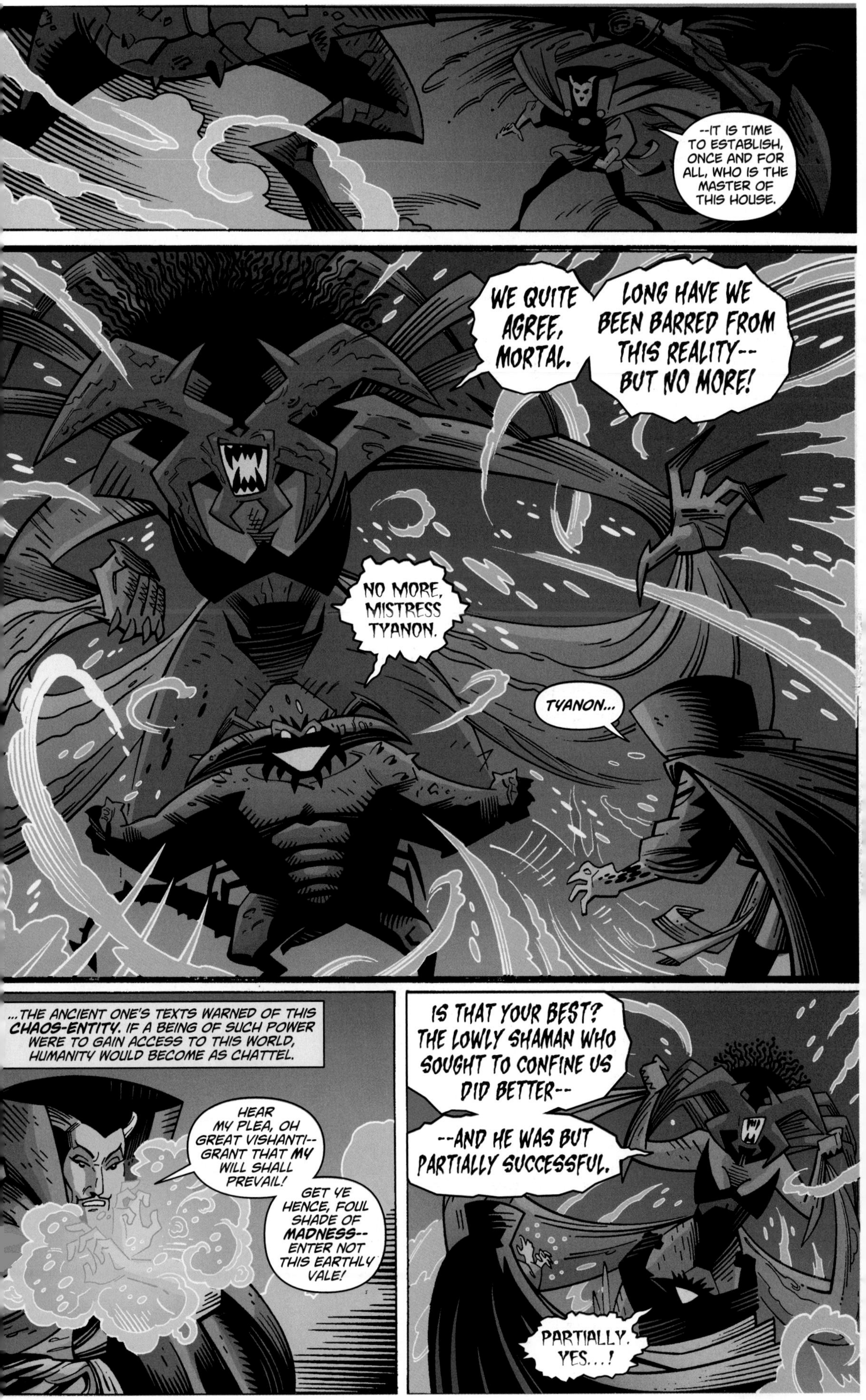
--IT IS TIME TO ESTABLISH, ONCE AND FOR ALL, WHO IS THE MASTER OF THIS HOUSE.
WE QUITE AGREE, MORTAL.
LONG HAVE WE BEEN BARRED FROM THIS REALITY-- BUT NO MORE!
NO MORE, MISTRESS TYANON.
TYANON...
...THE ANCIENT ONE'S TEXTS WARNED OF THIS CHAOS-ENTITY. IF A BEING OF SUCH POWER WERE TO GAIN ACCESS TO THIS WORLD, HUMANITY WOULD BECOME AS CHATTEL.
HEAR MY PLEA, OH GREAT VISHANTI-- GRANT THAT MY WILL SHALL PREVAIL!
GET YE HENCE, FOUL SHADE OF MADNESS-- ENTER NOT THIS EARTHLY VALE!
IS THAT YOUR BEST? THE LOWLY SHAMAN WHO SOUGHT TO CONFINE US DID BETTER--
--AND HE WAS BUT PARTIALLY SUCCESSFUL.
PARTIALLY. YES...!

YOUR EFFORT WAS LAUGHABLE.

TRY HARDER, WEAKLING-- IF YOU CAN!

MORTALS! THEY NEVER KNOW THEIR PLACE!

HAHR! FLING HIM ABOUT AGAIN, MISTRESS.

FIGHT FOR YOUR PITIFUL LIFE, YOU FOOL. FIGHT!

CASTING THAT SPELL WAS--DIFFICULT. DOES THE NERVE DAMAGE PLAGUE ME EVEN NOW?

SERAPHIM SHIELD ME...

WHY THE TAUNTS--? OF COURSE! CURSE ME FOR A NOVICE, THE CREATURE HAS BEEN FEEDING OFF MY SPELLS--

--GROWING TO FORM A LIVING PORTAL FOR TYANON. IF I KEEP USING MY MAGICKS IN THAT MANNER, I WILL ENSURE HER VICTORY.

YES...I SEE...

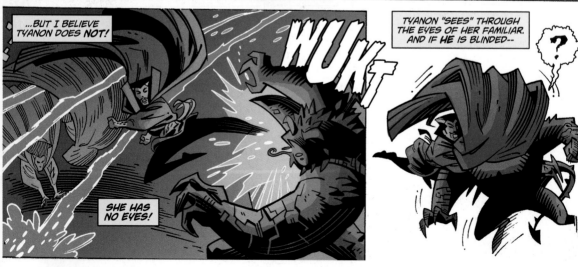

...BUT I BELIEVE TYANON DOES NOT!

SHE HAS NO EYES!

WUKT

TYANON "SEES" THROUGH THE EYES OF HER FAMILIAR. AND IF HE IS BLINDED--

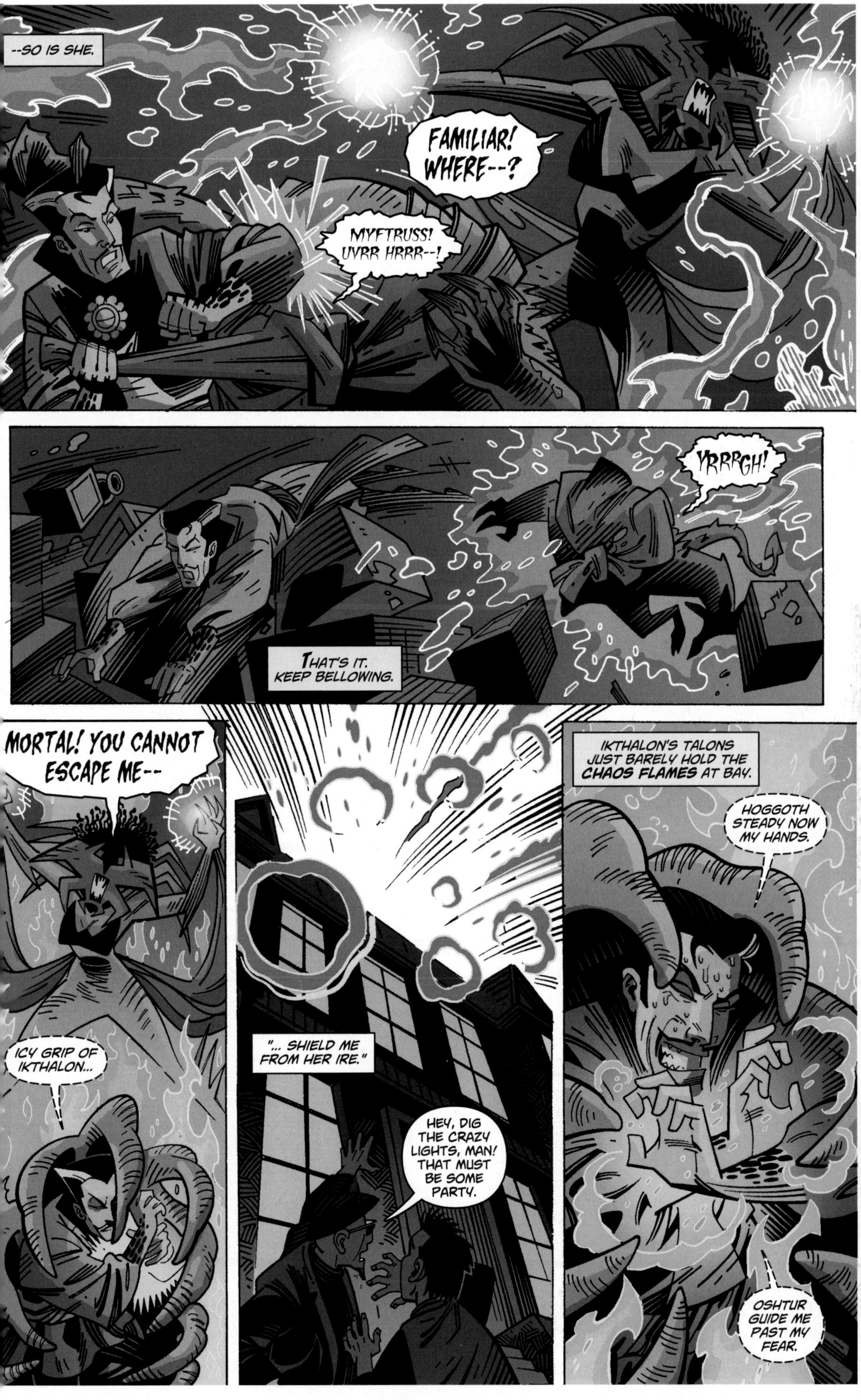
--SO IS SHE.
FAMILIAR! WHERE--?
MYFTRUSS! UVRR HRRR--!
YRRRGH!
THAT'S IT. KEEP BELLOWING.
MORTAL! YOU CANNOT ESCAPE ME--
ICY GRIP OF IKTHALON...
"... SHIELD ME FROM HER IRE."
HEY, DIG THE CRAZY LIGHTS, MAN! THAT MUST BE SOME PARTY.
IKTHALON'S TALONS JUST BARELY HOLD THE CHAOS FLAMES AT BAY.
HOGGOTH STEADY NOW MY HANDS.
OSHTUR GUIDE ME PAST MY FEAR.

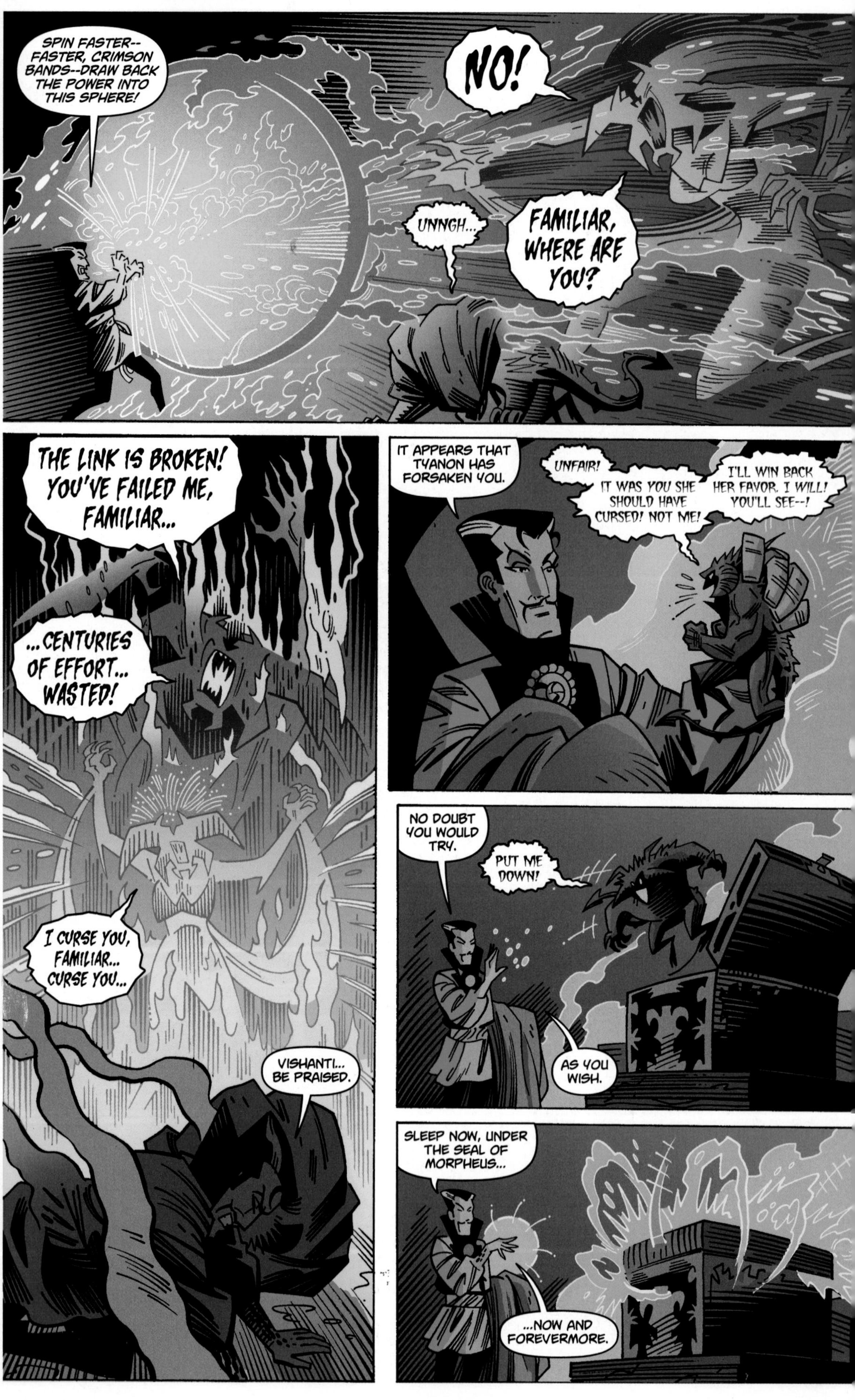
SPIN FASTER-- FASTER, CRIMSON BANDS--DRAW BACK THE POWER INTO THIS SPHERE!
NO!
UNNGH...
FAMILIAR, WHERE ARE YOU?
THE LINK IS BROKEN! YOU'VE FAILED ME, FAMILIAR...
...CENTURIES OF EFFORT... WASTED!
I CURSE YOU, FAMILIAR... CURSE YOU...
VISHANTI... BE PRAISED.
IT APPEARS THAT TYANON HAS FORSAKEN YOU.
UNFAIR!
IT WAS YOU SHE SHOULD HAVE CURSED! NOT ME!
I'LL WIN BACK HER FAVOR. I WILL! YOU'LL SEE--!
NO DOUBT YOU WOULD TRY.
PUT ME DOWN!
AS YOU WISH.
SLEEP NOW, UNDER THE SEAL OF MORPHEUS...
...NOW AND FOREVERMORE.

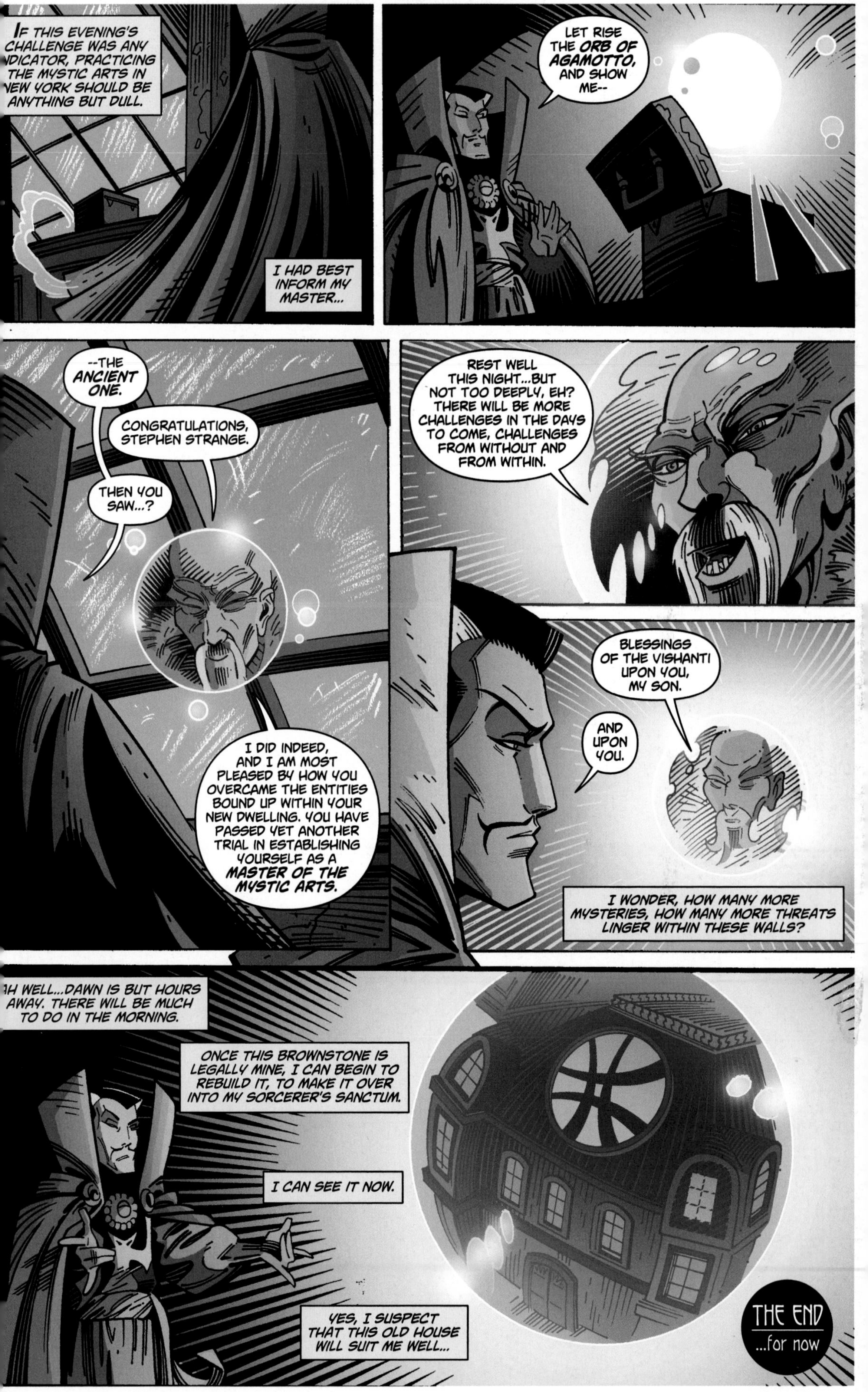
IF THIS EVENING'S CHALLENGE WAS ANY INDICATOR, PRACTICING THE MYSTIC ARTS IN NEW YORK SHOULD BE ANYTHING BUT DULL.
I HAD BEST INFORM MY MASTER...
LET RISE THE ORB OF AGAMOTTO, AND SHOW ME--
--THE ANCIENT ONE.
CONGRATULATIONS, STEPHEN STRANGE.
THEN YOU SAW...?
I DID INDEED, AND I AM MOST PLEASED BY HOW YOU OVERCAME THE ENTITIES BOUND UP WITHIN YOUR NEW DWELLING. YOU HAVE PASSED YET ANOTHER TRIAL IN ESTABLISHING YOURSELF AS A MASTER OF THE MYSTIC ARTS.
REST WELL THIS NIGHT...BUT NOT TOO DEEPLY, EH? THERE WILL BE MORE CHALLENGES IN THE DAYS TO COME, CHALLENGES FROM WITHOUT AND FROM WITHIN.
BLESSINGS OF THE VISHANTI UPON YOU, MY SON.
AND UPON YOU.
I WONDER, HOW MANY MORE MYSTERIES, HOW MANY MORE THREATS LINGER WITHIN THESE WALLS?
AH WELL...DAWN IS BUT HOURS AWAY. THERE WILL BE MUCH TO DO IN THE MORNING.
ONCE THIS BROWNSTONE IS LEGALLY MINE, I CAN BEGIN TO REBUILD IT, TO MAKE IT OVER INTO MY SORCERER'S SANCTUM.
I CAN SEE IT NOW.
YES, I SUSPECT THAT THIS OLD HOUSE WILL SUIT ME WELL...
THE END
...for now

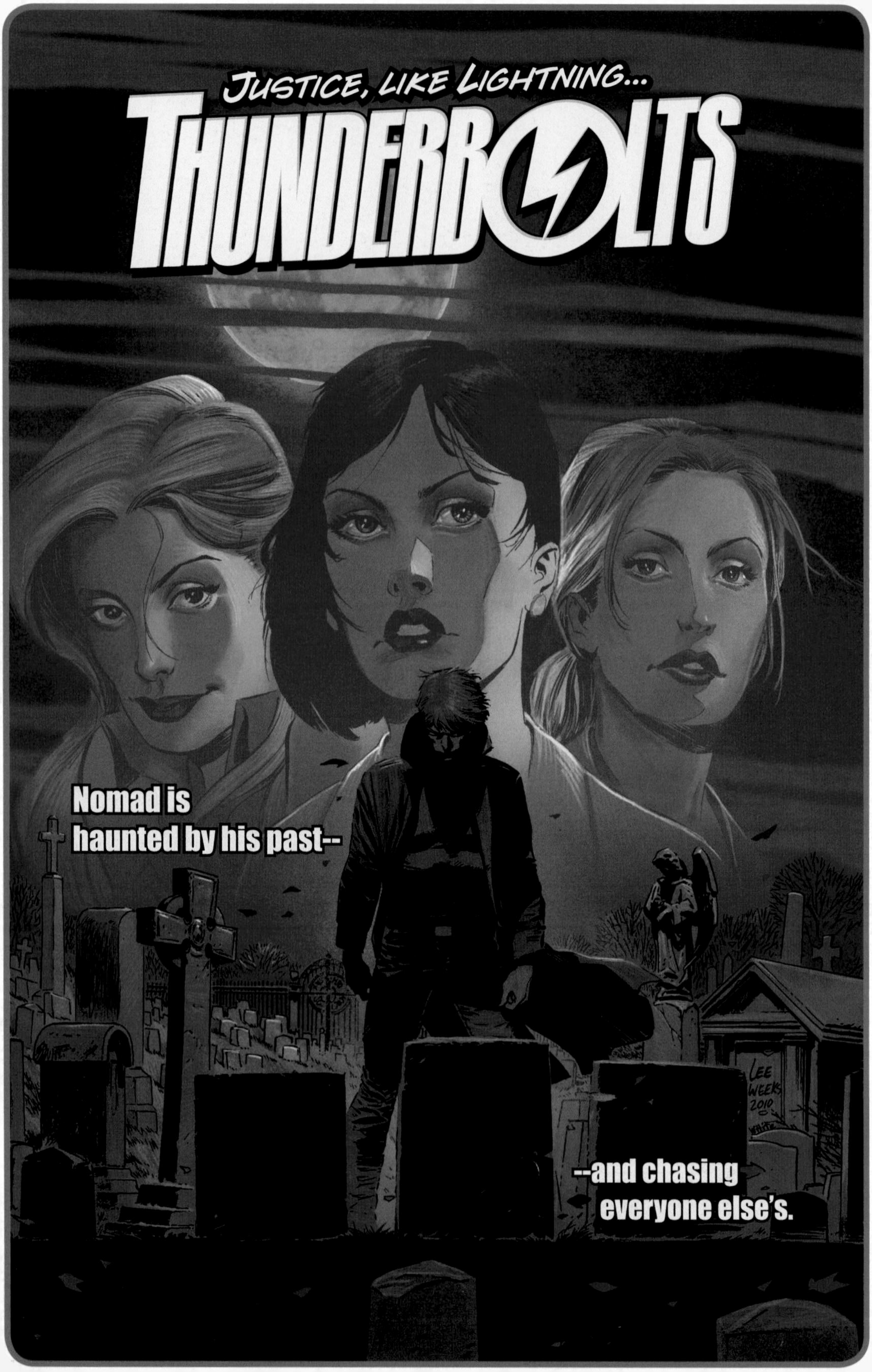
JUSTICE, LIKE LIGHTNING...
THUNDERBOLTS
Nomad is haunted by his past--
--and chasing everyone else's.
LEE WEEKS 2010
WHITE

The Thunderbolts were once the world's latest super hero team! But then, their darkest secret—that they were secretly The Masters of Evil—came to light! They went on the run, hunted by those they once protected! Jack Monroe hunted them, as Scourge, but eventually joined their cause for redemption. Now, in the aftermath, Jack Monroe is Nomad once again. And he still wonders: Is it possible for hardened criminals to find redemption? Or will they always return to their lives outside the law?

SECRETS OF THE VAULT!

It was a complete, but pleasant, surprise when Ellie contacted me to look over the finished lettering of this Thunderbolts issue. It's been years since I'd written the story, much less worked for Marvel. I'd planned this issue as an "inventory story," which basically is meant to sit in a drawer until the regular creative team needs a breather on the always-hectic monthly schedule.

This one sat in a drawer long enough that poor Jack Monroe got killed in the interim!

Former T-Bolts editor and current Marvel Demi-God, Tom Brevoort and I had wanted to follow up on the Scourge storyline that had run to much fanfare (okay, some fanfare) in order to see what Jack (Nomad) Monroe had been up to since cutting the strings that had been pulling him this way and that. As with most things I do, I also wanted to use the "wrap up" as a "set up" in case there would be other opportunities to write Nomad in the future.

Hindsight of time is always a tricky thing when I look at my old work, but overall, I like the status quo I'd set up for Jack in case he ever got a chance to wander the comics world again.

His death in Captain America was a bittersweet thing for me as a reader, in that it was very well-handled by the creative team of that title, but ultimately, I didn't like seeing a character I had such a strong emotional investment in get killed off at all, much less in the way he did.

Seeing this issue takes a bit of the sting out of that. Now I remember the path Jack Monroe could have gone on and he'll always live on in the perpetual fan-fiction that goes on in my head!

-- Fabian Nicieza (from somewhere in Gotham City)

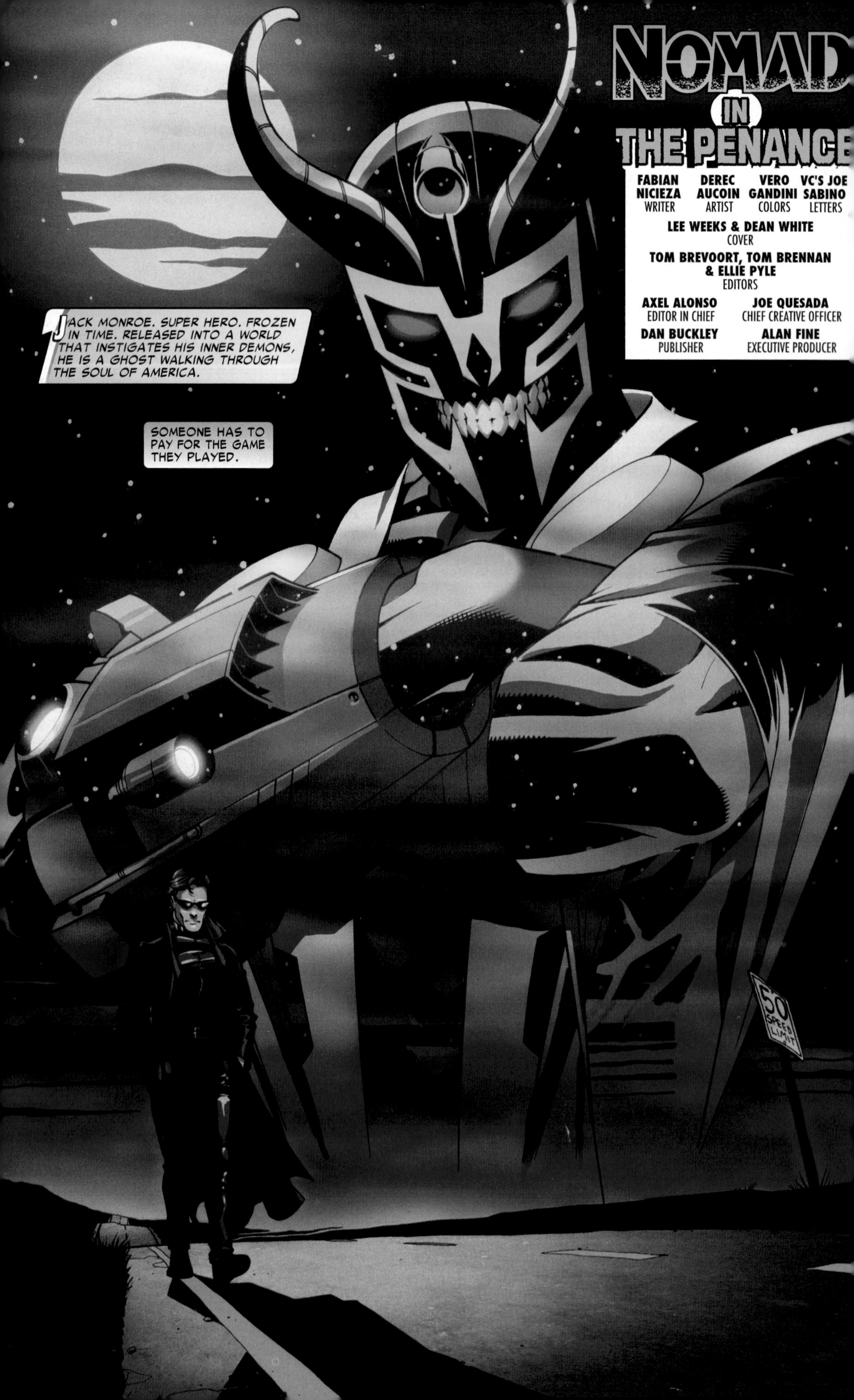
NOMAD
IN
THE PENANCE
FABIAN NICIEZA WRITER
DEREC AUCOIN ARTIST
VERO GANDINI COLORS
VC'S JOE SABINO LETTERS
LEE WEEKS & DEAN WHITE COVER
TOM BREVOORT, TOM BRENNAN & ELLIE PYLE EDITORS
AXEL ALONSO EDITOR IN CHIEF
JOE QUESADA CHIEF CREATIVE OFFICER
DAN BUCKLEY PUBLISHER
ALAN FINE EXECUTIVE PRODUCER
JACK MONROE. SUPER HERO. FROZEN IN TIME. RELEASED INTO A WORLD THAT INSTIGATES HIS INNER DEMONS, HE IS A GHOST WALKING THROUGH THE SOUL OF AMERICA.
SOMEONE HAS TO PAY FOR THE GAME THEY PLAYED.
50 SPEED LIMIT

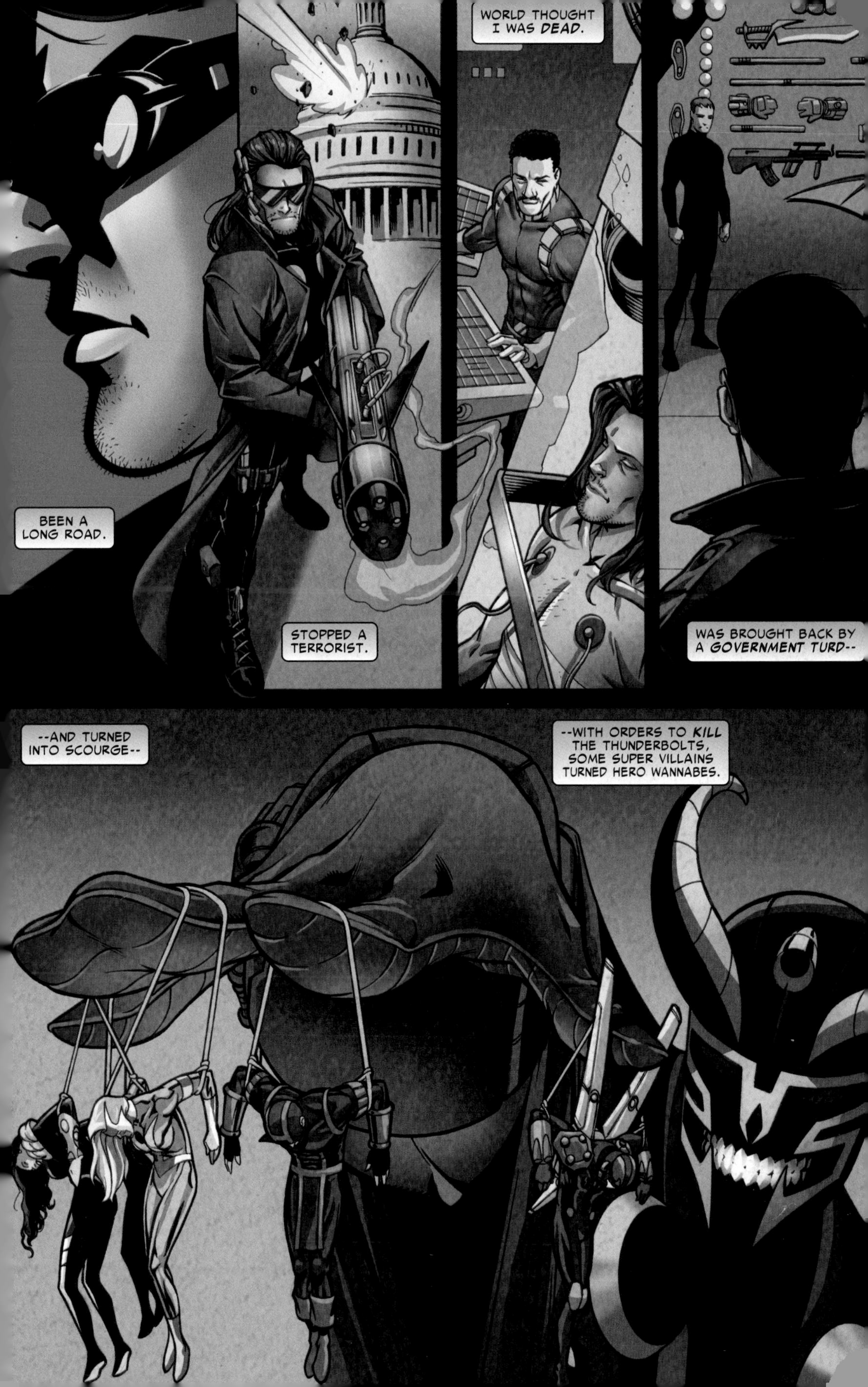
BEEN A LONG ROAD.
STOPPED A TERRORIST.
WORLD THOUGHT I WAS DEAD.
WAS BROUGHT BACK BY A GOVERNMENT TURD--
--AND TURNED INTO SCOURGE--
--WITH ORDERS TO KILL THE THUNDERBOLTS, SOME SUPER VILLAINS TURNED HERO WANNABES.

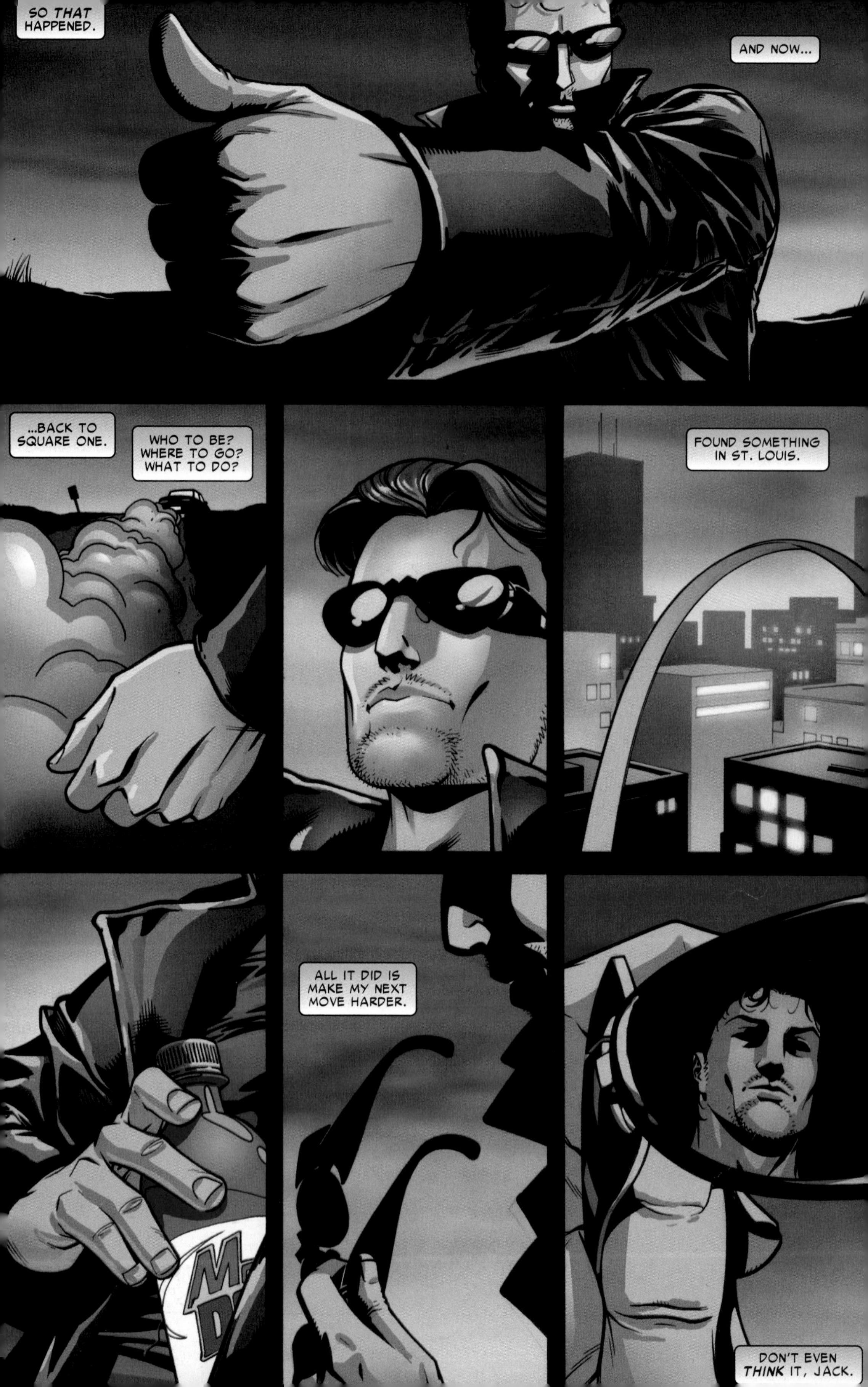
SO *THAT* HAPPENED.
AND NOW...
...BACK TO SQUARE ONE.
WHO TO BE? WHERE TO GO? WHAT TO DO?
FOUND SOMETHING IN ST. LOUIS.
ALL IT DID IS MAKE MY NEXT MOVE HARDER.
DON'T EVEN *THINK* IT, JACK.

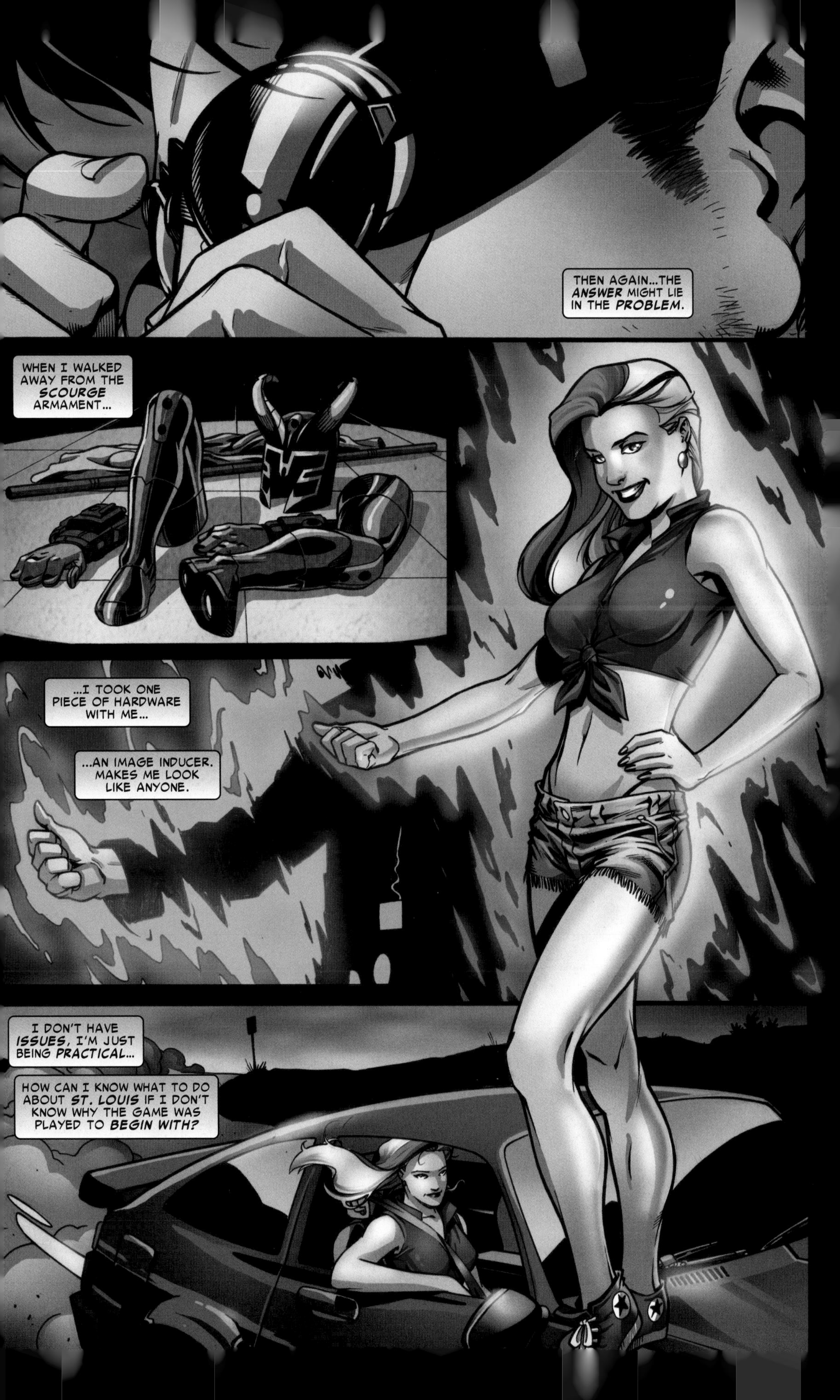
THEN AGAIN...THE *ANSWER* MIGHT LIE IN THE *PROBLEM.*
WHEN I WALKED AWAY FROM THE *SCOURGE* ARMAMENT...
...I TOOK ONE PIECE OF HARDWARE WITH ME...
...AN IMAGE INDUCER. MAKES ME LOOK LIKE ANYONE.
I DON'T HAVE *ISSUES,* I'M JUST BEING *PRACTICAL...*
HOW CAN I KNOW WHAT TO DO ABOUT *ST. LOUIS* IF I DON'T KNOW WHY THE GAME WAS PLAYED TO *BEGIN WITH?*

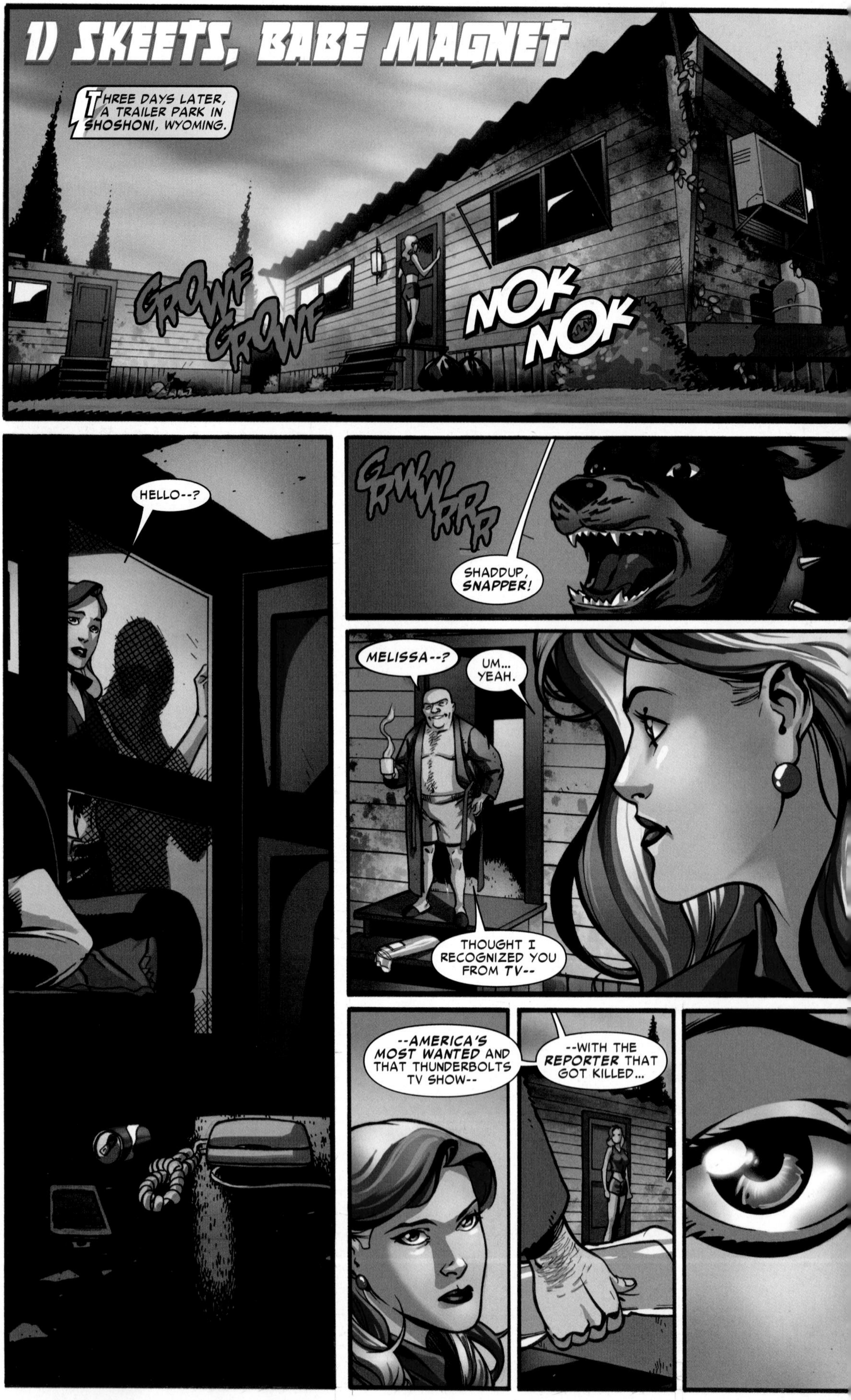

1) SKEETS, BABE MAGNET
THREE DAYS LATER, A TRAILER PARK IN SHOSHONI, WYOMING.
GROWF GROWF
NOK NOK
HELLO--?
GRWWRRR
SHADDUP, SNAPPER!
MELISSA--?
UM... YEAH.
THOUGHT I RECOGNIZED YOU FROM TV--
--AMERICA'S MOST WANTED AND THAT THUNDERBOLTS TV SHOW--
--WITH THE REPORTER THAT GOT KILLED...

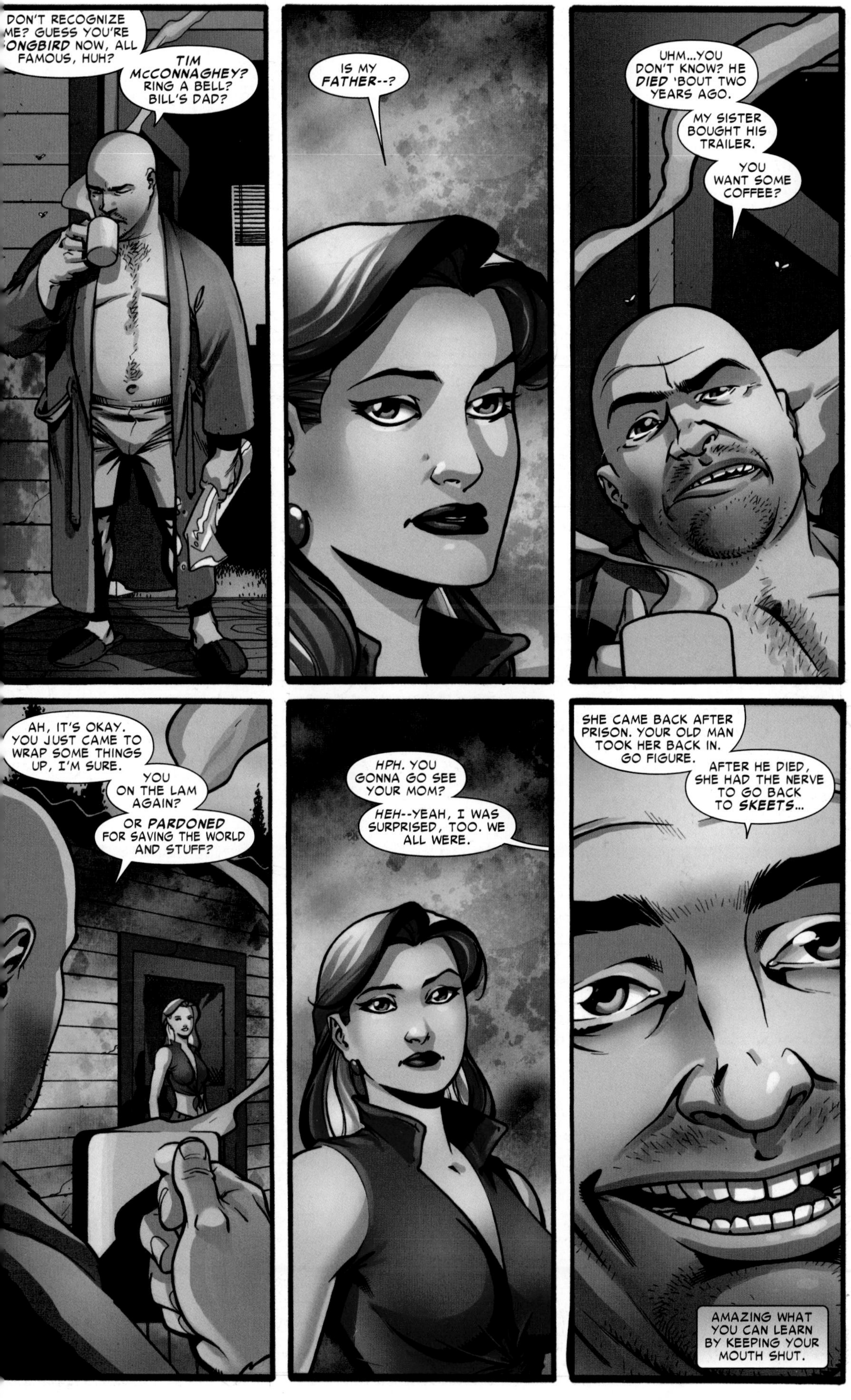
DON'T RECOGNIZE ME? GUESS YOU'RE SONGBIRD NOW, ALL FAMOUS, HUH?
TIM McCONNAGHEY? RING A BELL? BILL'S DAD?
IS MY FATHER--?
UHM...YOU DON'T KNOW? HE DIED 'BOUT TWO YEARS AGO.
MY SISTER BOUGHT HIS TRAILER.
YOU WANT SOME COFFEE?
AH, IT'S OKAY. YOU JUST CAME TO WRAP SOME THINGS UP, I'M SURE.
YOU ON THE LAM AGAIN?
OR PARDONED FOR SAVING THE WORLD AND STUFF?
HPH. YOU GONNA GO SEE YOUR MOM?
HEH--YEAH, I WAS SURPRISED, TOO. WE ALL WERE.
SHE CAME BACK AFTER PRISON. YOUR OLD MAN TOOK HER BACK IN. GO FIGURE.
AFTER HE DIED, SHE HAD THE NERVE TO GO BACK TO SKEETS...
AMAZING WHAT YOU CAN LEARN BY KEEPING YOUR MOUTH SHUT.

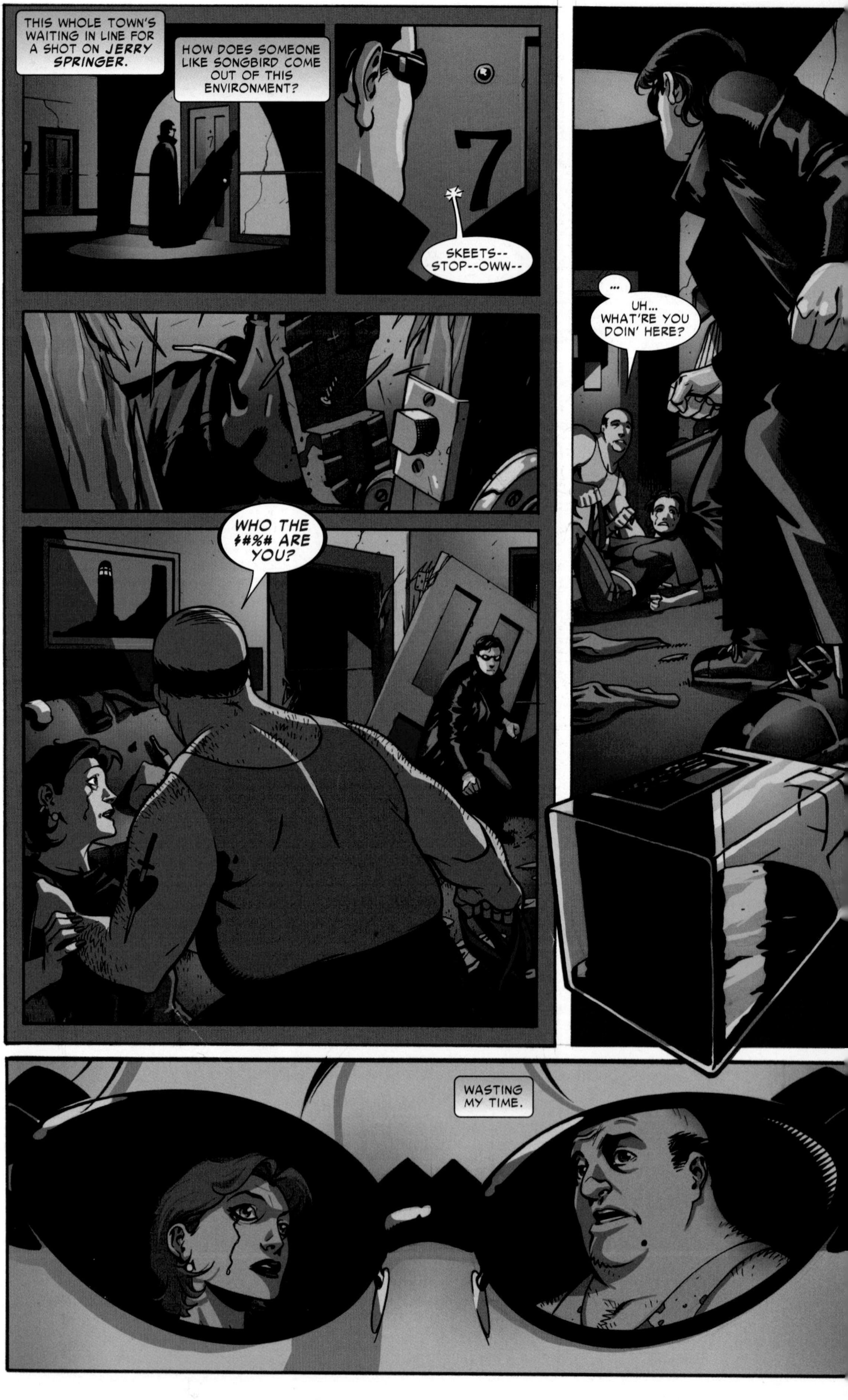
THIS WHOLE TOWN'S WAITING IN LINE FOR A SHOT ON JERRY SPRINGER.
HOW DOES SOMEONE LIKE SONGBIRD COME OUT OF THIS ENVIRONMENT?
7
SKEETS-- STOP--OWW--
WHO THE $#%# ARE YOU?
...
UH... WHAT'RE YOU DOIN' HERE?
WASTING MY TIME.

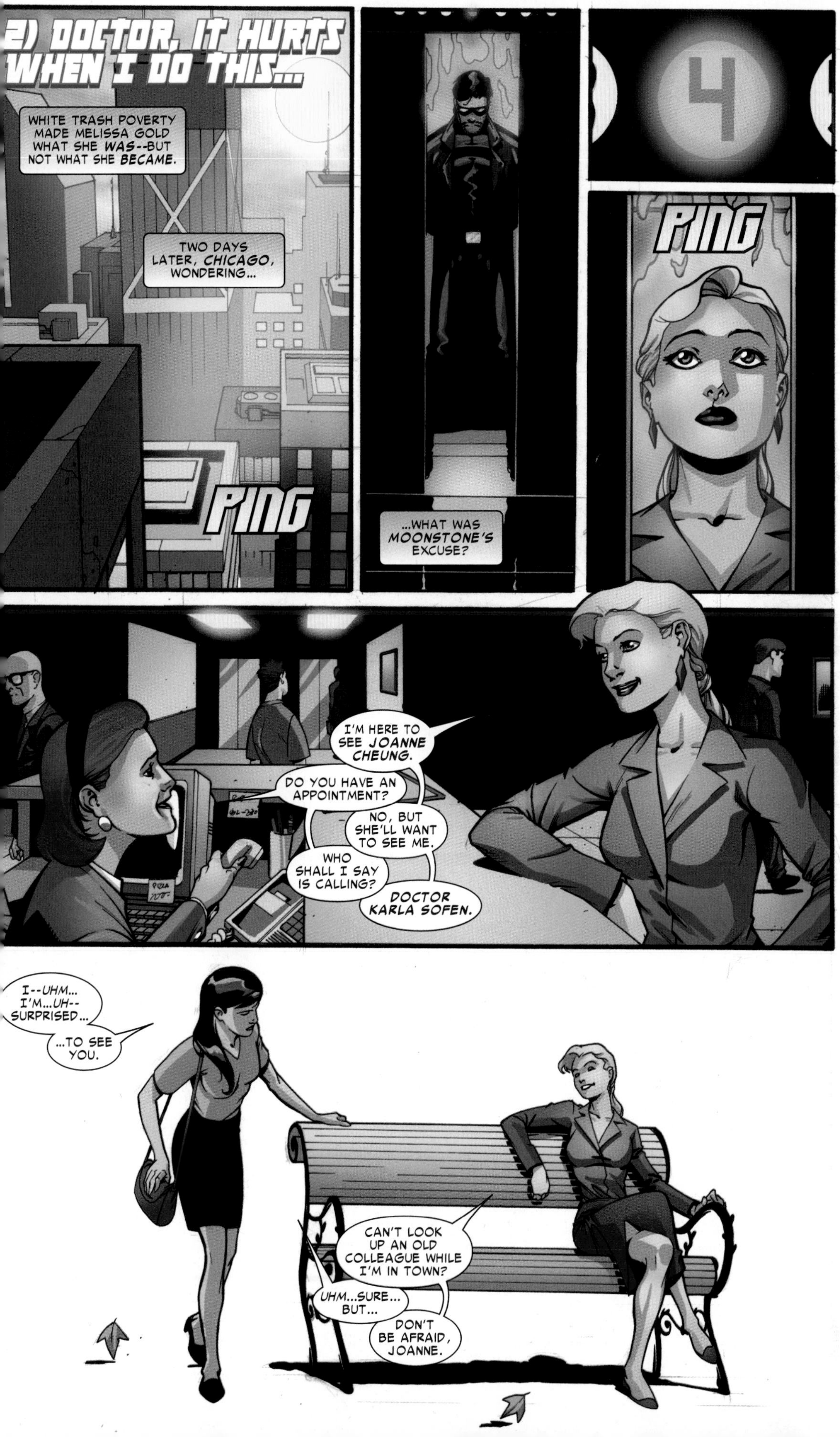
2) DOCTOR, IT HURTS WHEN I DO THIS...
WHITE TRASH POVERTY MADE MELISSA GOLD WHAT SHE WAS--BUT NOT WHAT SHE BECAME.
TWO DAYS LATER, CHICAGO, WONDERING...
PING
...WHAT WAS MOONSTONE'S EXCUSE?
4
PING
I'M HERE TO SEE JOANNE CHEUNG.
DO YOU HAVE AN APPOINTMENT?
NO, BUT SHE'LL WANT TO SEE ME.
WHO SHALL I SAY IS CALLING?
DOCTOR KARLA SOFEN.
I--UHM... I'M...UH-- SURPRISED...
...TO SEE YOU.
CAN'T LOOK UP AN OLD COLLEAGUE WHILE I'M IN TOWN?
UHM...SURE... BUT...
DON'T BE AFRAID, JOANNE.

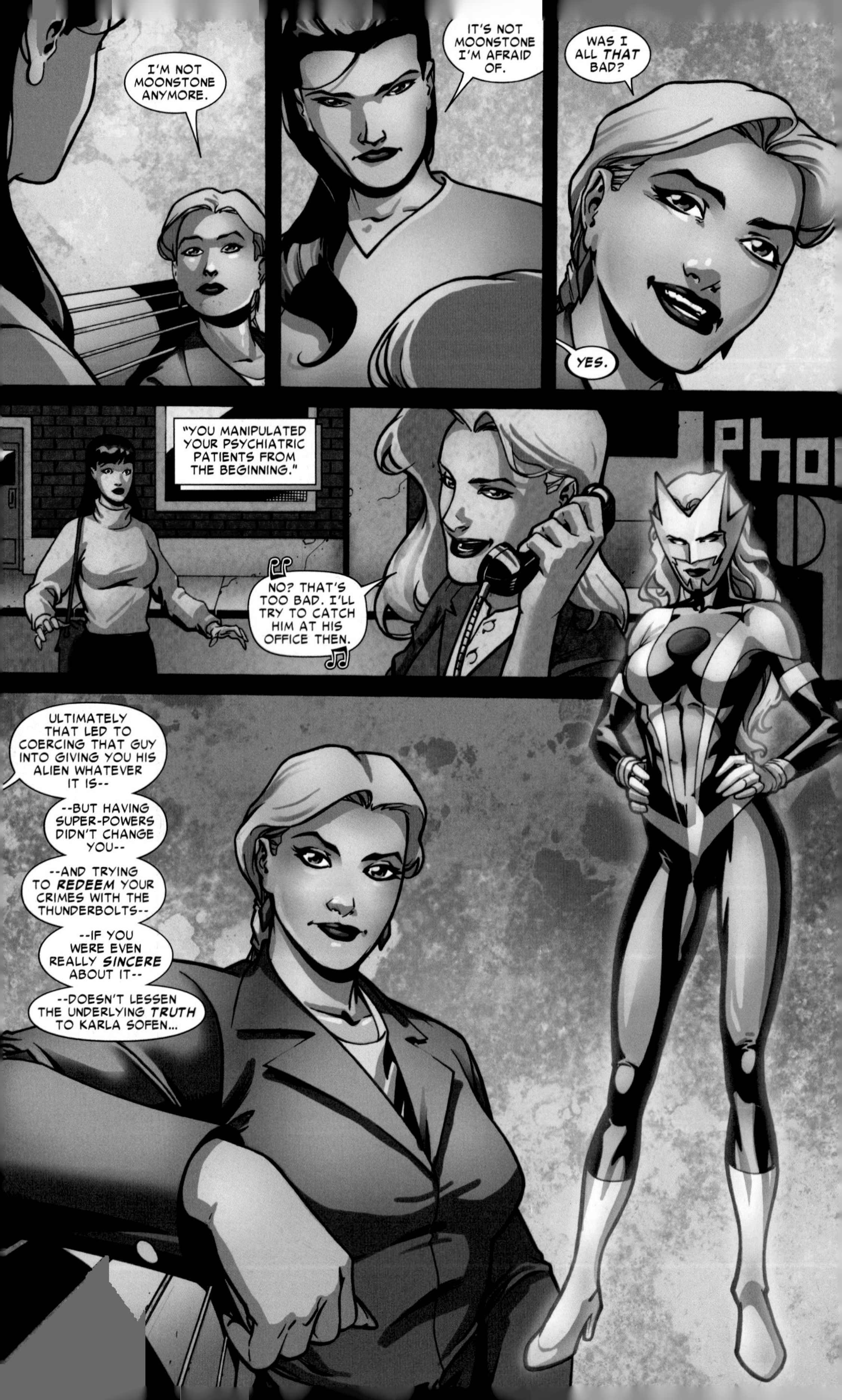
I'M NOT MOONSTONE ANYMORE.
IT'S NOT MOONSTONE I'M AFRAID OF.
WAS I ALL *THAT* BAD?
YES.
"YOU MANIPULATED YOUR PSYCHIATRIC PATIENTS FROM THE BEGINNING."
NO? THAT'S TOO BAD. I'LL TRY TO CATCH HIM AT HIS OFFICE THEN.
ULTIMATELY THAT LED TO COERCING THAT GUY INTO GIVING YOU HIS ALIEN WHATEVER IT IS--
--BUT HAVING SUPER-POWERS DIDN'T CHANGE YOU--
--AND TRYING TO *REDEEM* YOUR CRIMES WITH THE THUNDERBOLTS--
--IF YOU WERE EVEN REALLY *SINCERE* ABOUT IT--
--DOESN'T LESSEN THE UNDERLYING *TRUTH* TO KARLA SOFEN...

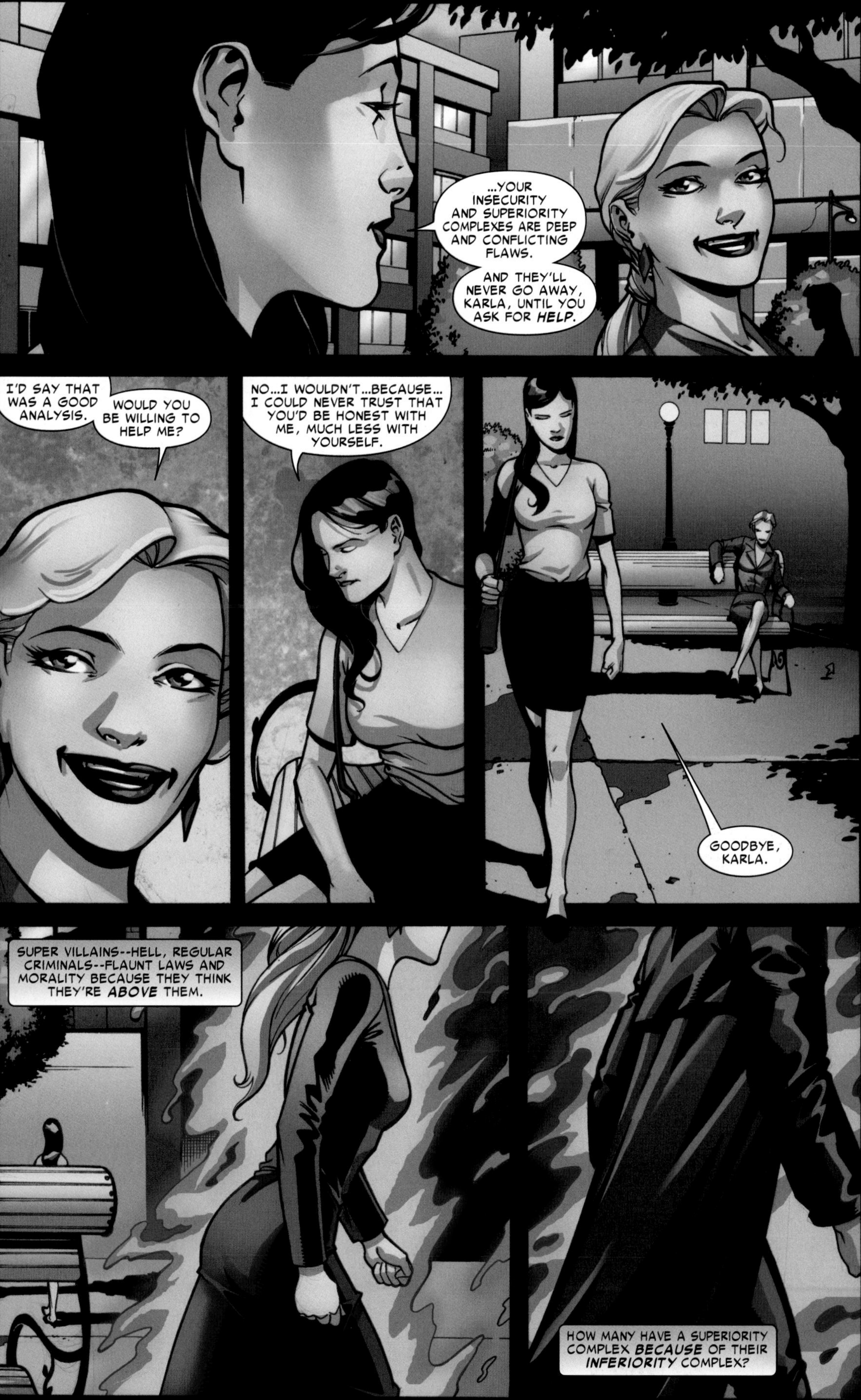
...YOUR INSECURITY AND SUPERIORITY COMPLEXES ARE DEEP AND CONFLICTING FLAWS.
AND THEY'LL NEVER GO AWAY, KARLA, UNTIL YOU ASK FOR HELP.
I'D SAY THAT WAS A GOOD ANALYSIS.
WOULD YOU BE WILLING TO HELP ME?
NO...I WOULDN'T...BECAUSE... I COULD NEVER TRUST THAT YOU'D BE HONEST WITH ME, MUCH LESS WITH YOURSELF.
GOODBYE, KARLA.
SUPER VILLAINS--HELL, REGULAR CRIMINALS--FLAUNT LAWS AND MORALITY BECAUSE THEY THINK THEY'RE ABOVE THEM.
HOW MANY HAVE A SUPERIORITY COMPLEX BECAUSE OF THEIR INFERIORITY COMPLEX?

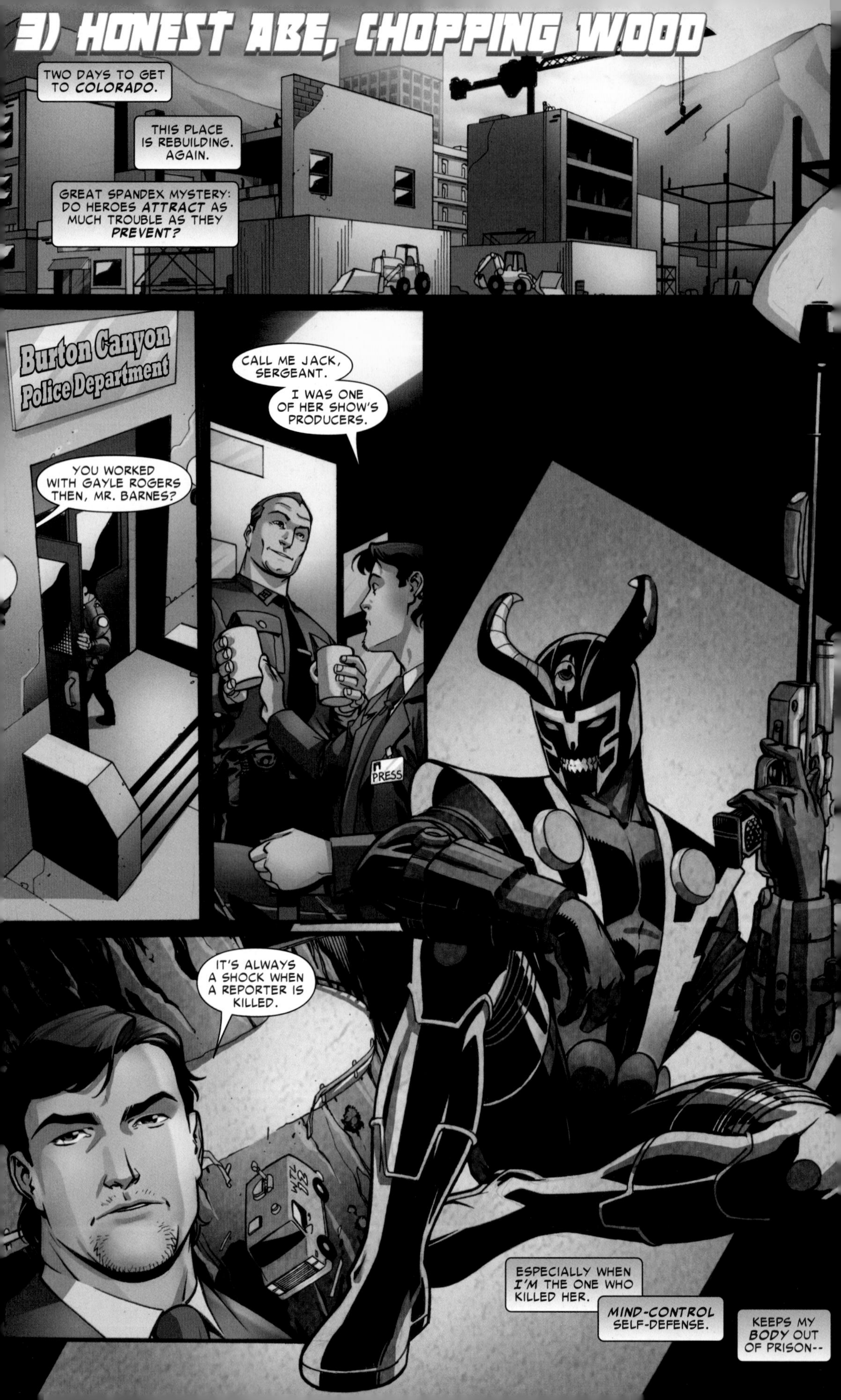
3) HONEST ABE, CHOPPING WOOD
TWO DAYS TO GET TO COLORADO.
THIS PLACE IS REBUILDING. AGAIN.
GREAT SPANDEX MYSTERY: DO HEROES ATTRACT AS MUCH TROUBLE AS THEY PREVENT?
Burton Canyon Police Department
YOU WORKED WITH GAYLE ROGERS THEN, MR. BARNES?
CALL ME JACK, SERGEANT.
I WAS ONE OF HER SHOW'S PRODUCERS.
PRESS
IT'S ALWAYS A SHOCK WHEN A REPORTER IS KILLED.
ESPECIALLY WHEN I'M THE ONE WHO KILLED HER.
MIND-CONTROL SELF-DEFENSE.
KEEPS MY BODY OUT OF PRISON--

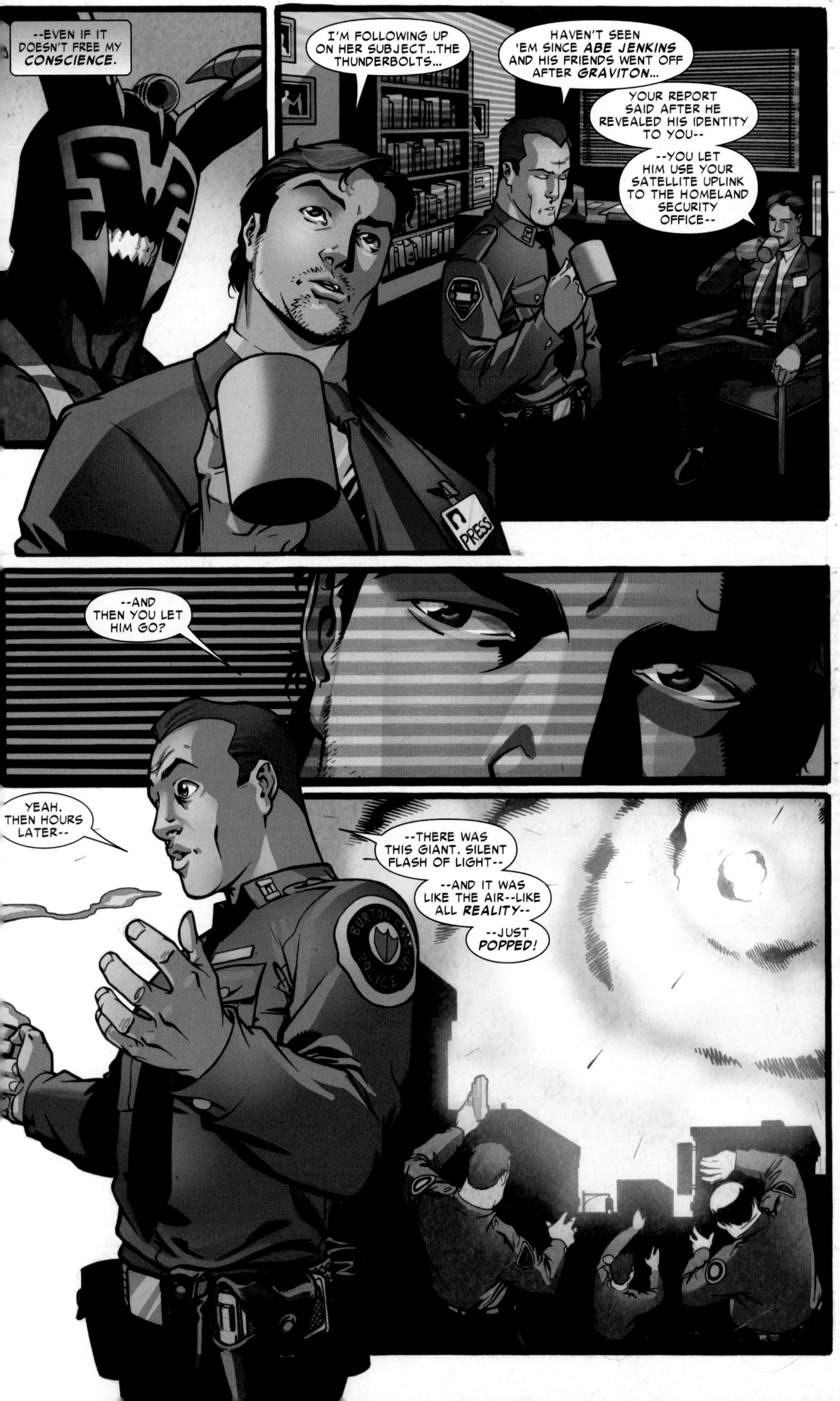

--EVEN IF IT DOESN'T FREE MY *CONSCIENCE*.
I'M FOLLOWING UP ON HER SUBJECT...THE THUNDERBOLTS...
HAVEN'T SEEN 'EM SINCE *ABE JENKINS* AND HIS FRIENDS WENT OFF AFTER *GRAVITON*...
YOUR REPORT SAID AFTER HE REVEALED HIS IDENTITY TO YOU--
--YOU LET HIM USE YOUR SATELLITE UPLINK TO THE HOMELAND SECURITY OFFICE--
PRESS
--AND THEN YOU LET HIM GO?
YEAH. THEN HOURS LATER--
--THERE WAS THIS GIANT. SILENT FLASH OF LIGHT--
--AND IT WAS LIKE THE AIR--LIKE ALL *REALITY*--
--JUST *POPPED!*
BURTON CANYON POLICE

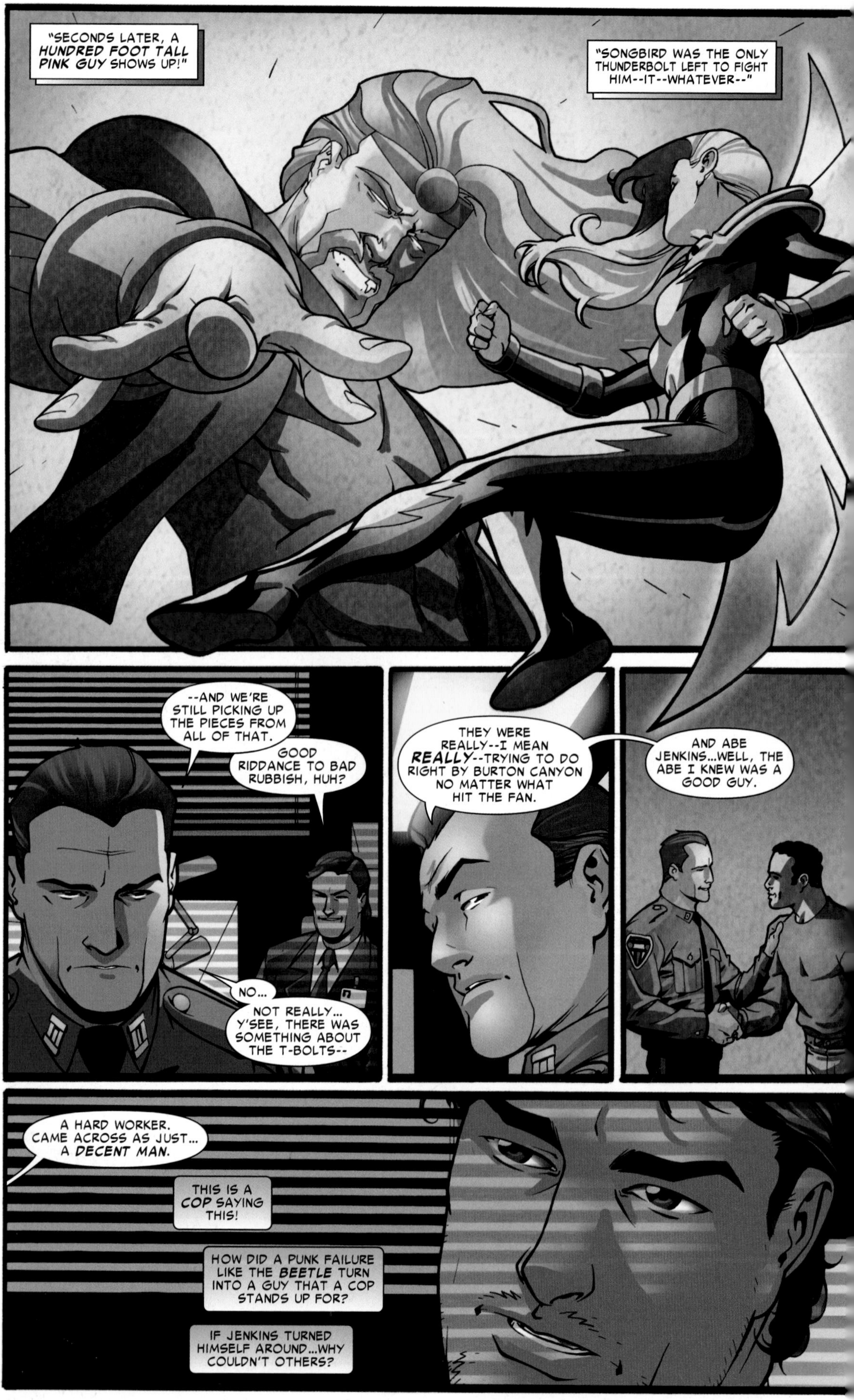
"SECONDS LATER, A HUNDRED FOOT TALL PINK GUY SHOWS UP!"
"SONGBIRD WAS THE ONLY THUNDERBOLT LEFT TO FIGHT HIM--IT--WHATEVER--"
--AND WE'RE STILL PICKING UP THE PIECES FROM ALL OF THAT.
GOOD RIDDANCE TO BAD RUBBISH, HUH?
NO...
NOT REALLY... Y'SEE, THERE WAS SOMETHING ABOUT THE T-BOLTS--
THEY WERE REALLY--I MEAN REALLY--TRYING TO DO RIGHT BY BURTON CANYON NO MATTER WHAT HIT THE FAN.
AND ABE JENKINS...WELL, THE ABE I KNEW WAS A GOOD GUY.
A HARD WORKER. CAME ACROSS AS JUST... A DECENT MAN.
THIS IS A COP SAYING THIS!
HOW DID A PUNK FAILURE LIKE THE BEETLE TURN INTO A GUY THAT A COP STANDS UP FOR?
IF JENKINS TURNED HIMSELF AROUND...WHY COULDN'T OTHERS?

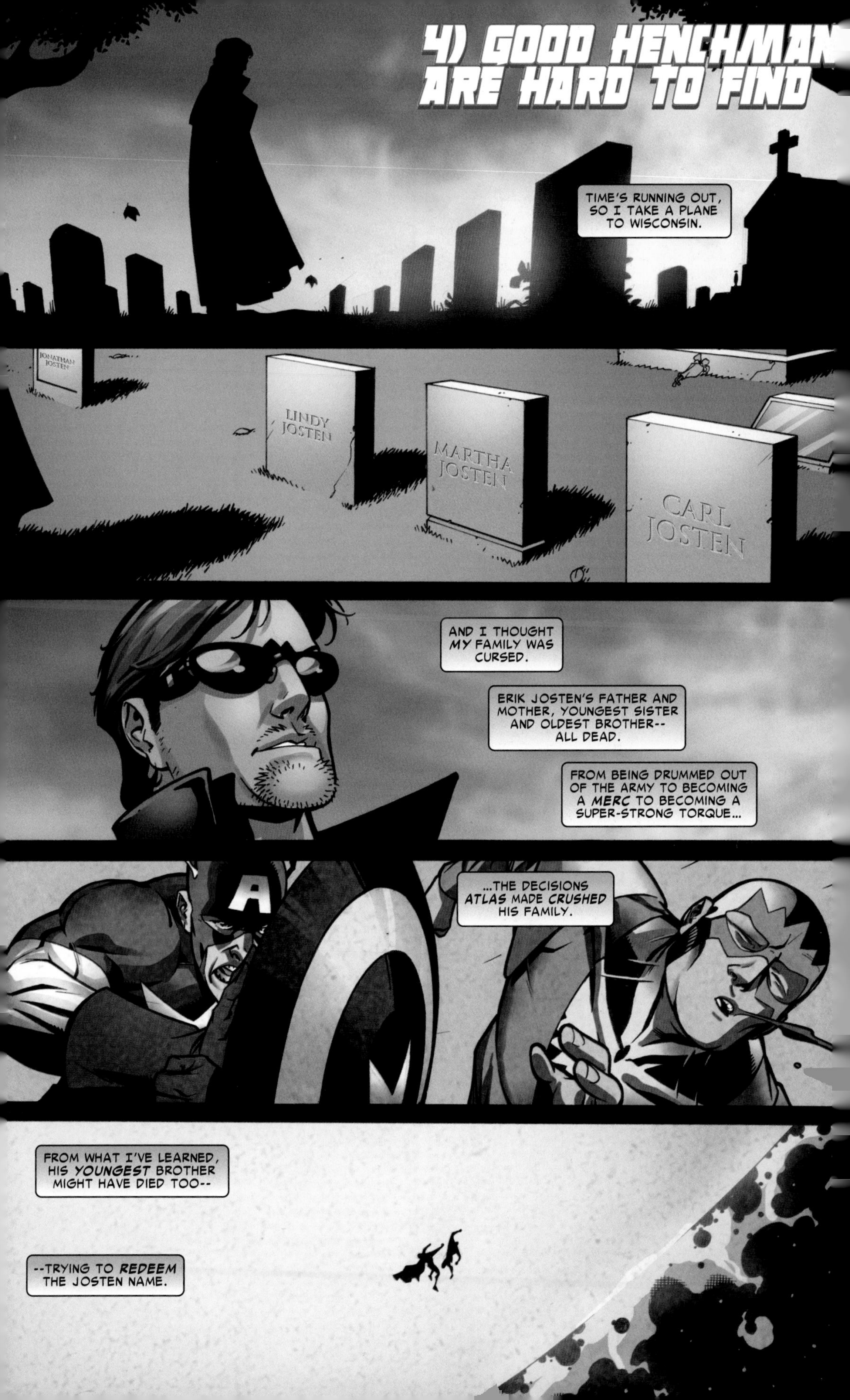
4) GOOD HENCHMAN ARE HARD TO FIND
TIME'S RUNNING OUT, SO I TAKE A PLANE TO WISCONSIN.
JONATHAN JOSTEN
LINDY JOSTEN
MARTHA JOSTEN
CARL JOSTEN
AND I THOUGHT MY FAMILY WAS CURSED.
ERIK JOSTEN'S FATHER AND MOTHER, YOUNGEST SISTER AND OLDEST BROTHER-- ALL DEAD.
FROM BEING DRUMMED OUT OF THE ARMY TO BECOMING A MERC TO BECOMING A SUPER-STRONG TORQUE...
...THE DECISIONS ATLAS MADE CRUSHED HIS FAMILY.
FROM WHAT I'VE LEARNED, HIS YOUNGEST BROTHER MIGHT HAVE DIED TOO--
--TRYING TO REDEEM THE JOSTEN NAME.

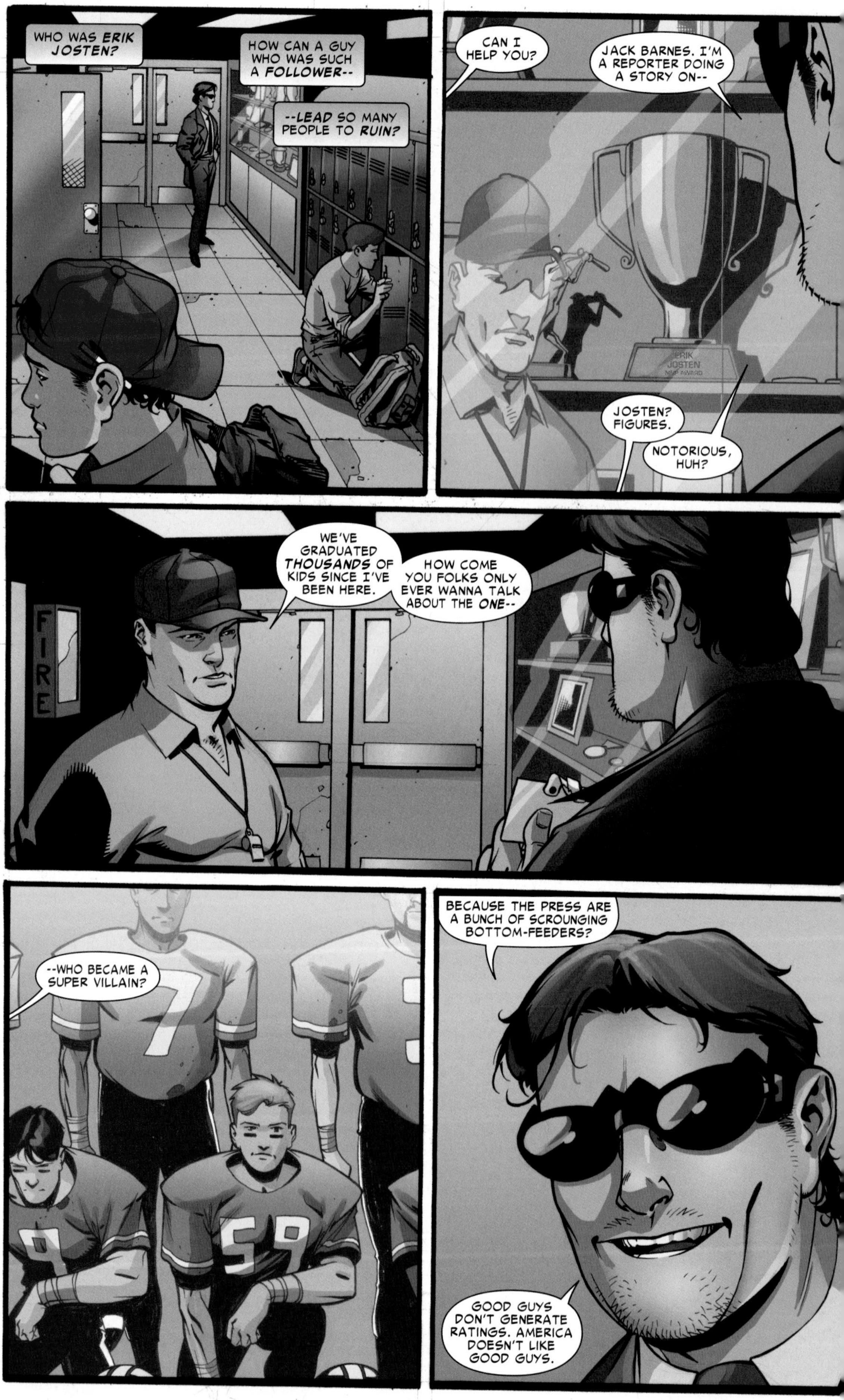
WHO WAS *ERIK JOSTEN?*
HOW CAN A GUY WHO WAS SUCH A *FOLLOWER*--
--*LEAD* SO MANY PEOPLE TO *RUIN?*
CAN I HELP YOU?
JACK BARNES. I'M A REPORTER DOING A STORY ON--
ERIK JOSTEN MVP AWARD
JOSTEN? FIGURES.
NOTORIOUS, HUH?
WE'VE GRADUATED *THOUSANDS* OF KIDS SINCE I'VE BEEN HERE.
HOW COME YOU FOLKS ONLY EVER WANNA TALK ABOUT THE *ONE*--
FIRE
--WHO BECAME A SUPER VILLAIN?
BECAUSE THE PRESS ARE A BUNCH OF SCROUNGING BOTTOM-FEEDERS?
GOOD GUYS DON'T GENERATE RATINGS. AMERICA DOESN'T LIKE GOOD GUYS.

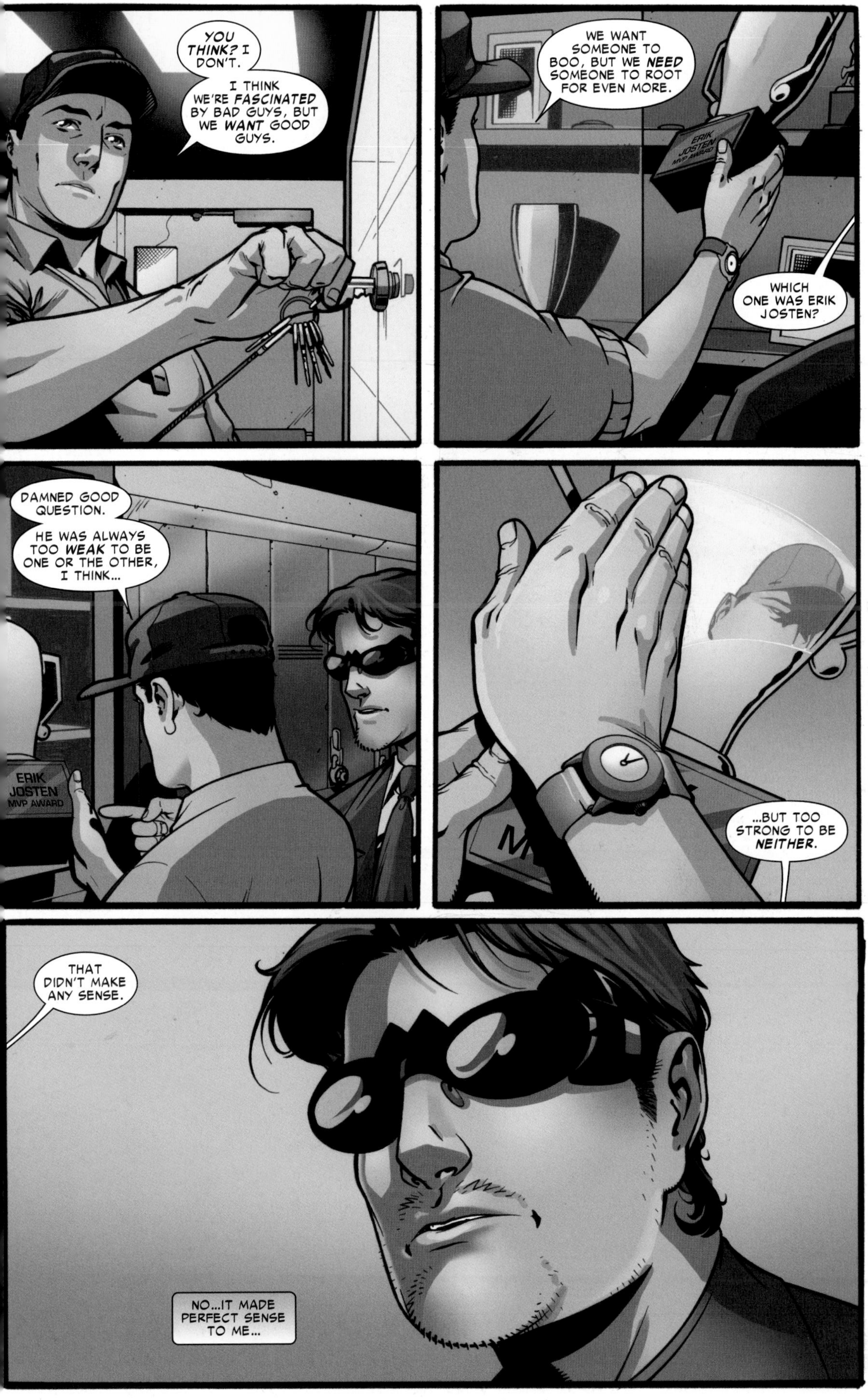
YOU THINK? I DON'T.
I THINK WE'RE FASCINATED BY BAD GUYS, BUT WE WANT GOOD GUYS.
WE WANT SOMEONE TO BOO, BUT WE NEED SOMEONE TO ROOT FOR EVEN MORE.
ERIK JOSTEN MVP AWARD
WHICH ONE WAS ERIK JOSTEN?
DAMNED GOOD QUESTION.
HE WAS ALWAYS TOO WEAK TO BE ONE OR THE OTHER, I THINK...
ERIK JOSTEN MVP AWARD
...BUT TOO STRONG TO BE NEITHER.
THAT DIDN'T MAKE ANY SENSE.
NO...IT MADE PERFECT SENSE TO ME...

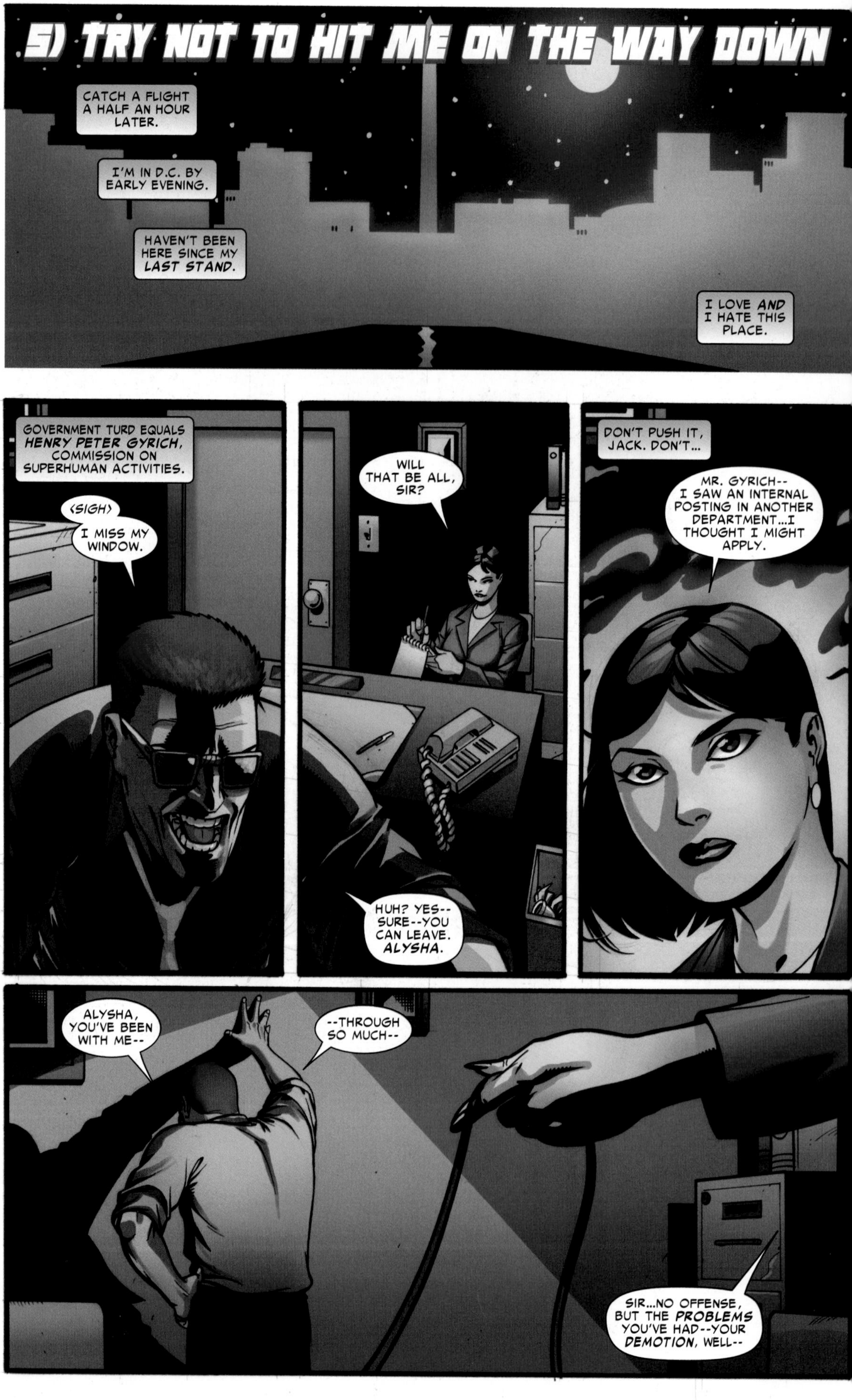
5) TRY NOT TO HIT ME ON THE WAY DOWN
CATCH A FLIGHT A HALF AN HOUR LATER.
I'M IN D.C. BY EARLY EVENING.
HAVEN'T BEEN HERE SINCE MY *LAST STAND*.
I LOVE *AND* I HATE THIS PLACE.
GOVERNMENT TURD EQUALS *HENRY PETER GYRICH*, COMMISSION ON SUPERHUMAN ACTIVITIES.
<SIGH> I MISS MY WINDOW.
WILL THAT BE ALL, SIR?
HUH? YES--SURE--YOU CAN LEAVE. *ALYSHA*.
DON'T PUSH IT, JACK. DON'T...
MR. GYRICH--I SAW AN INTERNAL POSTING IN ANOTHER DEPARTMENT...I THOUGHT I MIGHT APPLY.
ALYSHA, YOU'VE BEEN WITH ME--
--THROUGH SO MUCH--
SIR...NO OFFENSE, BUT THE *PROBLEMS* YOU'VE HAD--YOUR *DEMOTION*, WELL--

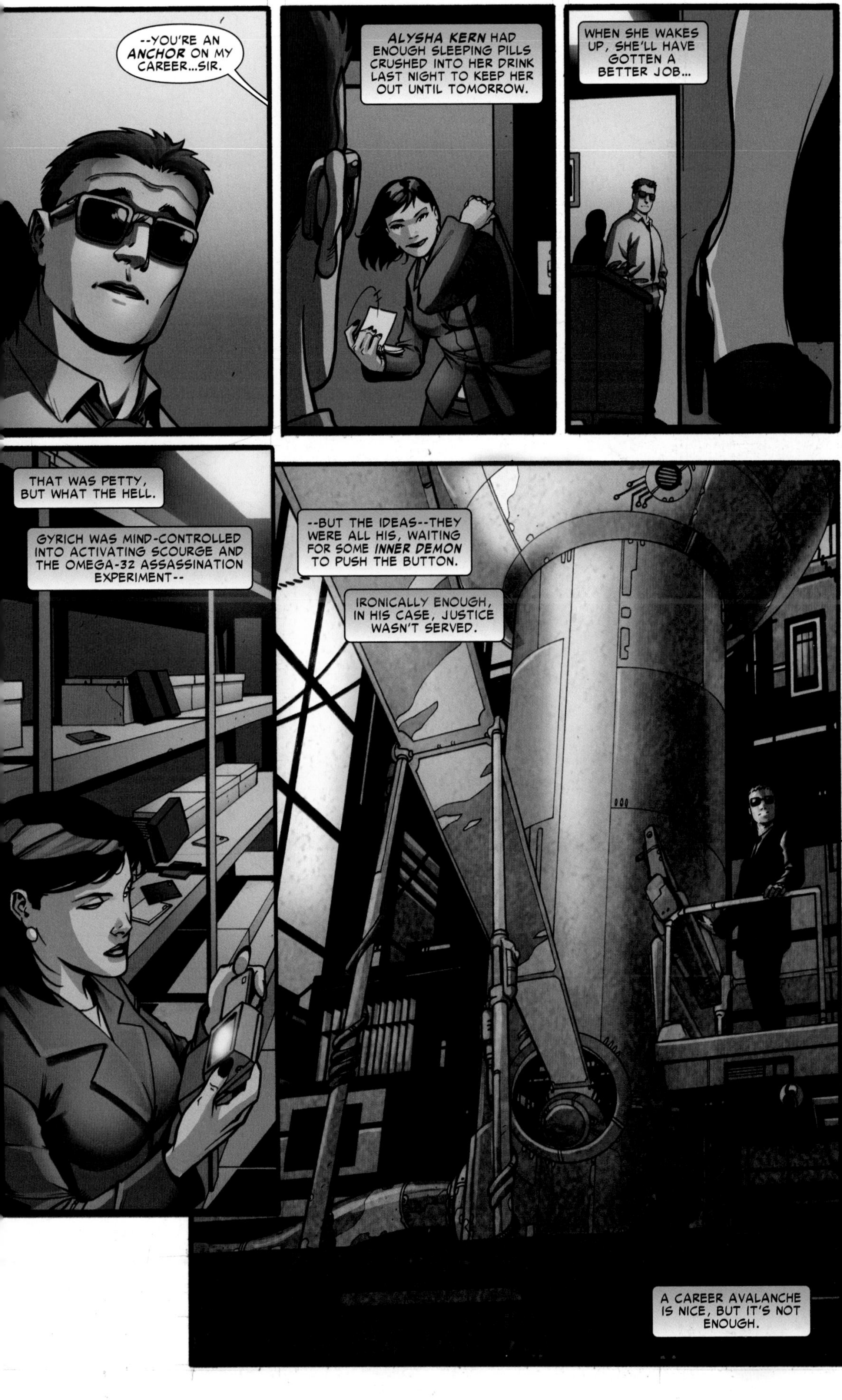
--YOU'RE AN ANCHOR ON MY CAREER...SIR.
ALYSHA KERN HAD ENOUGH SLEEPING PILLS CRUSHED INTO HER DRINK LAST NIGHT TO KEEP HER OUT UNTIL TOMORROW.
WHEN SHE WAKES UP, SHE'LL HAVE GOTTEN A BETTER JOB...
THAT WAS PETTY, BUT WHAT THE HELL.
GYRICH WAS MIND-CONTROLLED INTO ACTIVATING SCOURGE AND THE OMEGA-32 ASSASSINATION EXPERIMENT--
--BUT THE IDEAS--THEY WERE ALL HIS, WAITING FOR SOME INNER DEMON TO PUSH THE BUTTON.
IRONICALLY ENOUGH, IN HIS CASE, JUSTICE WASN'T SERVED.
A CAREER AVALANCHE IS NICE, BUT IT'S NOT ENOUGH.

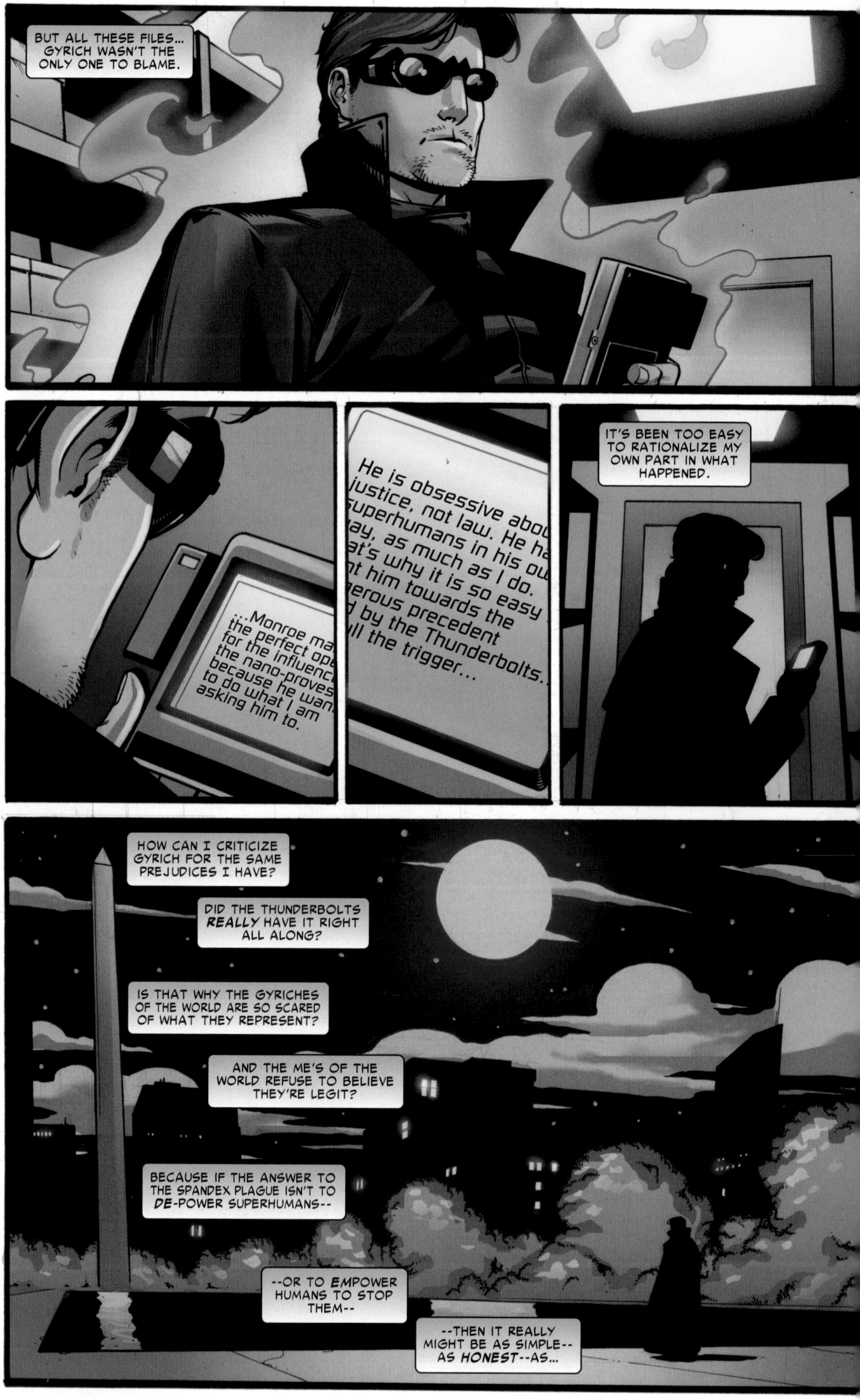
BUT ALL THESE FILES... GYRICH WASN'T THE ONLY ONE TO BLAME.
...Monroe ma
the perfect ope
for the influenc
the nano-proves
because he wan
to do what I am
asking him to.
He is obsessive abou
justice, not law. He ha
superhumans in his ow
way, as much as I do.
at's why it is so easy
nt him towards the
gerous precedent
d by the Thunderbolts..
ull the trigger...
IT'S BEEN TOO EASY TO RATIONALIZE MY OWN PART IN WHAT HAPPENED.
HOW CAN I CRITICIZE GYRICH FOR THE SAME PREJUDICES I HAVE?
DID THE THUNDERBOLTS REALLY HAVE IT RIGHT ALL ALONG?
IS THAT WHY THE GYRICHES OF THE WORLD ARE SO SCARED OF WHAT THEY REPRESENT?
AND THE ME'S OF THE WORLD REFUSE TO BELIEVE THEY'RE LEGIT?
BECAUSE IF THE ANSWER TO THE SPANDEX PLAGUE ISN'T TO DE-POWER SUPERHUMANS--
--OR TO EMPOWER HUMANS TO STOP THEM--
--THEN IT REALLY MIGHT BE AS SIMPLE-- AS HONEST--AS...

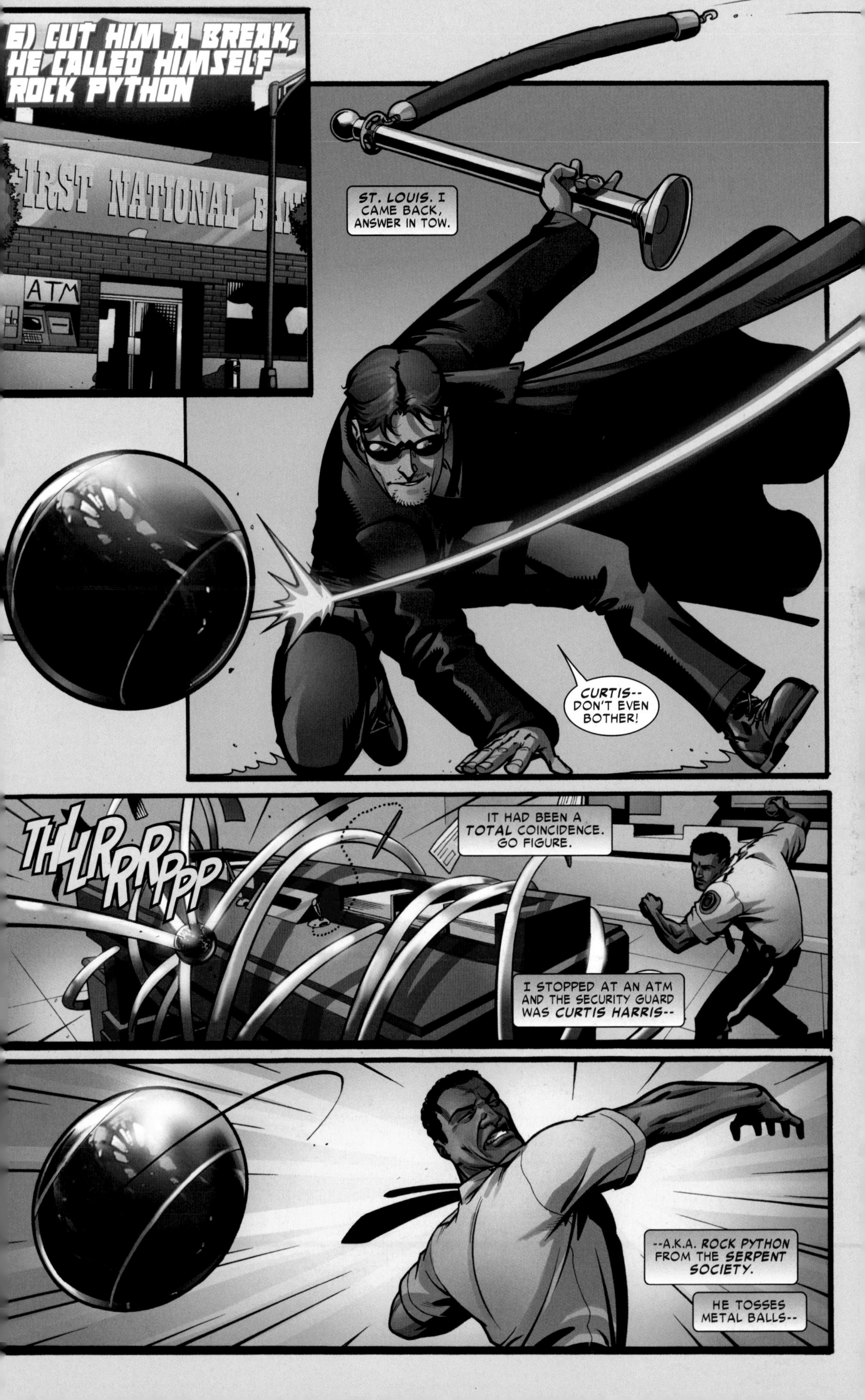
6) CUT HIM A BREAK, HE CALLED HIMSELF ROCK PYTHON
FIRST NATIONAL BA
ATM
ST. LOUIS. I CAME BACK, ANSWER IN TOW.
CURTIS-- DON'T EVEN BOTHER!
THLRRRPPP
IT HAD BEEN A TOTAL COINCIDENCE. GO FIGURE.
I STOPPED AT AN ATM AND THE SECURITY GUARD WAS CURTIS HARRIS--
--A.K.A. ROCK PYTHON FROM THE SERPENT SOCIETY.
HE TOSSES METAL BALLS--

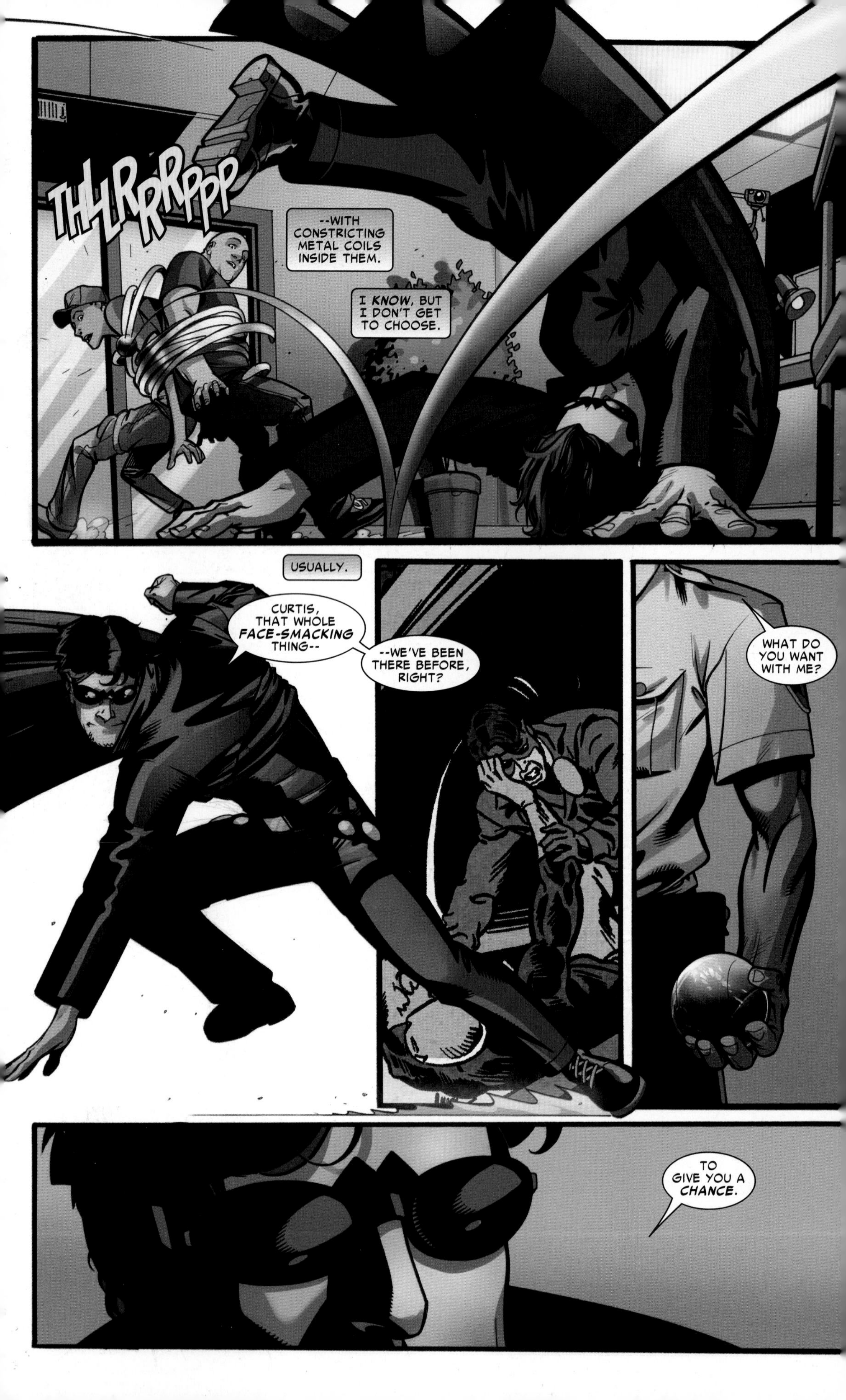
THHLRRRPPP
--WITH CONSTRICTING METAL COILS INSIDE THEM.
I KNOW, BUT I DON'T GET TO CHOOSE.
USUALLY.
CURTIS, THAT WHOLE FACE-SMACKING THING--
--WE'VE BEEN THERE BEFORE, RIGHT?
WHAT DO YOU WANT WITH ME?
TO GIVE YOU A CHANCE.

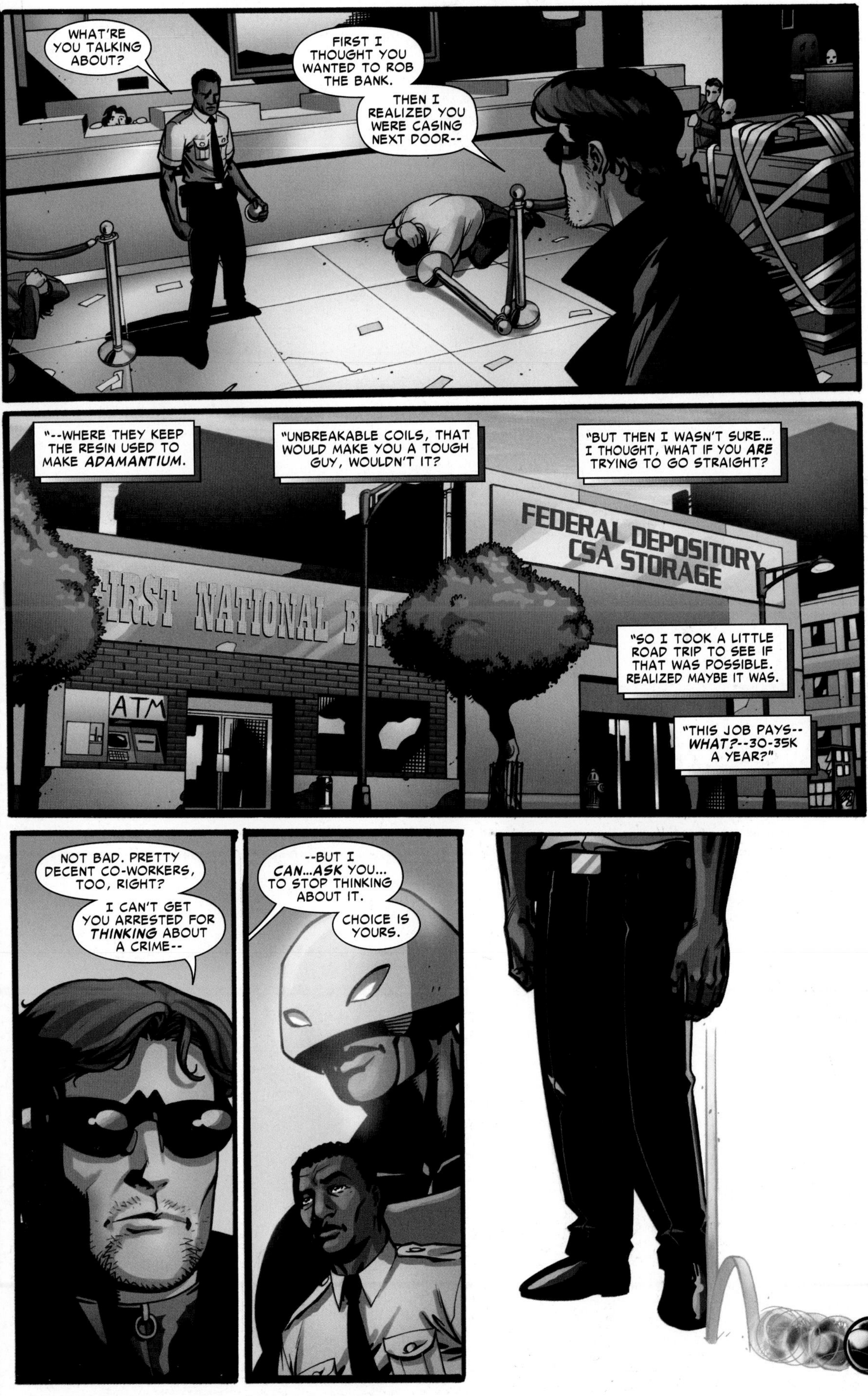
WHAT'RE YOU TALKING ABOUT?
FIRST I THOUGHT YOU WANTED TO ROB THE BANK.
THEN I REALIZED YOU WERE CASING NEXT DOOR--
"--WHERE THEY KEEP THE RESIN USED TO MAKE ADAMANTIUM.
"UNBREAKABLE COILS, THAT WOULD MAKE YOU A TOUGH GUY, WOULDN'T IT?
"BUT THEN I WASN'T SURE... I THOUGHT, WHAT IF YOU ARE TRYING TO GO STRAIGHT?
FEDERAL DEPOSITORY CSA STORAGE
IRST NATIONAL B
ATM
"SO I TOOK A LITTLE ROAD TRIP TO SEE IF THAT WAS POSSIBLE. REALIZED MAYBE IT WAS.
"THIS JOB PAYS-- WHAT?--30-35K A YEAR?"
NOT BAD. PRETTY DECENT CO-WORKERS, TOO, RIGHT?
I CAN'T GET YOU ARRESTED FOR THINKING ABOUT A CRIME--
--BUT I CAN...ASK YOU... TO STOP THINKING ABOUT IT.
CHOICE IS YOURS.

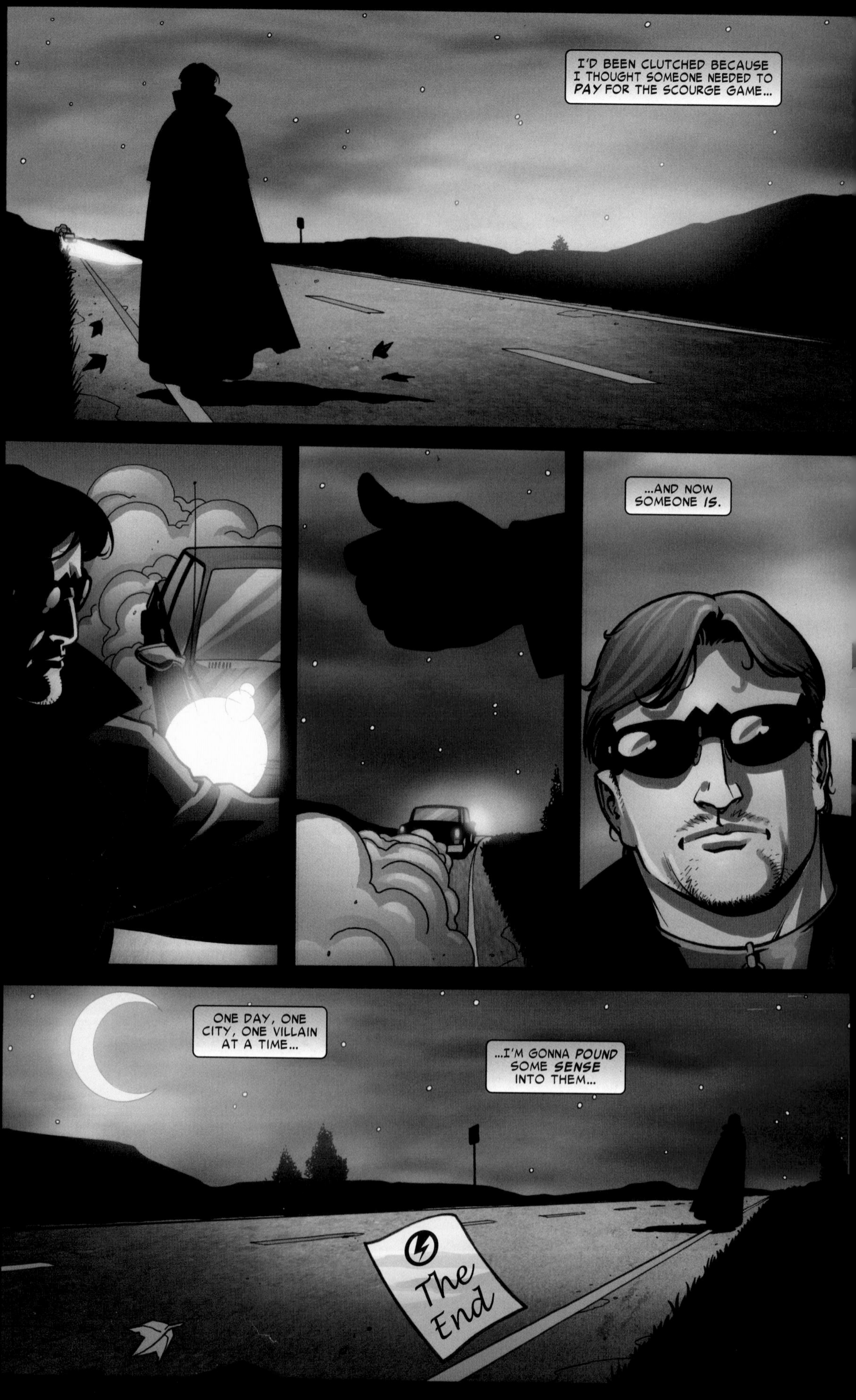
I'D BEEN CLUTCHED BECAUSE I THOUGHT SOMEONE NEEDED TO PAY FOR THE SCOURGE GAME...
...AND NOW SOMEONE IS.
ONE DAY, ONE CITY, ONE VILLAIN AT A TIME...
...I'M GONNA POUND SOME SENSE INTO THEM...
The End

JUSTICE, LIKE LIGHTNING...
THUNDERBOLTS

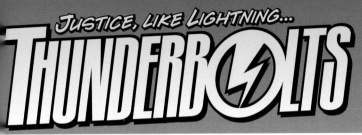

Hello, loyal Thunderbolts readers!

Thanks for joining us on this journey into Thunderbolts past and what might have been in the life of Jack Monroe. The plot for this comic dates back to 2001, so in order to find some appropriate letters for this page, we had to make use of modern technology. Special thanks to Spider-Man editor Stephen Wacker for extending the call to write in to his 4,585 followers on Twitter. (Fortunately, they responded much better to this than to his request that they each send him $50. I've assured him that it's just because they don't want him to get flush with cash and stop editing his books.)

Dear Marvel,

I am super excited to hear about you reprinting my favorite era of Thunderbolts! I read the old back issues recently, especially the issues by Fabian Nicieza, and thought they were just so cool. Jack Monroe as Nomad was such a interesting character because he was a leader of super-powered beings but was just a man with an incredible intelligence and drive. If he fights Rock Python in the issue you are printing, I will definitely be picking it up as I cannot get enough of this era's Thunderbolts. Please bring Jack Monroe back to the comics. Maybe he was also shot with a time bullet? Justice, like Lightning!

Mike Jaffe, Seattle, WA

Hi Mike,

Thanks so much for writing in. I hope the issue lived up to your expectations and you enjoyed it thoroughly. If you read Fabian Nicieza's lovely opening thoughts, then you already know that this isn't a reprint. It is actually a brand new issue (that just happens to have spent 10 years in the drawer of Tom Brevoort's desk. The top drawer, I'm sure.) And though Jack Monroe may live on in the "perpetual fan fiction" of Fabian's head, to my knowledge there just aren't that many time bullets out there. But apparently wanting us to bring Jack Monroe back from the dead is a common hope among people named Mike...

Dear Marvel,

I've been waiting patiently for roughly...17 years. That is when the final issue of the Nomad regular series ended. Nevermind the whole silly "Jack Monroe became Scourge and was killed" plot (it wouldn't be the first time chronology was ignored in comics), Jack Monroe is Nomad and we need him back. How is it possible that with almost every second tier character getting a reboot, limited series, graphic novel or developing screenplay, no one is talking about Nomad? The Captain America movie trailer is out so how is it that Nomad was forgotten?

The good news is, you can make it up to me. Firstly, release a reprint (maybe in graphic novel form) of the Jack Monroe Nomad storylines starting with the Fabian Nicieza storyline from Marvel Comics Presents #14 and Captain America Annual #9, the four-issue mini-series and the story from Captain America Annual #10. Once that is released, you can split the 25 issues into a series of graphic novels (the Dead Man's Hand storyline should include those issues of Daredevil and Punisher as well) and you have excellent promotion for a new series and a chance to cash in on the Captain America universe because Jack Monroe will either have to appear in the movie sequel or in his own smaller movie (along the lines of Blade and the rumored Iron Fist). He's basically The Road Warrior for the 21st century!

Now, while I won't need regular updates on the progression of the relaunch you can repay me by keeping me in the loop with the release of the new series and the film (in which I would like to assist with the screenplay, the casting of the lead and have a cameo role along the lines of Stan the Man).

Please, no thanks is necessary for this brilliant plan but let's get it going. Time's a wastin' don't you know.

Make Mine Marvel
Mike Trigiani

Wow, Mike. You put...a lot of thought into that. I'm sorry to say, we have no plans to resurrect Jack Monroe any time soon. I hope this doesn't interfere too much with the trajectory of your film career.

Dear Marvel,

Really the cool thing about TBolts for me is that it has always been a fantastic way to take villains who normally would be painfully two-dimensional and give them a platform to be as interesting as their heroic counterparts. You don't fall into the "anti-hero" trap of Punisher or Wolverine. Gritty and edgy aren't inherently cool. Heroes should be able to be heroes. Villains should be able to be villains. And there should be a space for that line to blur, but it shouldn't sacrifice the two traditional camps.

Mike Rozycki, Richmond, VA

Thanks for reading...Mike. The current series of Thunderbolts continues to play with these ideas and should have some exciting developments when disaster hits the Raft during Fear Itself!

Thunderbolts Crew-

I first started reading Thunderbolts with issue number 1. I was 12 at the time of the launch and it was the first new book I really latched onto. It will always hold a place in my heart as one of the first things I contributed my money to and made a hit. I still break out some of those old issues when the mood fits. They were funny, sad and just plain cool all at the same time, exactly what I grew to expect from a Marvel Comic. The thing that really got me hooked was the characters though. The great thing was that, even though they were bad guys, they weren't bloodthirsty killers, they weren't insane (Well, in the grand scheme of Marvel characters anyway). They were really just a bunch of screwups trying to make things right. They wanted to do the right thing even if they didn't always know what it was or how to do it. Even when Hawkeye showed up things never really turned out right but they kept on trying. Thanks for the years of great books about a bunch of no-good screwups.

Josh Sinason

And thank you, Josh, for abating my growing paranoia about a cult of Thunderbolts readers named Mike dedicated to bringing Jack Monroe back from the dead. You really got to the heart of what Thunderbolts is all about. I'm glad we've kept you as a faithful reader over the years.

And speaking of what Thunderbolts is all about, I will leave you all with a few thoughts from its creators:

"It was a fun book to work on, full of lots of interesting and exciting characters... both to read and to draw. It was a blast getting to design a whole new cast of characters...all the while knowing we were pulling the wool over everyone's eyes. The book was simply a lot of fun, and just kept evolving while we worked on it."

-Mark Bagley

"When we started THUNDERBOLTS, the concept was simple: The Master of Evil disguise themselves as heroes as part of a scheme to take over the world. Before the scheme's done, some of them discover they kinda like this 'hero' thing.

When we started, some readers said we wouldn't last 8 issues. Then that we wouldn't last 12. Then 25. Then 50. And I had to stop and think, "Geez, if we lasted 50 issues, that's not exactly a failure, is it?"

And now it's over ten years later, and over 150 issues, and T-BOLTS is going strong. I don't think that can be said about many new characters/teams/concepts to be introduced at Marvel after, say, 1975 or so. And here we are with a special issue publishing a fill-in story that never got used, of all things.

I'm pretty proud of THUNDERBOLTS. That Mark Bagley and I were able to create something that's lasted this long, that's been through such change, so many creators, so many twists, staying unpredictable and different the whole time. Thanks for sticking around--anyone wanna try for 250 issues? 500?"

-Kurt Busiek

We're shutting the vault for now, but keep an eye out for the next time it opens! (Especially if you're missing Johnny Storm.)

Said with a smile,
Ellie Pyle

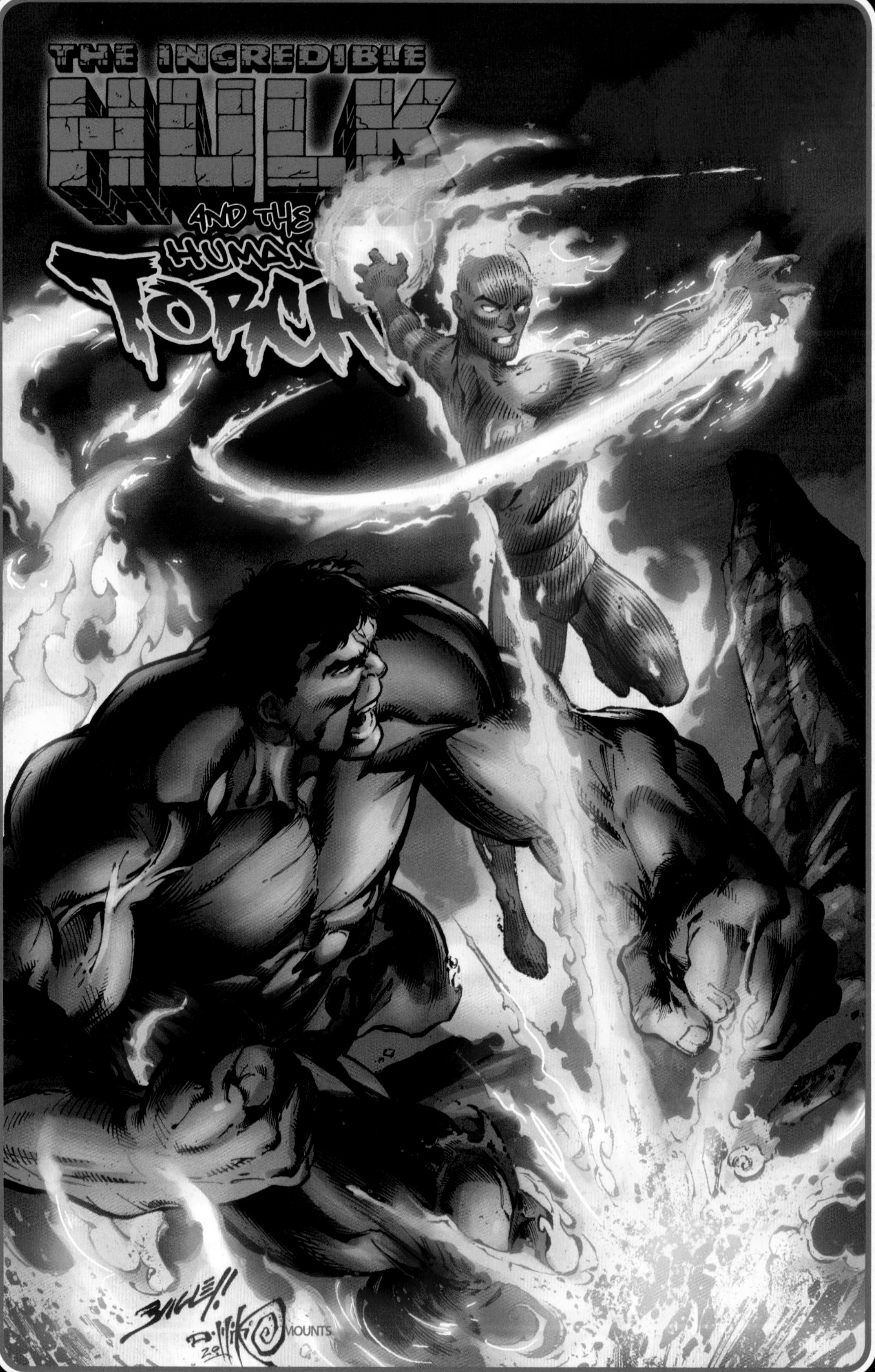
THE INCREDIBLE
HULK
AND THE
HUMAN
TORCH
MOUNTS

SECRETS OF THE VAULT!

TOGETHER AGAIN—FOR THE FIRST TIME! A MARVEL TEAM-UP 25 YEARS IN THE MAKING!

STEVE DITKO. "Sturdy" Steve. Second only to Jack Kirby in his artistic influence on the early 1960s Marvel Comics. Co-created Dr. Strange and a scrawny super hero you may have heard of named Spider-Man. A Legend.

It's not every day you get to work with a Legend. Sometimes you only get one chance.

My chance came in 1986. Mike Barr was the writer/editor of the Outsiders for DC Comics, and had a 7-page Black Lightning backup penciled by Ditko. He needed an inker. He asked me. I agreed instantly, enthusiastically. I could not have been more thrilled. Ditko was one of The Greats—his style instantly identifiable and undeniably unique—while I was just an eager, energetic young inker. It was a chance that I couldn't pass up.

But it was a chance that I screwed up. Being eager, energetic and young, I was also overcommitted. With too much to do and not enough hours in the day, something had to go. Sadly, reluctantly, it was the Ditko job.

Best thing that could have happened—for the backup story and for me.

Mike Barr quickly brought in Jerry Ordway to ink the story, an artist I'm about 1/10th as talented as even on my best day. The Ditko/Ordway art team was stunning, and far beyond anything I would have done. One of a number of times in my career that I was "replaced" by someone far, far better than I was.

Jump forward twenty-five years.

Tom Brevoort asks if I'd be interested in re-dialoguing and finishing the art to an old MARVEL TEAM-UP inventory story that had never been published. A story drawn by…Steve Ditko! And—in a freakish twist of fate—drawn about twenty-five years earlier, around the same time Ditko drew the backup I was supposed to ink! Of course I wanted to do it. I almost felt destined to do it.

And best of all: I'm a much better artist than I was back then. Not Ordway-good, but good enough to do some level of justice to Ditko's work.

Working on the story itself was always fun and at times challenging. Ditko usually drew seven or more panels on each of these pages, so by today's standards this would be a 40+ page story. This probably has something to do with Jack C. Harris' storyline—which is very dense—and Ditko's natural sense of pacing, which often leans toward more panels and smaller moments. The original dialogue was fine for the mid-80s, but needed to be stripped down and simplified for today's audience. I also decided to have Johnny Storm narrate the story—mostly because I like Johnny and really miss him now that he's gone. (At least, as "gone" as anyone in comics ever is—right, Bucky?)

Inking Ditko…have to admit, I was nervous. Like I said: he's a Legend. And I probably wasn't going to get another chance, so I wanted to do it right. Took a few pages, but I finally hit a stride I was happy with. It's hard to explain, but Ditko and my natural drawing styles are both somewhat… mannered, and because of that I connected with his work in ways I hadn't expected to. I also got a much deeper appreciation and understanding of why he's a Legend. His storytelling is crystal clear and impeccable. Everything—everything—the story needs is there in his art. He doesn't skimp, he doesn't take shortcuts. And his characters are so fun, so visually interesting, so…Ditko!

It's not every day you get to work with a Legend. Sometimes you only get one chance.

But sometimes—if you're unbelievably lucky—you get a second.

—**Karl Kesel**

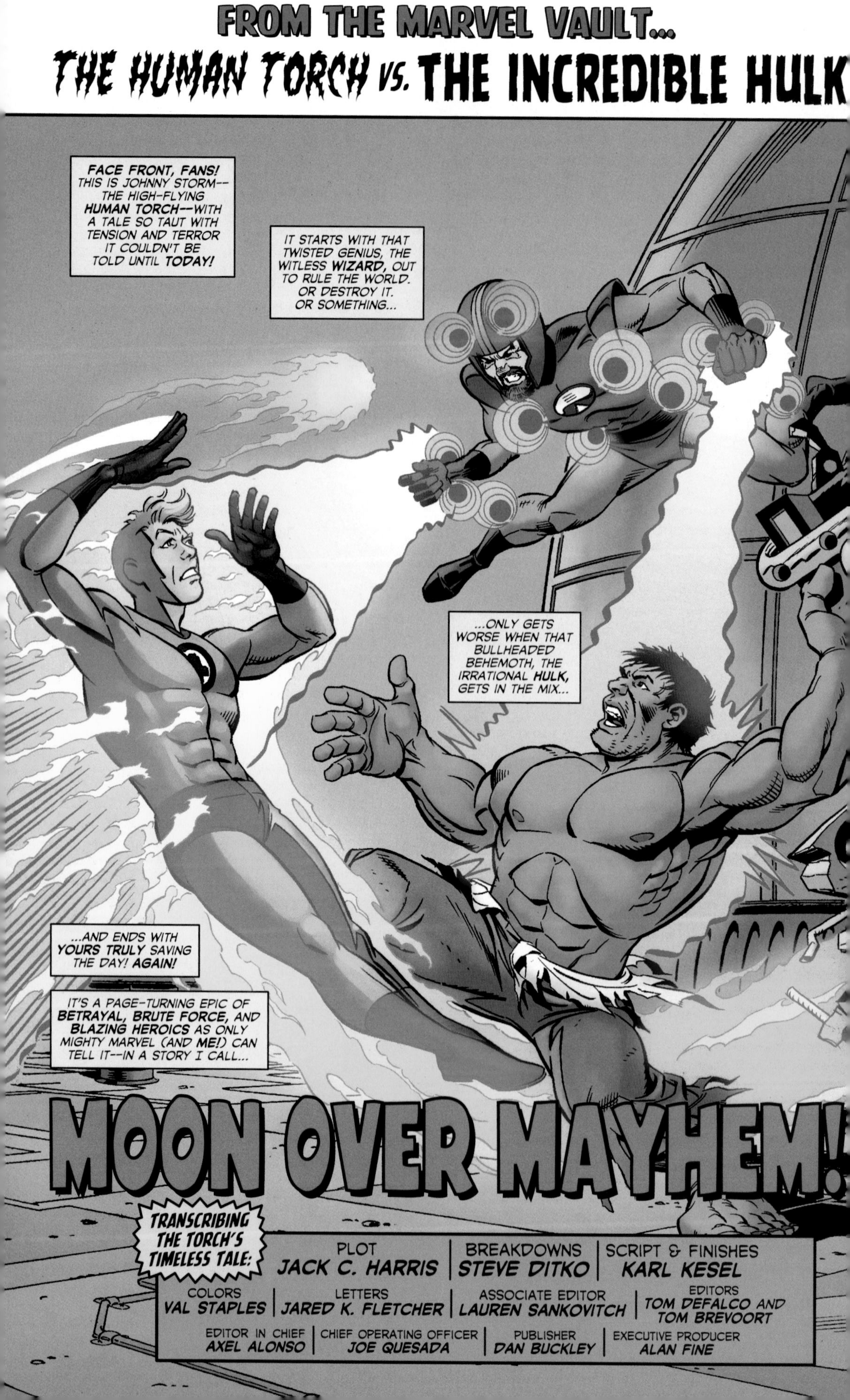

FROM THE MARVEL VAULT...
THE HUMAN TORCH VS. THE INCREDIBLE HULK
FACE FRONT, FANS! THIS IS JOHNNY STORM-- THE HIGH-FLYING HUMAN TORCH--WITH A TALE SO TAUT WITH TENSION AND TERROR IT COULDN'T BE TOLD UNTIL TODAY!
IT STARTS WITH THAT TWISTED GENIUS, THE WITLESS WIZARD, OUT TO RULE THE WORLD. OR DESTROY IT. OR SOMETHING...
...ONLY GETS WORSE WHEN THAT BULLHEADED BEHEMOTH, THE IRRATIONAL HULK, GETS IN THE MIX...
...AND ENDS WITH YOURS TRULY SAVING THE DAY! AGAIN!
IT'S A PAGE-TURNING EPIC OF BETRAYAL, BRUTE FORCE, AND BLAZING HEROICS AS ONLY MIGHTY MARVEL (AND ME!) CAN TELL IT--IN A STORY I CALL...
MOON OVER MAYHEM!
TRANSCRIBING THE TORCH'S TIMELESS TALE:
PLOT JACK C. HARRIS
BREAKDOWNS STEVE DITKO
SCRIPT & FINISHES KARL KESEL
COLORS VAL STAPLES
LETTERS JARED K. FLETCHER
ASSOCIATE EDITOR LAUREN SANKOVITCH
EDITORS TOM DEFALCO AND TOM BREVOORT
EDITOR IN CHIEF AXEL ALONSO
CHIEF OPERATING OFFICER JOE QUESADA
PUBLISHER DAN BUCKLEY
EXECUTIVE PRODUCER ALAN FINE

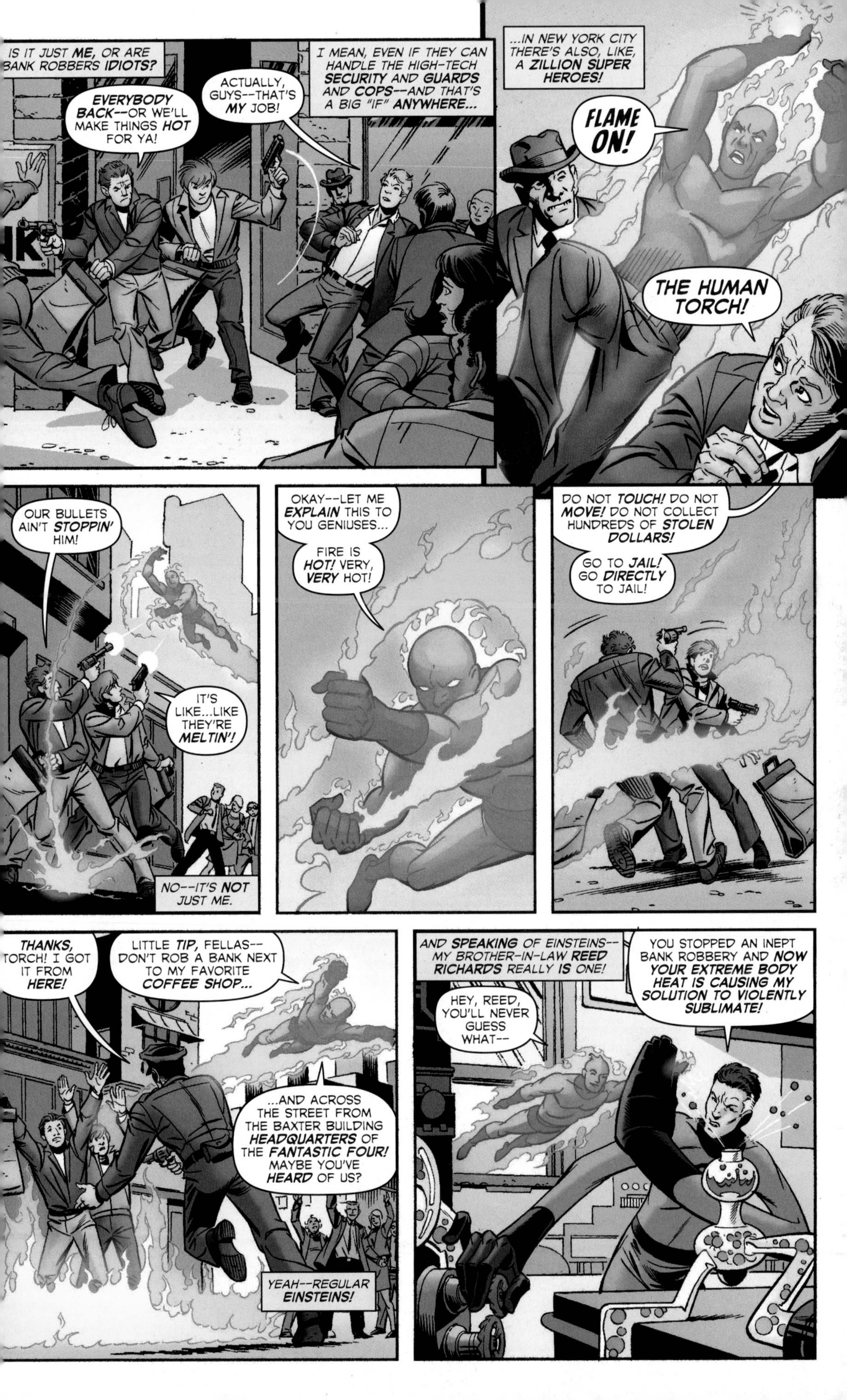
IS IT JUST ME, OR ARE BANK ROBBERS IDIOTS?
EVERYBODY BACK--OR WE'LL MAKE THINGS HOT FOR YA!
ACTUALLY, GUYS--THAT'S MY JOB!
I MEAN, EVEN IF THEY CAN HANDLE THE HIGH-TECH SECURITY AND GUARDS AND COPS--AND THAT'S A BIG "IF" ANYWHERE...
...IN NEW YORK CITY THERE'S ALSO, LIKE, A ZILLION SUPER HEROES!
FLAME ON!
THE HUMAN TORCH!
OUR BULLETS AIN'T STOPPIN' HIM!
IT'S LIKE...LIKE THEY'RE MELTIN'!
NO--IT'S NOT JUST ME.
OKAY--LET ME EXPLAIN THIS TO YOU GENIUSES...
FIRE IS HOT! VERY, VERY HOT!
DO NOT TOUCH! DO NOT MOVE! DO NOT COLLECT HUNDREDS OF STOLEN DOLLARS!
GO TO JAIL! GO DIRECTLY TO JAIL!
THANKS, TORCH! I GOT IT FROM HERE!
LITTLE TIP, FELLAS--DON'T ROB A BANK NEXT TO MY FAVORITE COFFEE SHOP...
...AND ACROSS THE STREET FROM THE BAXTER BUILDING HEADQUARTERS OF THE FANTASTIC FOUR! MAYBE YOU'VE HEARD OF US?
YEAH--REGULAR EINSTEINS!
AND SPEAKING OF EINSTEINS--MY BROTHER-IN-LAW REED RICHARDS REALLY IS ONE!
HEY, REED, YOU'LL NEVER GUESS WHAT--
YOU STOPPED AN INEPT BANK ROBBERY AND NOW YOUR EXTREME BODY HEAT IS CAUSING MY SOLUTION TO VIOLENTLY SUBLIMATE!

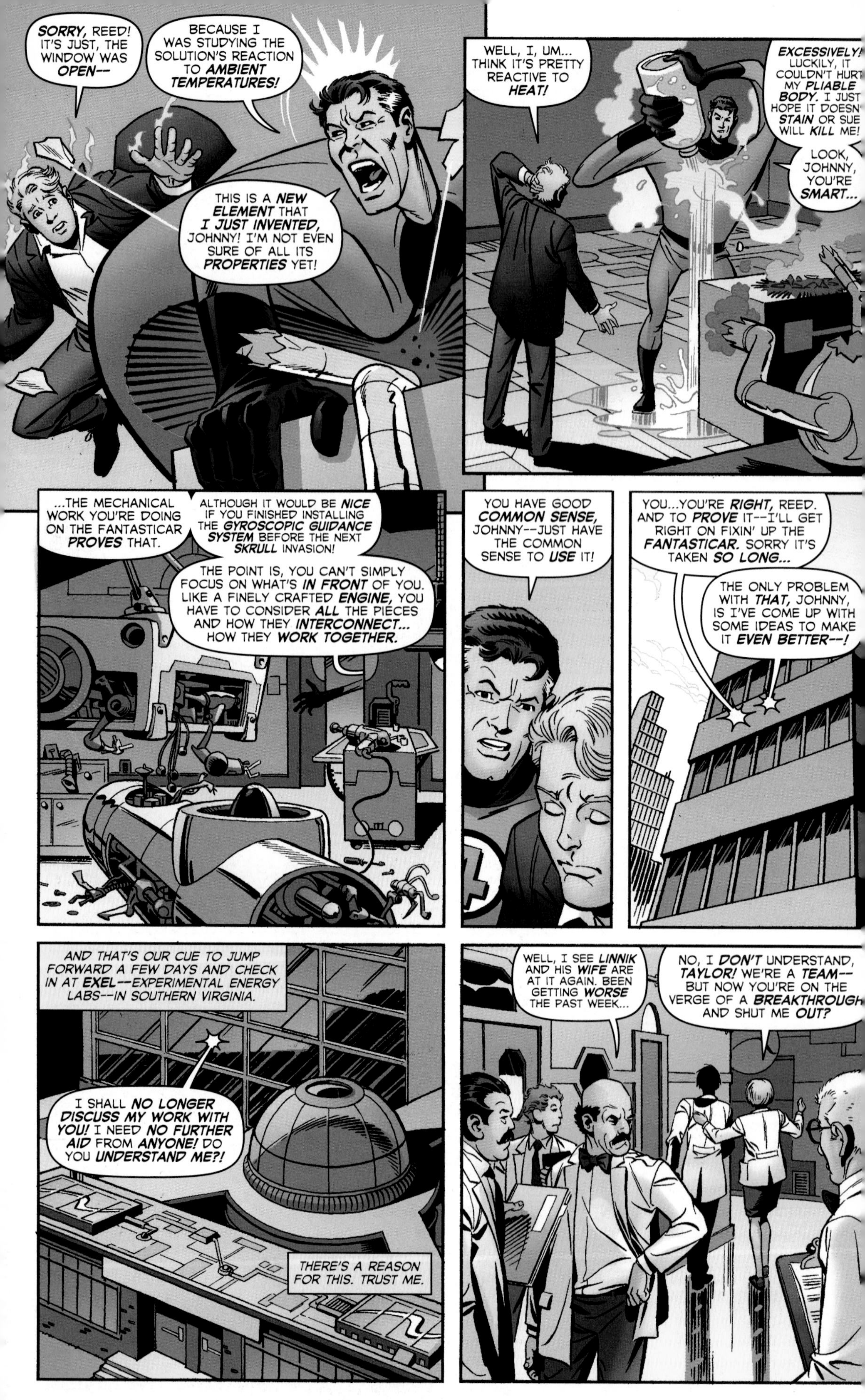
SORRY, REED! IT'S JUST, THE WINDOW WAS OPEN--
BECAUSE I WAS STUDYING THE SOLUTION'S REACTION TO AMBIENT TEMPERATURES!
THIS IS A NEW ELEMENT THAT I JUST INVENTED, JOHNNY! I'M NOT EVEN SURE OF ALL ITS PROPERTIES YET!
WELL, I, UM... THINK IT'S PRETTY REACTIVE TO HEAT!
EXCESSIVELY! LUCKILY, IT COULDN'T HURT MY PLIABLE BODY. I JUST HOPE IT DOESN' STAIN OR SUE WILL KILL ME!
LOOK, JOHNNY, YOU'RE SMART...
...THE MECHANICAL WORK YOU'RE DOING ON THE FANTASTICAR PROVES THAT.
ALTHOUGH IT WOULD BE NICE IF YOU FINISHED INSTALLING THE GYROSCOPIC GUIDANCE SYSTEM BEFORE THE NEXT SKRULL INVASION!
THE POINT IS, YOU CAN'T SIMPLY FOCUS ON WHAT'S IN FRONT OF YOU. LIKE A FINELY CRAFTED ENGINE, YOU HAVE TO CONSIDER ALL THE PIECES AND HOW THEY INTERCONNECT... HOW THEY WORK TOGETHER.
YOU HAVE GOOD COMMON SENSE, JOHNNY--JUST HAVE THE COMMON SENSE TO USE IT!
YOU...YOU'RE RIGHT, REED. AND TO PROVE IT--I'LL GET RIGHT ON FIXIN' UP THE FANTASTICAR. SORRY IT'S TAKEN SO LONG...
THE ONLY PROBLEM WITH THAT, JOHNNY, IS I'VE COME UP WITH SOME IDEAS TO MAKE IT EVEN BETTER--!
AND THAT'S OUR CUE TO JUMP FORWARD A FEW DAYS AND CHECK IN AT EXEL--EXPERIMENTAL ENERGY LABS--IN SOUTHERN VIRGINIA.
I SHALL NO LONGER DISCUSS MY WORK WITH YOU! I NEED NO FURTHER AID FROM ANYONE! DO YOU UNDERSTAND ME?!
THERE'S A REASON FOR THIS. TRUST ME.
WELL, I SEE LINNIK AND HIS WIFE ARE AT IT AGAIN. BEEN GETTING WORSE THE PAST WEEK...
NO, I DON'T UNDERSTAND, TAYLOR! WE'RE A TEAM-- BUT NOW YOU'RE ON THE VERGE OF A BREAKTHROUGH AND SHUT ME OUT?

CASSIE—TAPPING INTO THE MOON'S *MAGNETIC ENERGY* IS...IS MORE *DANGEROUS* THAN WE REALIZED! I *REFUSE* TO *EXPOSE* YOU TO THAT LEVEL OF *RISK!*

THAT'S *BULL*, TAYLOR. THE PROCESS IS COMPLETELY *SAFE.* OUR CALCULATIONS *PROVED—*

AND I'VE MOVED FAR *BEYOND* THOSE CALCULATIONS! BEYOND WHAT *ANYONE* AT *EXEL* COULD EVEN *COMPREHEND!*

I'VE CHANGED THE LAB'S *KEY-CODE,* CASSIE. IT'S NOW *OFF-LIMITS* TO YOU. THIS IS *BETTER—*FOR *BOTH* OF US!

TAYLOR— *DON'T!* AT LEAST LET ME...

...DOUBLE-CHECK YOUR WORK...

SOMEONE BETTER BE LOOKING OVER LINNIK'S SHOULDER! RESEARCH AUTONOMY IS *ONE* THING, BUT—

MAYBE *REED RICHARDS* COULD TAKE A PEEK. I HEAR HE'S IMPRESSED WITH OUR *FRICTIONLESS GYROSCOPE* AND IS COMING DOWN TO INSPECT IT...

SEE? IT ALL COMES TOGETHER!

BUT WHAT *IS* UP WITH DOC LINNIK? STRESSED-OUT...EXPERIMENTING WITH UNKNOWN FORCES...AND THAT WEIRD WIDOW'S-PEAK HAIRLINE OF HIS?

YOU ASK ME, THIS HAS *SUPER VILLAIN SECRET ORIGIN* WRITTEN ALL OVER IT!

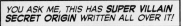

ALL FOR THE *BEST*...ALL FOR THE *BEST*...

THING IS, THAT ROLE'S *ALREADY TAKEN.*

QUIT YOUR MOURNFUL *MUTTERING,* LINNIK—AND GET TO *WORK!* YOU'RE *LATE!*

LATE? YES...

TOO LATE FOR MY *MARRIAGE,* I FEAR. THE WAY CASSIE *LOOKS* AT ME...

THAT WILL *CHANGE.* SOON THE ENTIRE *WORLD* WILL LOOK AT US *DIFFERENTLY!*

WE ARE ON THE EDGE OF *GREATNESS!* THIS DISCOVERY WILL LIFT US *ABOVE ALL OTHERS!* WE WILL HAVE THE RESPECT AND ADMIRATION WE HAVE *ALWAYS DESERVED!*

ANY WOMAN WHO DOESN'T UNDERSTAND *THAT—*I *WOULDN'T WANT* BY MY SIDE!

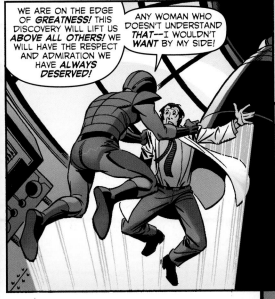

FOR I AM NO *ORDINARY* MAN—*I AM THE WIZARD!*

ALSO KNOWN AS THE POSTER BOY FOR "THE THIN LINE BETWEEN *GENIUS AND INSANITY.*"

WISH I'D *KNOWN* HE WAS BEHIND ALL THIS. WOULD'VE SAVED A *WORLD OF HURT*...

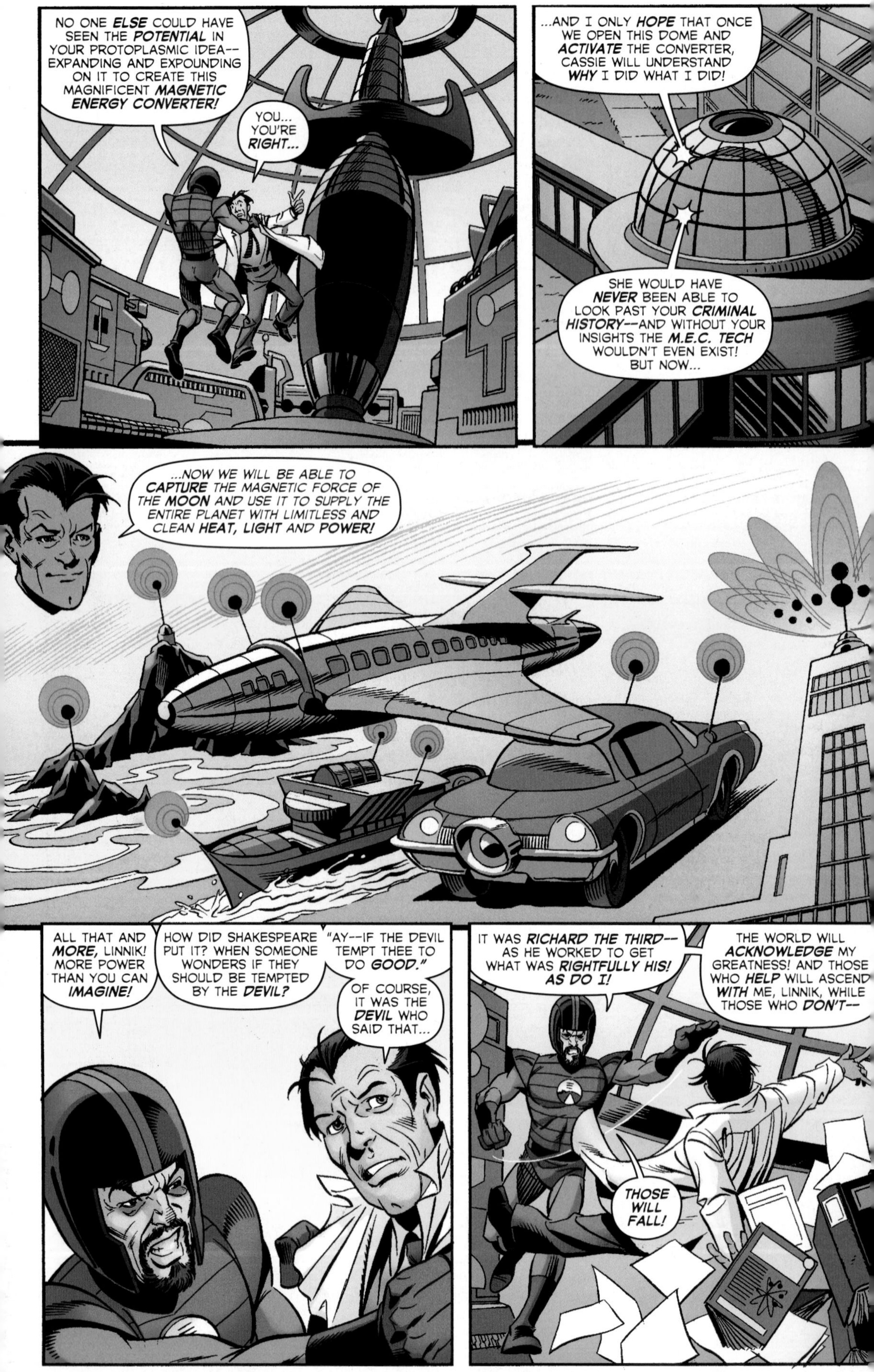
NO ONE ELSE COULD HAVE SEEN THE POTENTIAL IN YOUR PROTOPLASMIC IDEA-- EXPANDING AND EXPOUNDING ON IT TO CREATE THIS MAGNIFICENT MAGNETIC ENERGY CONVERTER!
YOU... YOU'RE RIGHT...
...AND I ONLY HOPE THAT ONCE WE OPEN THIS DOME AND ACTIVATE THE CONVERTER, CASSIE WILL UNDERSTAND WHY I DID WHAT I DID!
SHE WOULD HAVE NEVER BEEN ABLE TO LOOK PAST YOUR CRIMINAL HISTORY--AND WITHOUT YOUR INSIGHTS THE M.E.C. TECH WOULDN'T EVEN EXIST! BUT NOW...
...NOW WE WILL BE ABLE TO CAPTURE THE MAGNETIC FORCE OF THE MOON AND USE IT TO SUPPLY THE ENTIRE PLANET WITH LIMITLESS AND CLEAN HEAT, LIGHT AND POWER!
ALL THAT AND MORE, LINNIK! MORE POWER THAN YOU CAN IMAGINE!
HOW DID SHAKESPEARE PUT IT? WHEN SOMEONE WONDERS IF THEY SHOULD BE TEMPTED BY THE DEVIL?
"AY--IF THE DEVIL TEMPT THEE TO DO GOOD."
OF COURSE, IT WAS THE DEVIL WHO SAID THAT...
IT WAS RICHARD THE THIRD-- AS HE WORKED TO GET WHAT WAS RIGHTFULLY HIS! AS DO I!
THE WORLD WILL ACKNOWLEDGE MY GREATNESS! AND THOSE WHO HELP WILL ASCEND WITH ME, LINNIK, WHILE THOSE WHO DON'T--
THOSE WILL FALL!

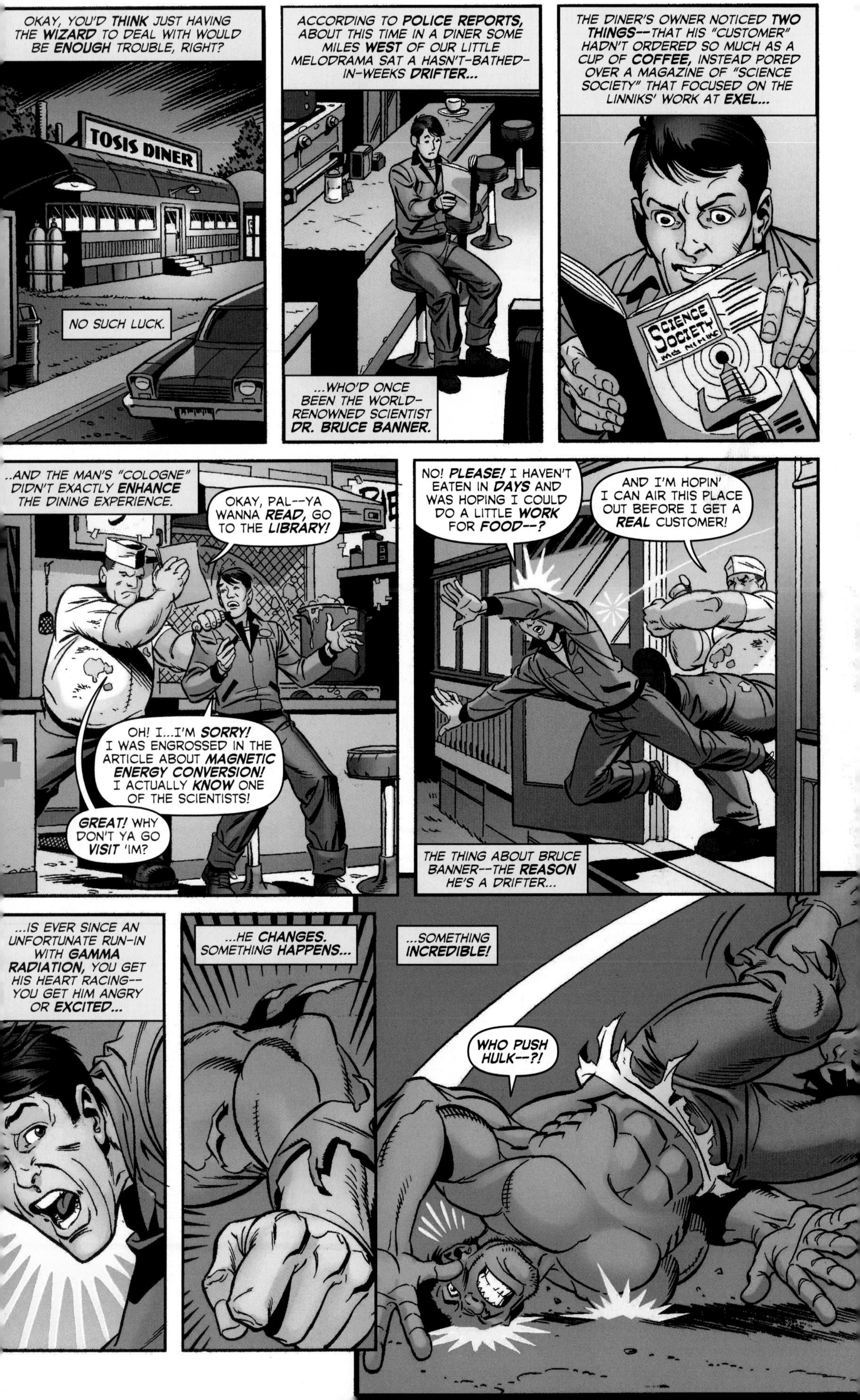
OKAY, YOU'D THINK JUST HAVING THE WIZARD TO DEAL WITH WOULD BE ENOUGH TROUBLE, RIGHT?
TOSIS DINER
NO SUCH LUCK.
ACCORDING TO POLICE REPORTS, ABOUT THIS TIME IN A DINER SOME MILES WEST OF OUR LITTLE MELODRAMA SAT A HASN'T-BATHED-IN-WEEKS DRIFTER...
...WHO'D ONCE BEEN THE WORLD-RENOWNED SCIENTIST DR. BRUCE BANNER.
THE DINER'S OWNER NOTICED TWO THINGS--THAT HIS "CUSTOMER" HADN'T ORDERED SO MUCH AS A CUP OF COFFEE, INSTEAD PORED OVER A MAGAZINE OF "SCIENCE SOCIETY" THAT FOCUSED ON THE LINNIKS' WORK AT EXEL...
SCIENCE SOCIETY
..AND THE MAN'S "COLOGNE" DIDN'T EXACTLY ENHANCE THE DINING EXPERIENCE.
OKAY, PAL--YA WANNA READ, GO TO THE LIBRARY!
OH! I...I'M SORRY! I WAS ENGROSSED IN THE ARTICLE ABOUT MAGNETIC ENERGY CONVERSION! I ACTUALLY KNOW ONE OF THE SCIENTISTS!
GREAT! WHY DON'T YA GO VISIT 'IM?
NO! PLEASE! I HAVEN'T EATEN IN DAYS AND WAS HOPING I COULD DO A LITTLE WORK FOR FOOD--?
AND I'M HOPIN' I CAN AIR THIS PLACE OUT BEFORE I GET A REAL CUSTOMER!
THE THING ABOUT BRUCE BANNER--THE REASON HE'S A DRIFTER...
...IS EVER SINCE AN UNFORTUNATE RUN-IN WITH GAMMA RADIATION, YOU GET HIS HEART RACING--YOU GET HIM ANGRY OR EXCITED...
...HE CHANGES. SOMETHING HAPPENS...
...SOMETHING INCREDIBLE!
WHO PUSH HULK--?!

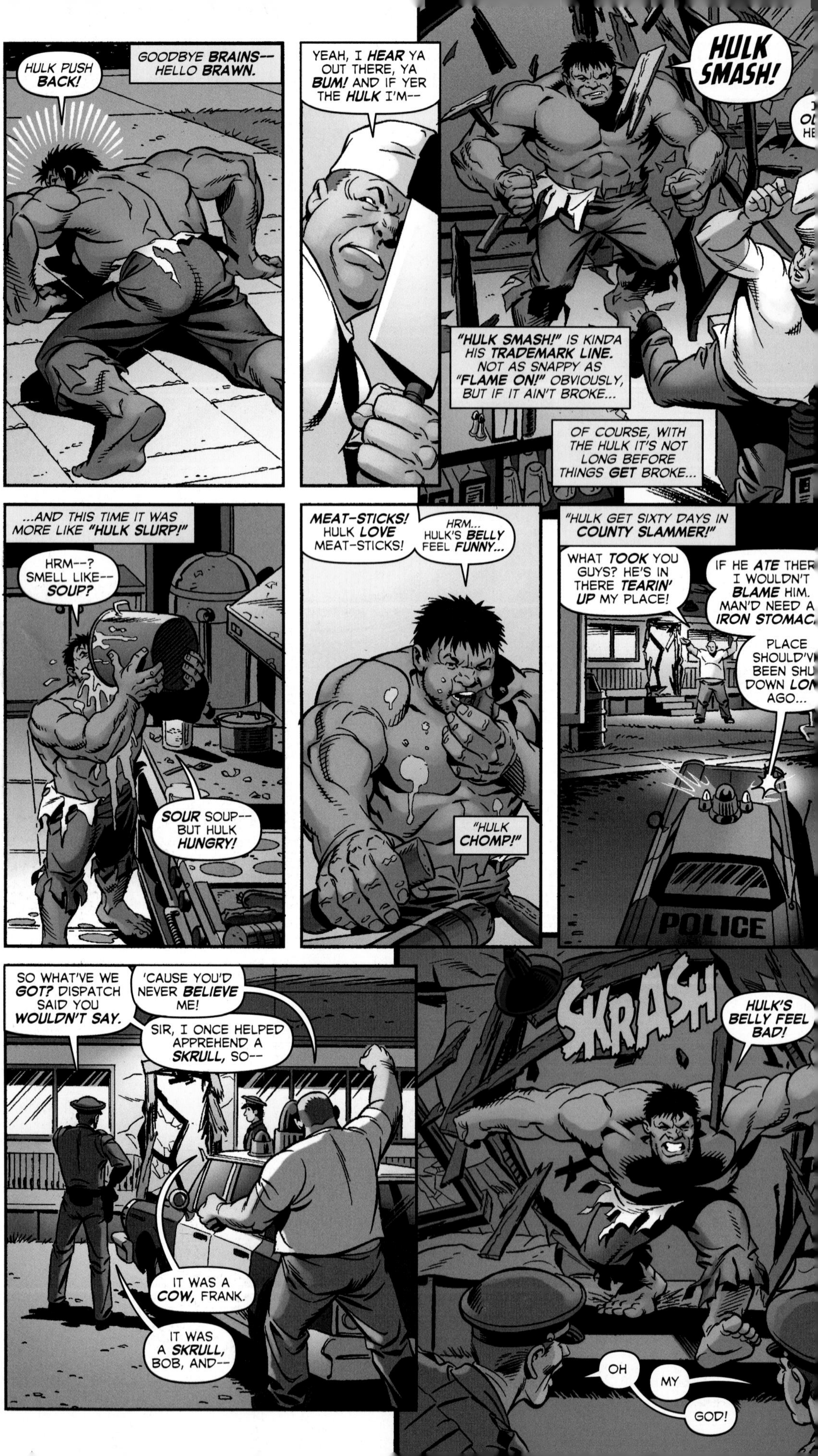

HULK PUSH BACK!
GOODBYE BRAINS-- HELLO BRAWN.
YEAH, I HEAR YA OUT THERE, YA BUM! AND IF YER THE HULK I'M--
HULK SMASH!
"HULK SMASH!" IS KINDA HIS TRADEMARK LINE. NOT AS SNAPPY AS "FLAME ON!" OBVIOUSLY, BUT IF IT AIN'T BROKE...
OF COURSE, WITH THE HULK IT'S NOT LONG BEFORE THINGS GET BROKE...
...AND THIS TIME IT WAS MORE LIKE "HULK SLURP!"
HRM--? SMELL LIKE-- SOUP?
SOUR SOUP-- BUT HULK HUNGRY!
MEAT-STICKS! HULK LOVE MEAT-STICKS!
HRM... HULK'S BELLY FEEL FUNNY...
"HULK CHOMP!"
"HULK GET SIXTY DAYS IN COUNTY SLAMMER!"
WHAT TOOK YOU GUYS? HE'S IN THERE TEARIN' UP MY PLACE!
IF HE ATE THER I WOULDN'T BLAME HIM. MAN'D NEED A IRON STOMAC
PLACE SHOULD'V BEEN SHU DOWN LON AGO...
POLICE
SO WHAT'VE WE GOT? DISPATCH SAID YOU WOULDN'T SAY.
'CAUSE YOU'D NEVER BELIEVE ME!
SIR, I ONCE HELPED APPREHEND A SKRULL, SO--
IT WAS A COW, FRANK.
IT WAS A SKRULL, BOB, AND--
SKRASH
HULK'S BELLY FEEL BAD!
OH
MY
GOD!

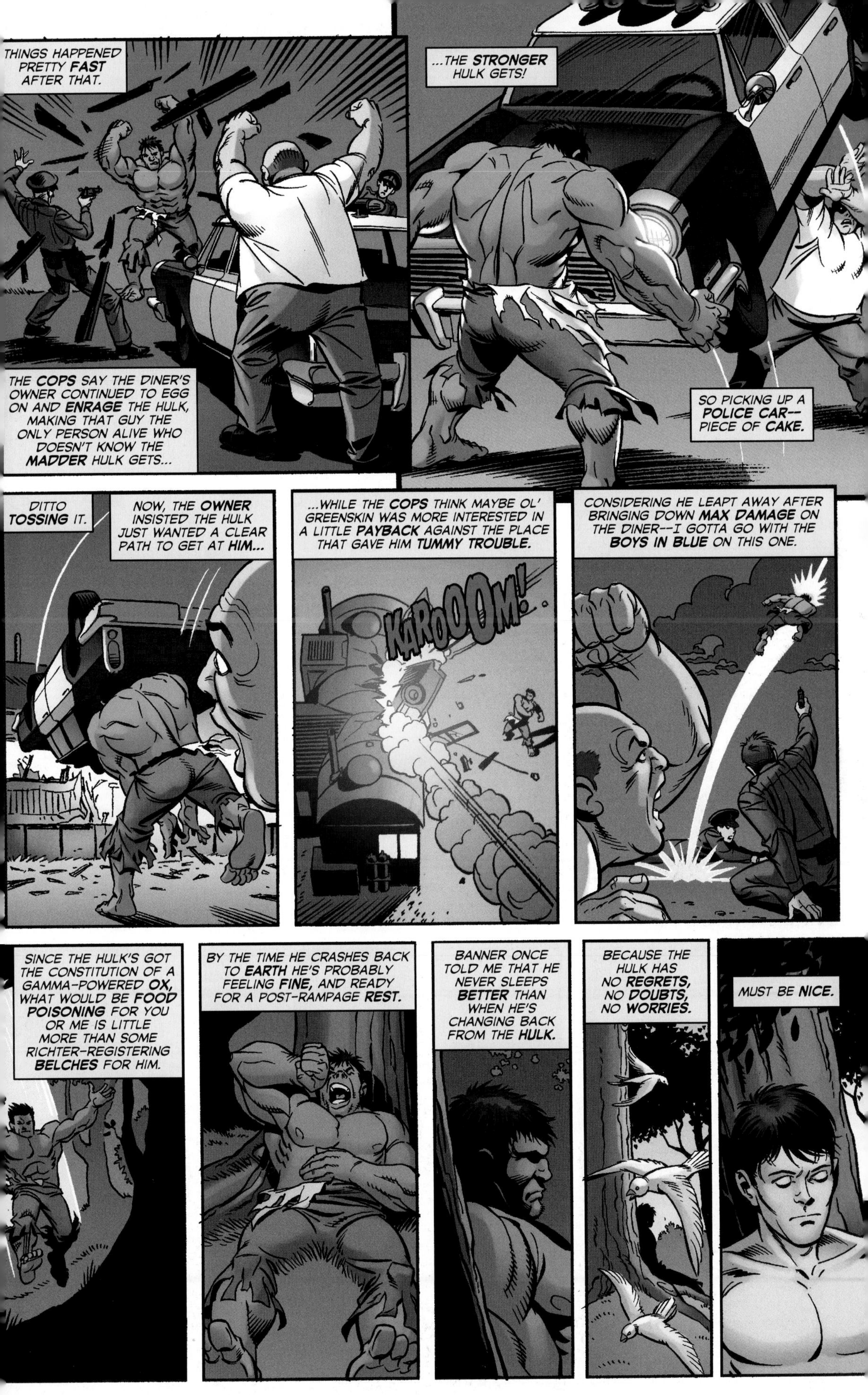
THINGS HAPPENED PRETTY FAST AFTER THAT.
THE COPS SAY THE DINER'S OWNER CONTINUED TO EGG ON AND ENRAGE THE HULK, MAKING THAT GUY THE ONLY PERSON ALIVE WHO DOESN'T KNOW THE MADDER HULK GETS...
...THE STRONGER HULK GETS!
SO PICKING UP A POLICE CAR-- PIECE OF CAKE.
DITTO TOSSING IT.
NOW, THE OWNER INSISTED THE HULK JUST WANTED A CLEAR PATH TO GET AT HIM...
...WHILE THE COPS THINK MAYBE OL' GREENSKIN WAS MORE INTERESTED IN A LITTLE PAYBACK AGAINST THE PLACE THAT GAVE HIM TUMMY TROUBLE.
KAROOOOM!
CONSIDERING HE LEAPT AWAY AFTER BRINGING DOWN MAX DAMAGE ON THE DINER--I GOTTA GO WITH THE BOYS IN BLUE ON THIS ONE.
SINCE THE HULK'S GOT THE CONSTITUTION OF A GAMMA-POWERED OX, WHAT WOULD BE FOOD POISONING FOR YOU OR ME IS LITTLE MORE THAN SOME RICHTER-REGISTERING BELCHES FOR HIM.
BY THE TIME HE CRASHES BACK TO EARTH HE'S PROBABLY FEELING FINE, AND READY FOR A POST-RAMPAGE REST.
BANNER ONCE TOLD ME THAT HE NEVER SLEEPS BETTER THAN WHEN HE'S CHANGING BACK FROM THE HULK.
BECAUSE THE HULK HAS NO REGRETS, NO DOUBTS, NO WORRIES.
MUST BE NICE.

NOT THAT I'D CHANGE **PLACES** WITH HIM--WAKING UP GOD KNOWS **WHERE**, NOT KNOWING HOW I **GOT** THERE, NOT KNOWING WHAT I **DID**...

I'D MAKE IT MY MISSION TO **GET OUT** OF THAT KIND OF HELL, A.S.A.P.--SO IN NO TIME I'D BE DOING CRAZY, **DESPERATE** THINGS.

JUST LIKE **BANNER**.

JUST LIKE WHAT HE DID **NEXT**.

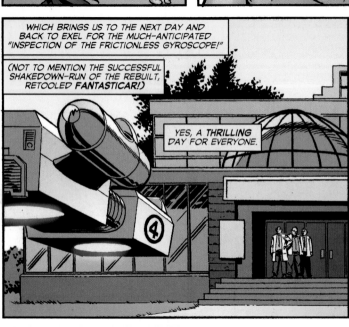

WHICH BRINGS US TO THE NEXT DAY AND BACK TO EXEL FOR THE MUCH-ANTICIPATED "INSPECTION OF THE FRICTIONLESS GYROSCOPE!"

(NOT TO MENTION THE SUCCESSFUL SHAKEDOWN-RUN OF THE REBUILT, RETOOLED **FANTASTICAR!**)

YES, A **THRILLING** DAY FOR EVERYONE.

WELL...**ALMOST** EVERYONE...

THE FANTASTIC FOUR? HERE?! **NOW!?!**

THIS IS **YOUR** DOING, LINNIK!

YOU WAITED UNTIL CONSTRUCTION OF THE CONVERTER WAS **NEARLY COMPLETE**--THEN **BETRAYED** ME TO MY **GREATEST FOES** SO YOU COULD TAKE **ALL** THE CREDIT!

WHAT? **NO!** I--I HAVEN'T BREATHED A **WORD**--!

AND YOU CERTAINLY WON'T BREATHE **ANOTHER!**

TRAGIC--HOW YOU ACCIDENTALLY FELL TO YOUR **DEATH** FROM THIS HEIGHT!

NO! **DON'T!** I'LL DO WHATEVER YOU **WANT!**

ANYTHING! JUST **NAME** IT!

PERHAPS, LINNIK...

YES-- PERHAPS I STILL HAVE A **USE** FOR YOU...

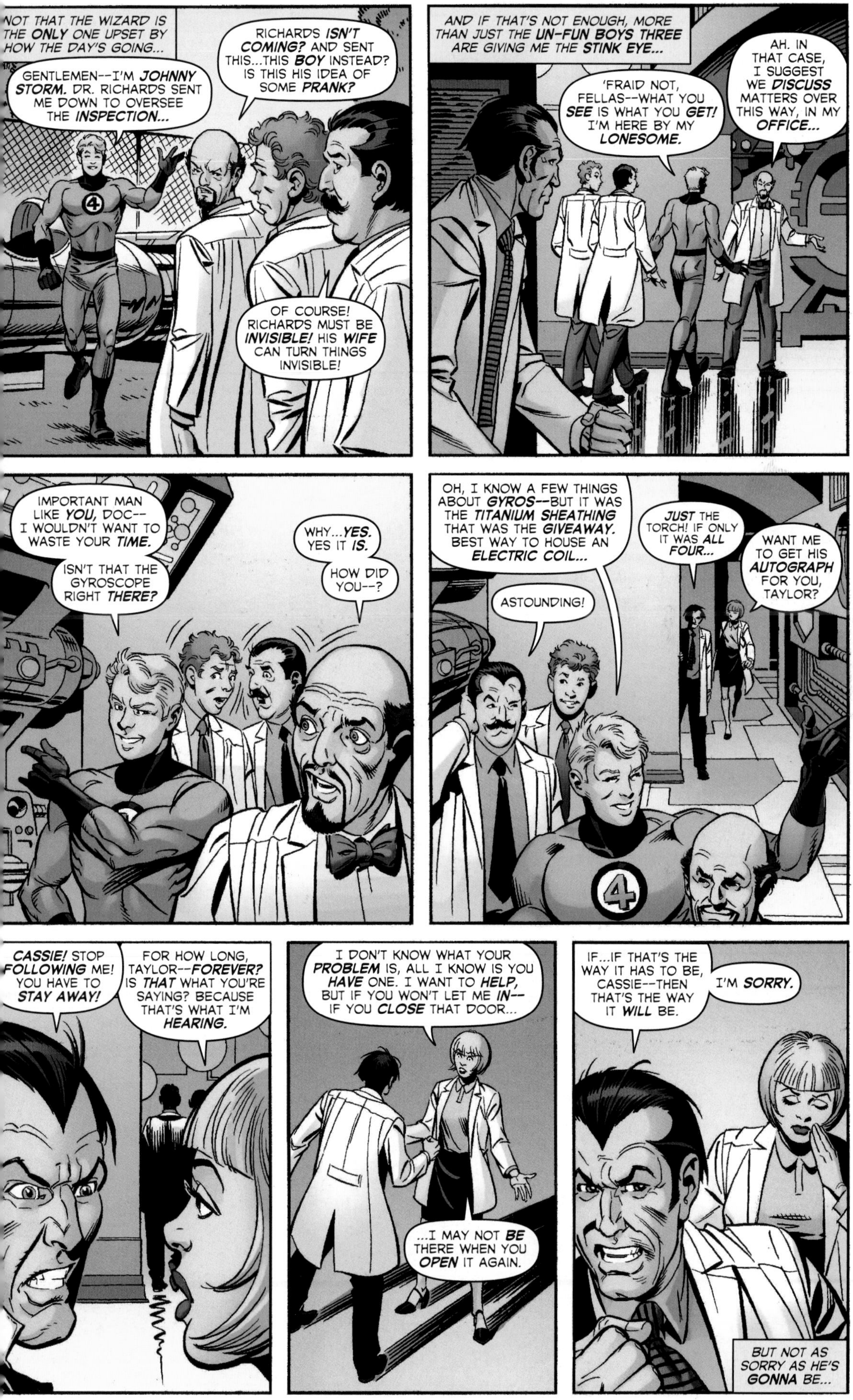
NOT THAT THE WIZARD IS THE ONLY ONE UPSET BY HOW THE DAY'S GOING...
GENTLEMEN--I'M JOHNNY STORM. DR. RICHARDS SENT ME DOWN TO OVERSEE THE INSPECTION...
RICHARDS ISN'T COMING? AND SENT THIS...THIS BOY INSTEAD? IS THIS HIS IDEA OF SOME PRANK?
OF COURSE! RICHARDS MUST BE INVISIBLE! HIS WIFE CAN TURN THINGS INVISIBLE!
AND IF THAT'S NOT ENOUGH, MORE THAN JUST THE UN-FUN BOYS THREE ARE GIVING ME THE STINK EYE...
'FRAID NOT, FELLAS--WHAT YOU SEE IS WHAT YOU GET! I'M HERE BY MY LONESOME.
AH. IN THAT CASE, I SUGGEST WE DISCUSS MATTERS OVER THIS WAY, IN MY OFFICE...
IMPORTANT MAN LIKE YOU, DOC-- I WOULDN'T WANT TO WASTE YOUR TIME.
ISN'T THAT THE GYROSCOPE RIGHT THERE?
WHY...YES. YES IT IS.
HOW DID YOU--?
OH, I KNOW A FEW THINGS ABOUT GYROS--BUT IT WAS THE TITANIUM SHEATHING THAT WAS THE GIVEAWAY. BEST WAY TO HOUSE AN ELECTRIC COIL...
ASTOUNDING!
JUST THE TORCH! IF ONLY IT WAS ALL FOUR...
WANT ME TO GET HIS AUTOGRAPH FOR YOU, TAYLOR?
CASSIE! STOP FOLLOWING ME! YOU HAVE TO STAY AWAY!
FOR HOW LONG, TAYLOR--FOREVER? IS THAT WHAT YOU'RE SAYING? BECAUSE THAT'S WHAT I'M HEARING.
I DON'T KNOW WHAT YOUR PROBLEM IS, ALL I KNOW IS YOU HAVE ONE. I WANT TO HELP, BUT IF YOU WON'T LET ME IN-- IF YOU CLOSE THAT DOOR...
...I MAY NOT BE THERE WHEN YOU OPEN IT AGAIN.
IF...IF THAT'S THE WAY IT HAS TO BE, CASSIE--THEN THAT'S THE WAY IT WILL BE.
I'M SORRY.
BUT NOT AS SORRY AS HE'S GONNA BE...

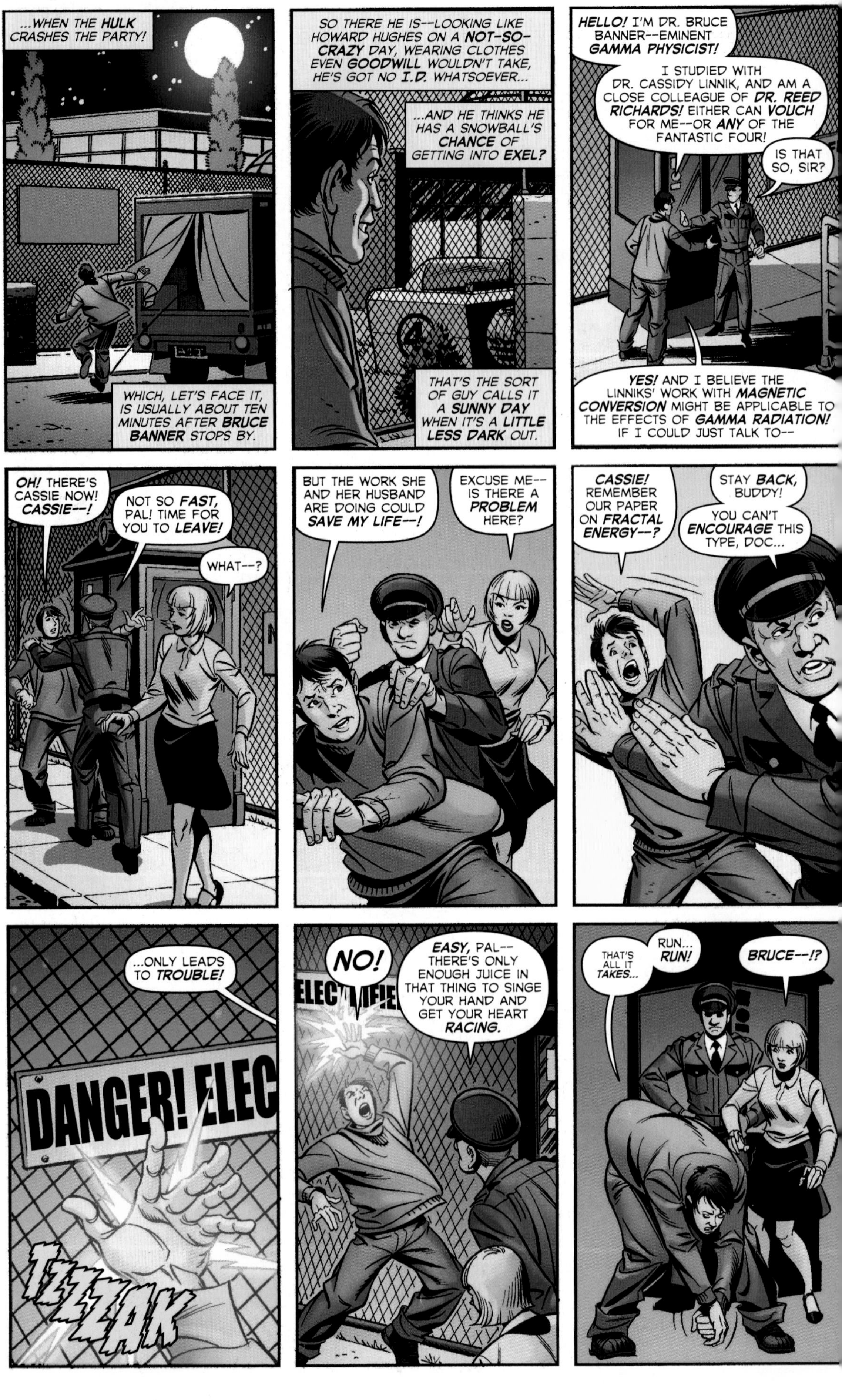
...WHEN THE HULK CRASHES THE PARTY!
WHICH, LET'S FACE IT, IS USUALLY ABOUT TEN MINUTES AFTER BRUCE BANNER STOPS BY.
SO THERE HE IS--LOOKING LIKE HOWARD HUGHES ON A NOT-SO-CRAZY DAY, WEARING CLOTHES EVEN GOODWILL WOULDN'T TAKE, HE'S GOT NO I.D. WHATSOEVER...
...AND HE THINKS HE HAS A SNOWBALL'S CHANCE OF GETTING INTO EXEL?
THAT'S THE SORT OF GUY CALLS IT A SUNNY DAY WHEN IT'S A LITTLE LESS DARK OUT.
HELLO! I'M DR. BRUCE BANNER--EMINENT GAMMA PHYSICIST!
I STUDIED WITH DR. CASSIDY LINNIK, AND AM A CLOSE COLLEAGUE OF DR. REED RICHARDS! EITHER CAN VOUCH FOR ME--OR ANY OF THE FANTASTIC FOUR!
IS THAT SO, SIR?
YES! AND I BELIEVE THE LINNIKS' WORK WITH MAGNETIC CONVERSION MIGHT BE APPLICABLE TO THE EFFECTS OF GAMMA RADIATION! IF I COULD JUST TALK TO--
OH! THERE'S CASSIE NOW! CASSIE--!
NOT SO FAST, PAL! TIME FOR YOU TO LEAVE!
WHAT--?
BUT THE WORK SHE AND HER HUSBAND ARE DOING COULD SAVE MY LIFE--!
EXCUSE ME-- IS THERE A PROBLEM HERE?
CASSIE! REMEMBER OUR PAPER ON FRACTAL ENERGY--?
STAY BACK, BUDDY!
YOU CAN'T ENCOURAGE THIS TYPE, DOC...
...ONLY LEADS TO TROUBLE!
DANGER! ELEC
TZZZAK
NO!
EASY, PAL-- THERE'S ONLY ENOUGH JUICE IN THAT THING TO SINGE YOUR HAND AND GET YOUR HEART RACING.
THAT'S ALL IT TAKES...
RUN... RUN!
BRUCE--!?

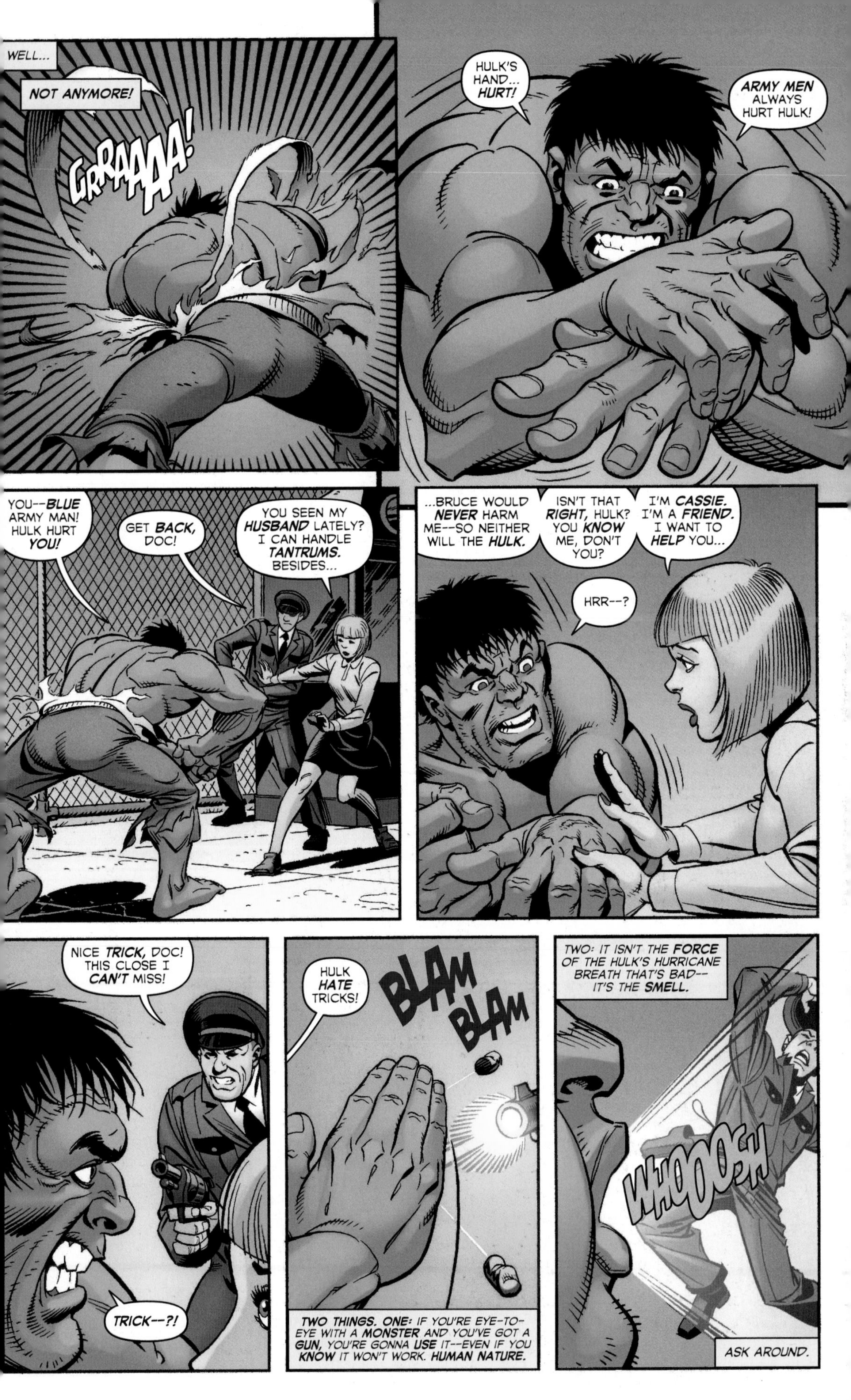
WELL...
NOT ANYMORE!
GRRAAAA!
HULK'S HAND... HURT!
ARMY MEN ALWAYS HURT HULK!
YOU--BLUE ARMY MAN! HULK HURT YOU!
GET BACK, DOC!
YOU SEEN MY HUSBAND LATELY? I CAN HANDLE TANTRUMS. BESIDES...
...BRUCE WOULD NEVER HARM ME--SO NEITHER WILL THE HULK.
ISN'T THAT RIGHT, HULK? YOU KNOW ME, DON'T YOU?
I'M CASSIE. I'M A FRIEND. I WANT TO HELP YOU...
HRR--?
NICE TRICK, DOC! THIS CLOSE I CAN'T MISS!
TRICK--?!
HULK HATE TRICKS!
BLAM BLAM
TWO THINGS. ONE: IF YOU'RE EYE-TO-EYE WITH A MONSTER AND YOU'VE GOT A GUN, YOU'RE GONNA USE IT--EVEN IF YOU KNOW IT WON'T WORK. HUMAN NATURE.
TWO: IT ISN'T THE FORCE OF THE HULK'S HURRICANE BREATH THAT'S BAD--IT'S THE SMELL.
WHOOOSH
ASK AROUND.

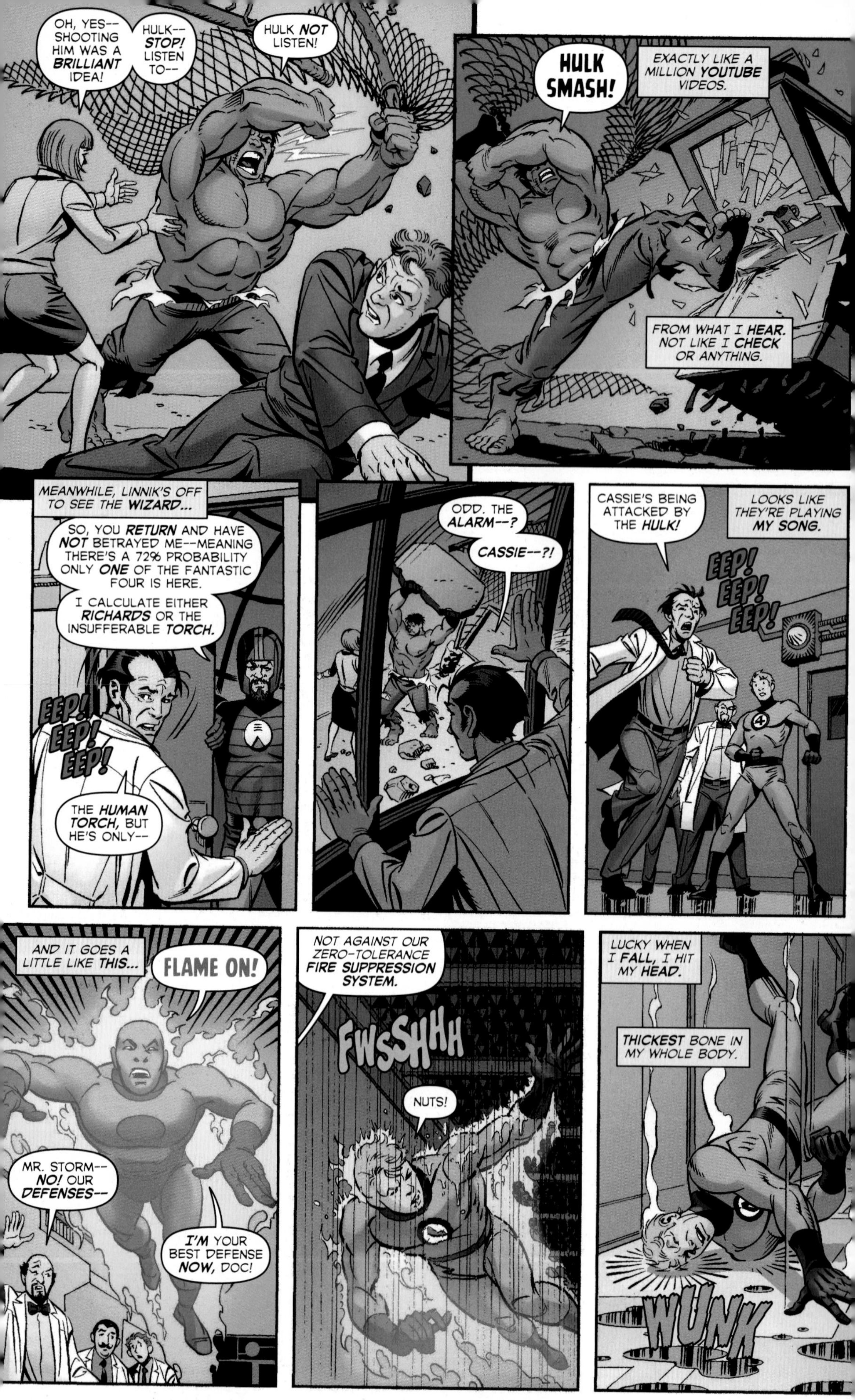
OH, YES--SHOOTING HIM WAS A BRILLIANT IDEA!
HULK--STOP! LISTEN TO--
HULK NOT LISTEN!
HULK SMASH!
EXACTLY LIKE A MILLION YOUTUBE VIDEOS.
FROM WHAT I HEAR. NOT LIKE I CHECK OR ANYTHING.
MEANWHILE, LINNIK'S OFF TO SEE THE WIZARD...
SO, YOU RETURN AND HAVE NOT BETRAYED ME--MEANING THERE'S A 72% PROBABILITY ONLY ONE OF THE FANTASTIC FOUR IS HERE.
I CALCULATE EITHER RICHARDS OR THE INSUFFERABLE TORCH.
EEP! EEP! EEP!
THE HUMAN TORCH, BUT HE'S ONLY--
ODD. THE ALARM--?
CASSIE--?!
CASSIE'S BEING ATTACKED BY THE HULK!
LOOKS LIKE THEY'RE PLAYING MY SONG.
EEP! EEP! EEP!
AND IT GOES A LITTLE LIKE THIS...
FLAME ON!
MR. STORM--NO! OUR DEFENSES--
I'M YOUR BEST DEFENSE NOW, DOC!
NOT AGAINST OUR ZERO-TOLERANCE FIRE SUPPRESSION SYSTEM.
FWSSHHH
NUTS!
LUCKY WHEN I FALL, I HIT MY HEAD.
THICKEST BONE IN MY WHOLE BODY.
WUNK

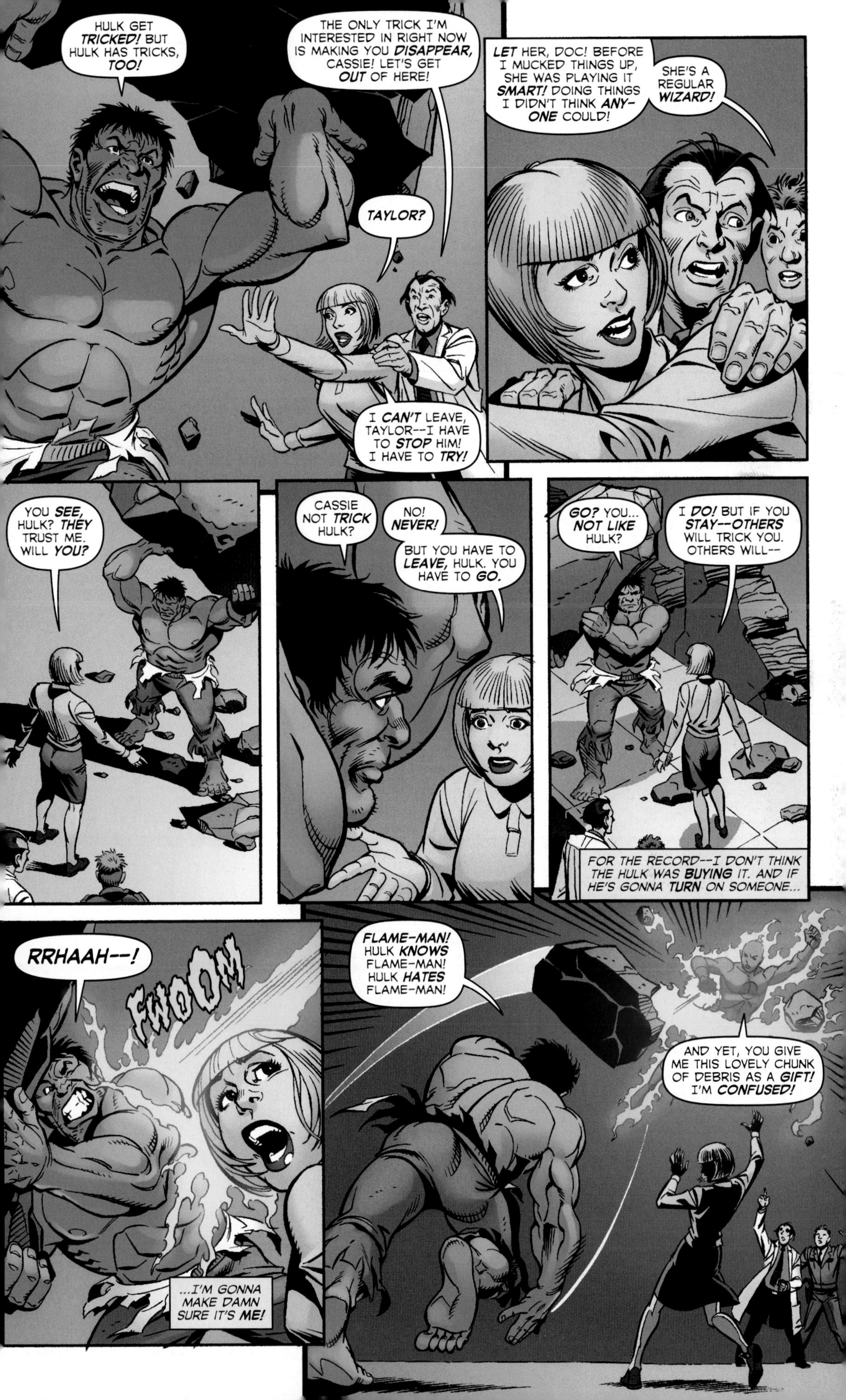

HULK GET TRICKED! BUT HULK HAS TRICKS, TOO!
THE ONLY TRICK I'M INTERESTED IN RIGHT NOW IS MAKING YOU DISAPPEAR, CASSIE! LET'S GET OUT OF HERE!
TAYLOR?
I CAN'T LEAVE, TAYLOR--I HAVE TO STOP HIM! I HAVE TO TRY!
LET HER, DOC! BEFORE I MUCKED THINGS UP, SHE WAS PLAYING IT SMART! DOING THINGS I DIDN'T THINK ANY-ONE COULD!
SHE'S A REGULAR WIZARD!
YOU SEE, HULK? THEY TRUST ME. WILL YOU?
CASSIE NOT TRICK HULK?
NO! NEVER!
BUT YOU HAVE TO LEAVE, HULK. YOU HAVE TO GO.
GO? YOU... NOT LIKE HULK?
I DO! BUT IF YOU STAY--OTHERS WILL TRICK YOU. OTHERS WILL--
FOR THE RECORD--I DON'T THINK THE HULK WAS BUYING IT. AND IF HE'S GONNA TURN ON SOMEONE...
RRHAAH--!
FWOOM
...I'M GONNA MAKE DAMN SURE IT'S ME!
FLAME-MAN! HULK KNOWS FLAME-MAN! HULK HATES FLAME-MAN!
AND YET, YOU GIVE ME THIS LOVELY CHUNK OF DEBRIS AS A GIFT! I'M CONFUSED!

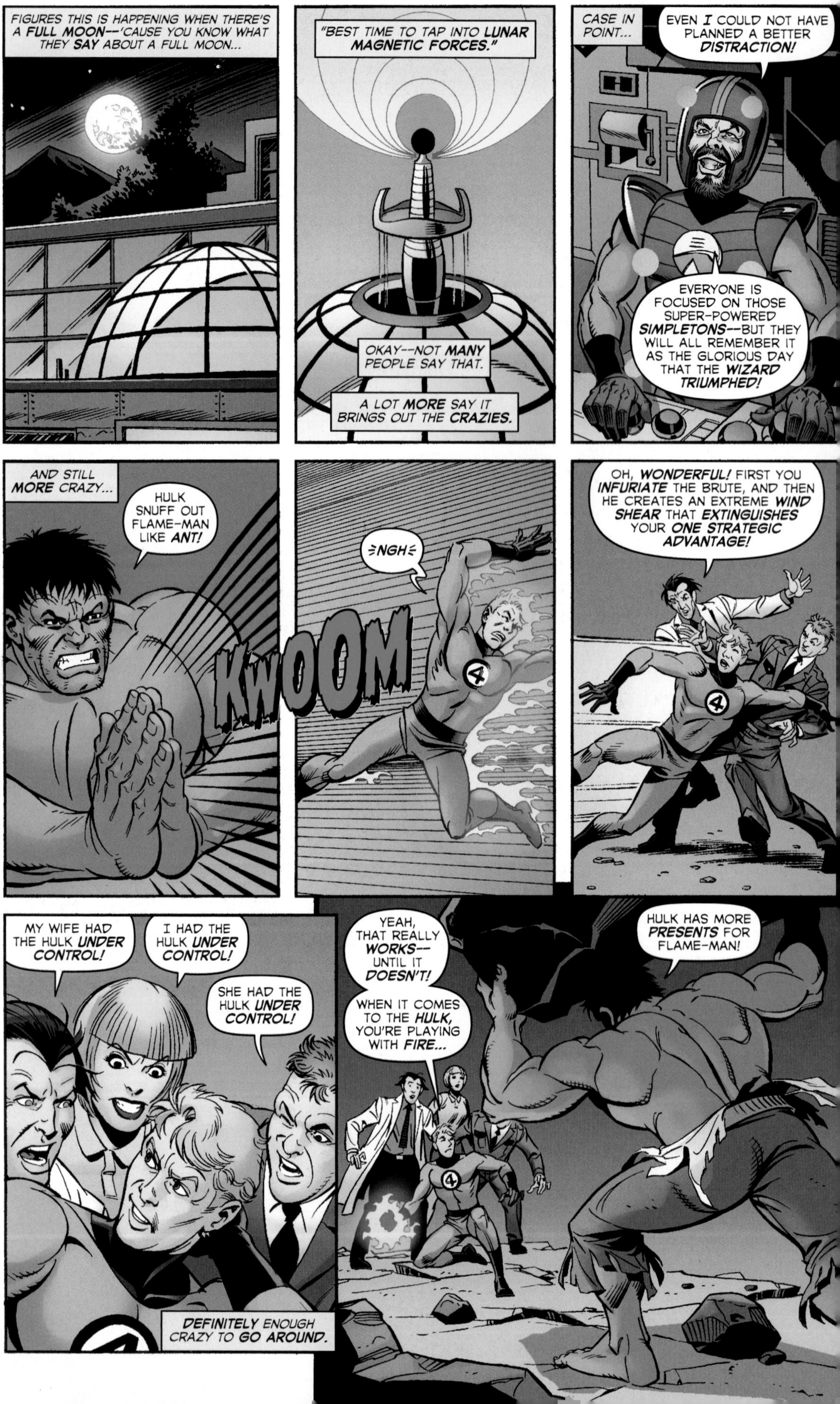
FIGURES THIS IS HAPPENING WHEN THERE'S A FULL MOON--'CAUSE YOU KNOW WHAT THEY SAY ABOUT A FULL MOON...
"BEST TIME TO TAP INTO LUNAR MAGNETIC FORCES."
OKAY--NOT MANY PEOPLE SAY THAT.
A LOT MORE SAY IT BRINGS OUT THE CRAZIES.
CASE IN POINT...
EVEN I COULD NOT HAVE PLANNED A BETTER DISTRACTION!
EVERYONE IS FOCUSED ON THOSE SUPER-POWERED SIMPLETONS--BUT THEY WILL ALL REMEMBER IT AS THE GLORIOUS DAY THAT THE WIZARD TRIUMPHED!
AND STILL MORE CRAZY...
HULK SNUFF OUT FLAME-MAN LIKE ANT!
KWOOOM
NGH
OH, WONDERFUL! FIRST YOU INFURIATE THE BRUTE, AND THEN HE CREATES AN EXTREME WIND SHEAR THAT EXTINGUISHES YOUR ONE STRATEGIC ADVANTAGE!
MY WIFE HAD THE HULK UNDER CONTROL!
I HAD THE HULK UNDER CONTROL!
SHE HAD THE HULK UNDER CONTROL!
DEFINITELY ENOUGH CRAZY TO GO AROUND.
YEAH, THAT REALLY WORKS-- UNTIL IT DOESN'T!
WHEN IT COMES TO THE HULK, YOU'RE PLAYING WITH FIRE...
HULK HAS MORE PRESENTS FOR FLAME-MAN!

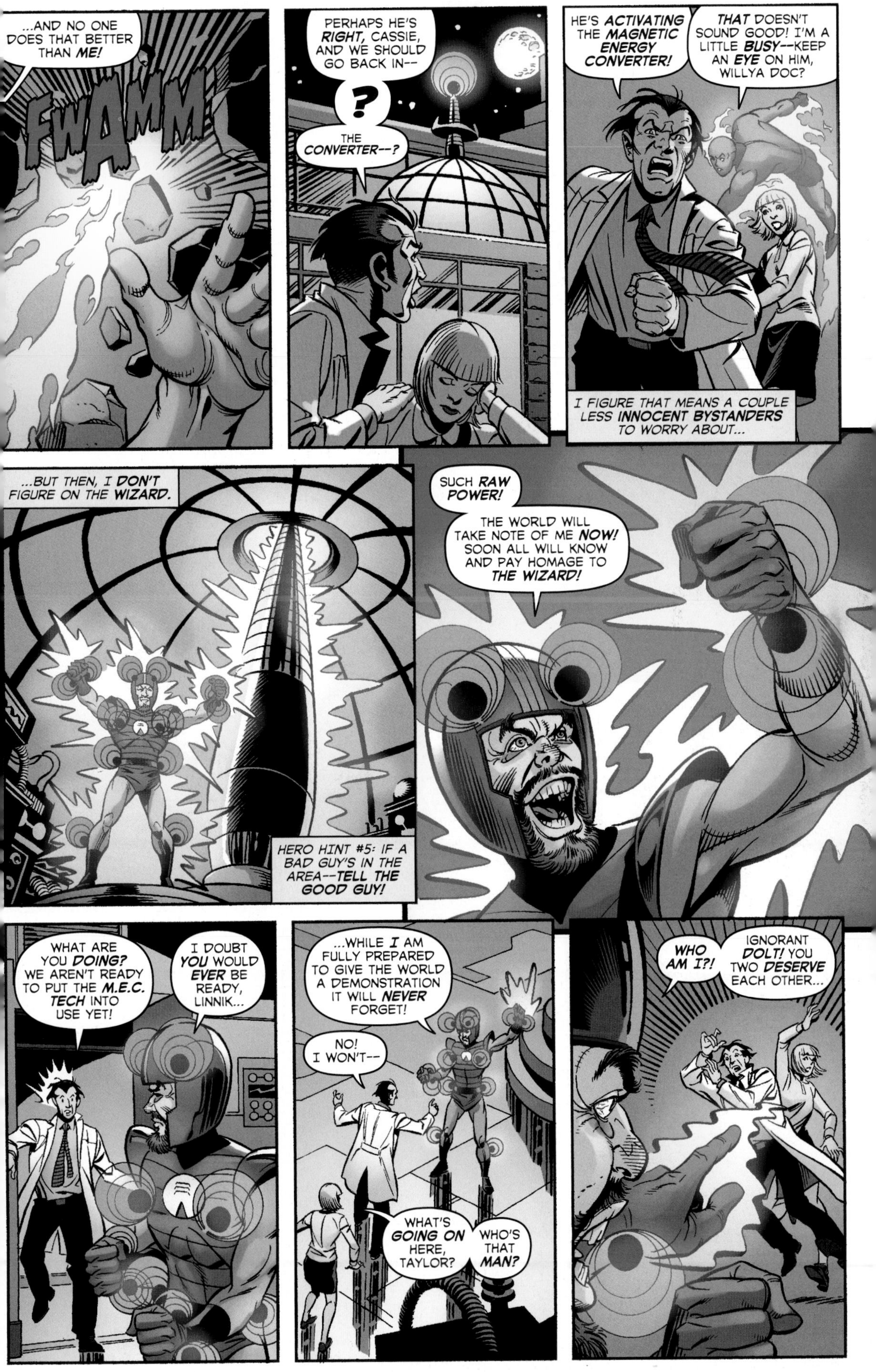
...AND NO ONE DOES THAT BETTER THAN ME!
FWAMM!
PERHAPS HE'S RIGHT, CASSIE, AND WE SHOULD GO BACK IN--
?
THE CONVERTER--?
HE'S ACTIVATING THE MAGNETIC ENERGY CONVERTER!
THAT DOESN'T SOUND GOOD! I'M A LITTLE BUSY--KEEP AN EYE ON HIM, WILLYA DOC?
I FIGURE THAT MEANS A COUPLE LESS INNOCENT BYSTANDERS TO WORRY ABOUT...
...BUT THEN, I DON'T FIGURE ON THE WIZARD.
HERO HINT #5: IF A BAD GUY'S IN THE AREA--TELL THE GOOD GUY!
SUCH RAW POWER!
THE WORLD WILL TAKE NOTE OF ME NOW! SOON ALL WILL KNOW AND PAY HOMAGE TO THE WIZARD!
WHAT ARE YOU DOING? WE AREN'T READY TO PUT THE M.E.C. TECH INTO USE YET!
I DOUBT YOU WOULD EVER BE READY, LINNIK...
...WHILE I AM FULLY PREPARED TO GIVE THE WORLD A DEMONSTRATION IT WILL NEVER FORGET!
NO! I WON'T--
WHAT'S GOING ON HERE, TAYLOR?
WHO'S THAT MAN?
WHO AM I?!
IGNORANT DOLT! YOU TWO DESERVE EACH OTHER...

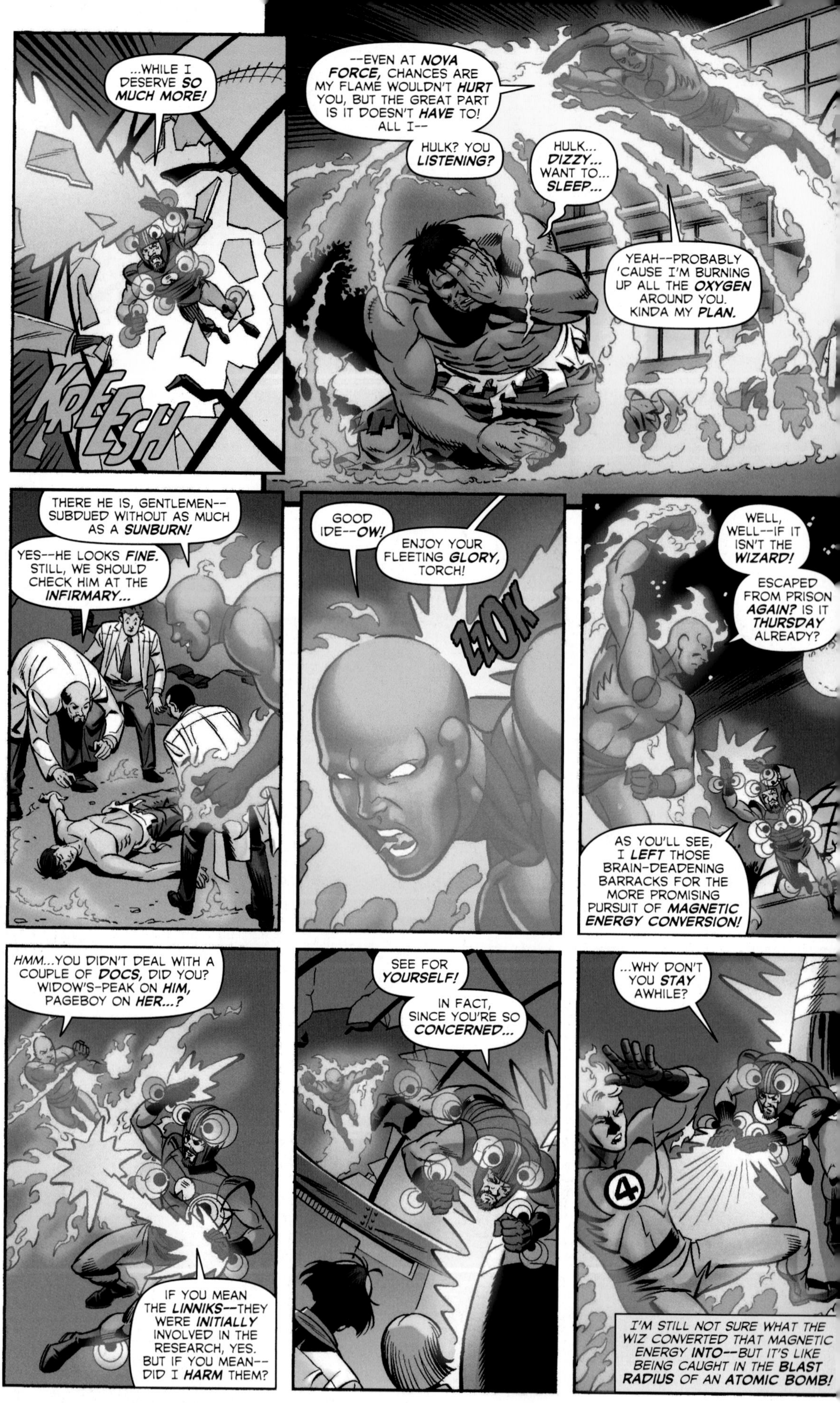

...WHILE I DESERVE SO MUCH MORE!
KREESH
--EVEN AT NOVA FORCE, CHANCES ARE MY FLAME WOULDN'T HURT YOU, BUT THE GREAT PART IS IT DOESN'T HAVE TO! ALL I--
HULK? YOU LISTENING?
HULK... DIZZY... WANT TO... SLEEP...
YEAH--PROBABLY 'CAUSE I'M BURNING UP ALL THE OXYGEN AROUND YOU. KINDA MY PLAN.
THERE HE IS, GENTLEMEN--SUBDUED WITHOUT AS MUCH AS A SUNBURN!
YES--HE LOOKS FINE. STILL, WE SHOULD CHECK HIM AT THE INFIRMARY...
GOOD IDE--OW!
ENJOY YOUR FLEETING GLORY, TORCH!
ZZOK
WELL, WELL--IF IT ISN'T THE WIZARD!
ESCAPED FROM PRISON AGAIN? IS IT THURSDAY ALREADY?
AS YOU'LL SEE, I LEFT THOSE BRAIN-DEADENING BARRACKS FOR THE MORE PROMISING PURSUIT OF MAGNETIC ENERGY CONVERSION!
HMM...YOU DIDN'T DEAL WITH A COUPLE OF DOCS, DID YOU? WIDOW'S-PEAK ON HIM, PAGEBOY ON HER...?
IF YOU MEAN THE LINNIKS--THEY WERE INITIALLY INVOLVED IN THE RESEARCH, YES. BUT IF YOU MEAN--DID I HARM THEM?
SEE FOR YOURSELF!
IN FACT, SINCE YOU'RE SO CONCERNED...
...WHY DON'T YOU STAY AWHILE?
4
I'M STILL NOT SURE WHAT THE WIZ CONVERTED THAT MAGNETIC ENERGY INTO--BUT IT'S LIKE BEING CAUGHT IN THE BLAST RADIUS OF AN ATOMIC BOMB!

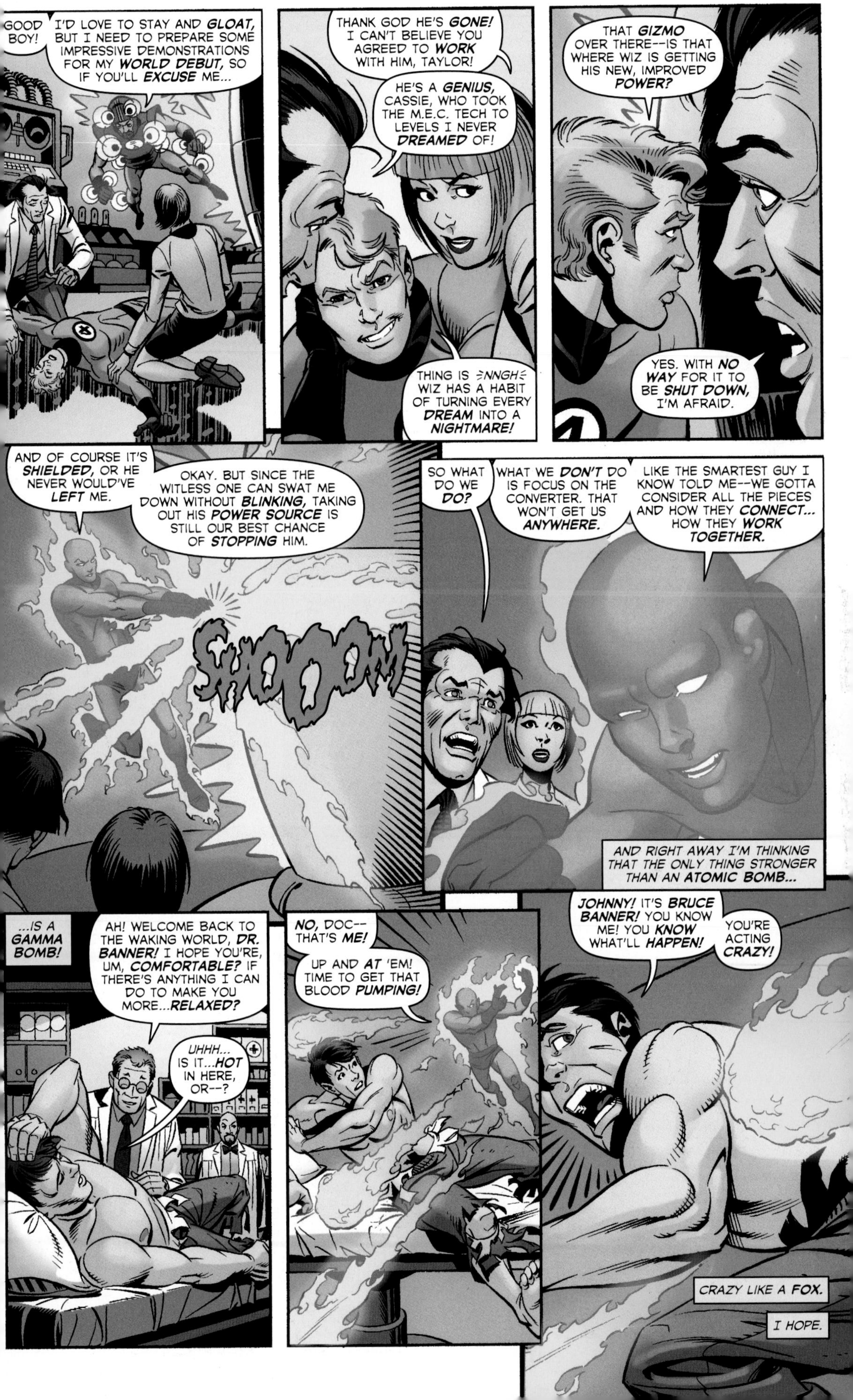
GOOD BOY!
I'D LOVE TO STAY AND GLOAT, BUT I NEED TO PREPARE SOME IMPRESSIVE DEMONSTRATIONS FOR MY WORLD DEBUT, SO IF YOU'LL EXCUSE ME...
THANK GOD HE'S GONE! I CAN'T BELIEVE YOU AGREED TO WORK WITH HIM, TAYLOR!
HE'S A GENIUS, CASSIE, WHO TOOK THE M.E.C. TECH TO LEVELS I NEVER DREAMED OF!
THING IS =NNGH= WIZ HAS A HABIT OF TURNING EVERY DREAM INTO A NIGHTMARE!
THAT GIZMO OVER THERE--IS THAT WHERE WIZ IS GETTING HIS NEW, IMPROVED POWER?
YES. WITH NO WAY FOR IT TO BE SHUT DOWN, I'M AFRAID.
AND OF COURSE IT'S SHIELDED, OR HE NEVER WOULD'VE LEFT ME.
OKAY. BUT SINCE THE WITLESS ONE CAN SWAT ME DOWN WITHOUT BLINKING, TAKING OUT HIS POWER SOURCE IS STILL OUR BEST CHANCE OF STOPPING HIM.
SHOOOM
SO WHAT DO WE DO?
WHAT WE DON'T DO IS FOCUS ON THE CONVERTER. THAT WON'T GET US ANYWHERE.
LIKE THE SMARTEST GUY I KNOW TOLD ME--WE GOTTA CONSIDER ALL THE PIECES AND HOW THEY CONNECT... HOW THEY WORK TOGETHER.
AND RIGHT AWAY I'M THINKING THAT THE ONLY THING STRONGER THAN AN ATOMIC BOMB...
...IS A GAMMA BOMB!
AH! WELCOME BACK TO THE WAKING WORLD, DR. BANNER! I HOPE YOU'RE, UM, COMFORTABLE? IF THERE'S ANYTHING I CAN DO TO MAKE YOU MORE...RELAXED?
UHHH... IS IT...HOT IN HERE, OR--?
NO, DOC-- THAT'S ME!
UP AND AT 'EM! TIME TO GET THAT BLOOD PUMPING!
JOHNNY! IT'S BRUCE BANNER! YOU KNOW ME! YOU KNOW WHAT'LL HAPPEN!
YOU'RE ACTING CRAZY!
CRAZY LIKE A FOX.
I HOPE.

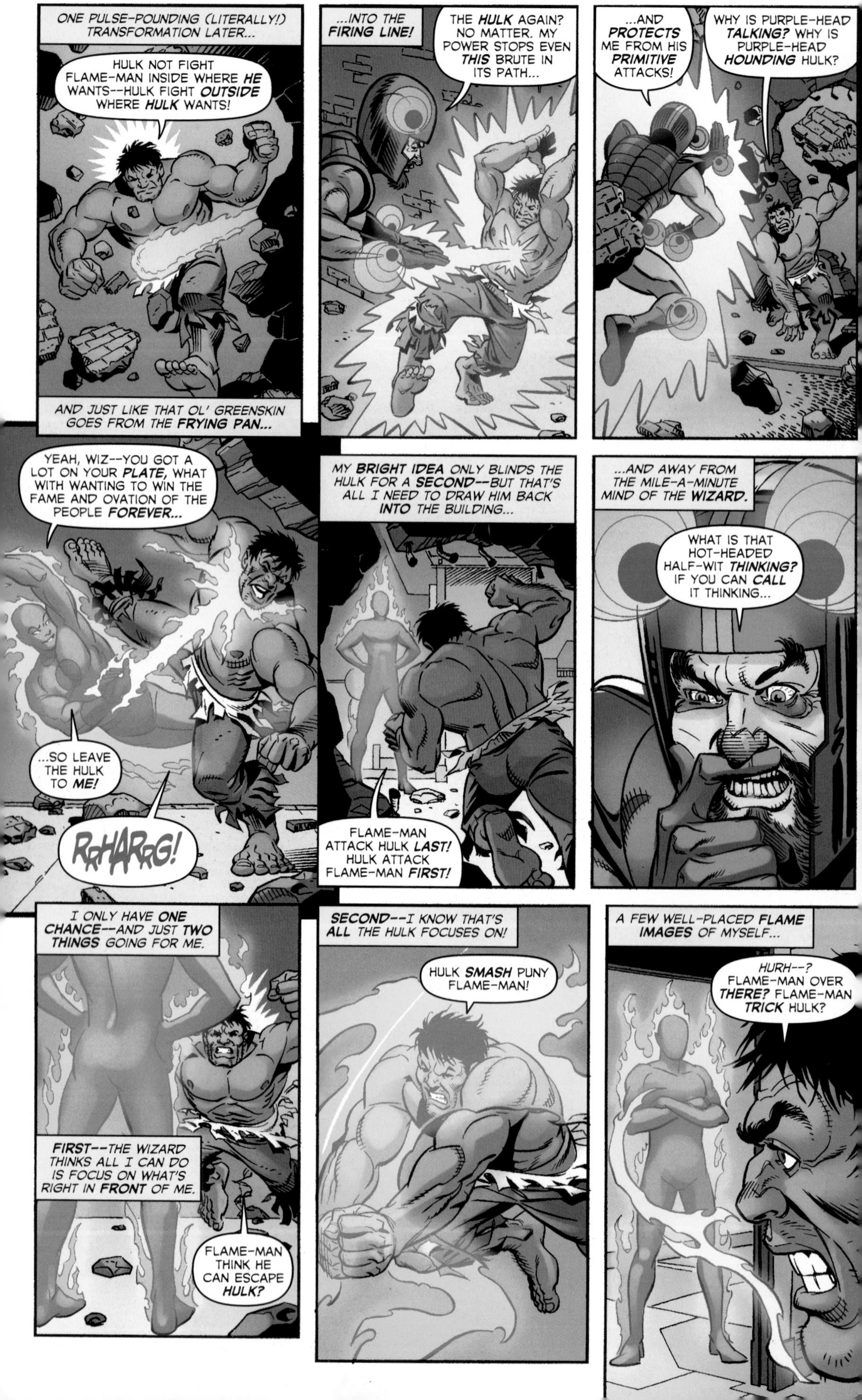
ONE PULSE-POUNDING (LITERALLY!) TRANSFORMATION LATER...
HULK NOT FIGHT FLAME-MAN INSIDE WHERE HE WANTS--HULK FIGHT OUTSIDE WHERE HULK WANTS!
AND JUST LIKE THAT OL' GREENSKIN GOES FROM THE FRYING PAN...
...INTO THE FIRING LINE!
THE HULK AGAIN? NO MATTER. MY POWER STOPS EVEN THIS BRUTE IN ITS PATH...
...AND PROTECTS ME FROM HIS PRIMITIVE ATTACKS!
WHY IS PURPLE-HEAD TALKING? WHY IS PURPLE-HEAD HOUNDING HULK?
YEAH, WIZ--YOU GOT A LOT ON YOUR PLATE, WHAT WITH WANTING TO WIN THE FAME AND OVATION OF THE PEOPLE FOREVER...
...SO LEAVE THE HULK TO ME!
RRHARRG!
MY BRIGHT IDEA ONLY BLINDS THE HULK FOR A SECOND--BUT THAT'S ALL I NEED TO DRAW HIM BACK INTO THE BUILDING...
FLAME-MAN ATTACK HULK LAST! HULK ATTACK FLAME-MAN FIRST!
...AND AWAY FROM THE MILE-A-MINUTE MIND OF THE WIZARD.
WHAT IS THAT HOT-HEADED HALF-WIT THINKING? IF YOU CAN CALL IT THINKING...
I ONLY HAVE ONE CHANCE--AND JUST TWO THINGS GOING FOR ME.
FIRST--THE WIZARD THINKS ALL I CAN DO IS FOCUS ON WHAT'S RIGHT IN FRONT OF ME.
FLAME-MAN THINK HE CAN ESCAPE HULK?
SECOND--I KNOW THAT'S ALL THE HULK FOCUSES ON!
HULK SMASH PUNY FLAME-MAN!
A FEW WELL-PLACED FLAME IMAGES OF MYSELF...
HURH--? FLAME-MAN OVER THERE? FLAME-MAN TRICK HULK?

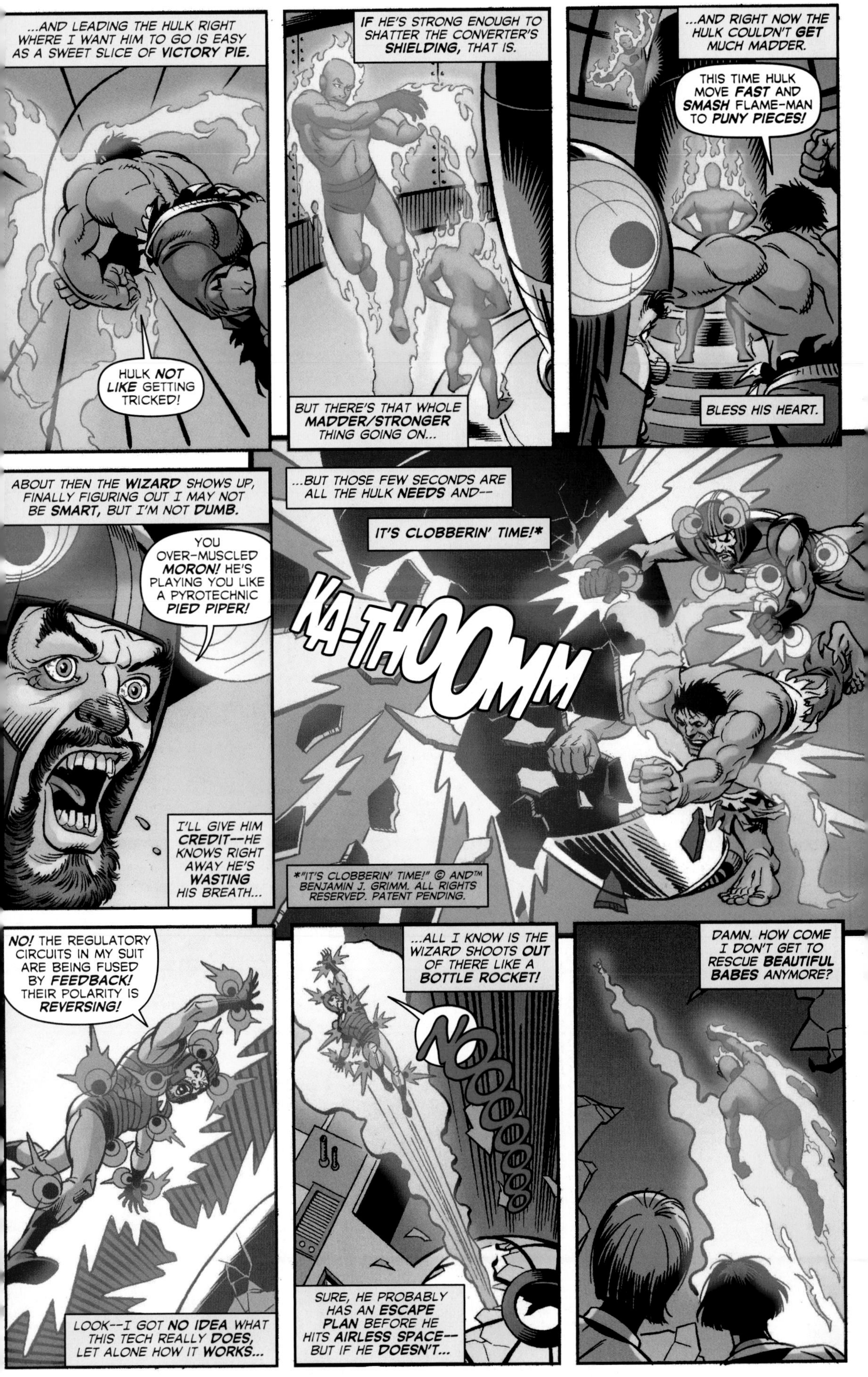
...AND LEADING THE HULK RIGHT WHERE I WANT HIM TO GO IS EASY AS A SWEET SLICE OF VICTORY PIE.
HULK NOT LIKE GETTING TRICKED!
IF HE'S STRONG ENOUGH TO SHATTER THE CONVERTER'S SHIELDING, THAT IS.
BUT THERE'S THAT WHOLE MADDER/STRONGER THING GOING ON...
...AND RIGHT NOW THE HULK COULDN'T GET MUCH MADDER.
THIS TIME HULK MOVE FAST AND SMASH FLAME-MAN TO PUNY PIECES!
BLESS HIS HEART.
ABOUT THEN THE WIZARD SHOWS UP, FINALLY FIGURING OUT I MAY NOT BE SMART, BUT I'M NOT DUMB.
YOU OVER-MUSCLED MORON! HE'S PLAYING YOU LIKE A PYROTECHNIC PIED PIPER!
I'LL GIVE HIM CREDIT--HE KNOWS RIGHT AWAY HE'S WASTING HIS BREATH...
...BUT THOSE FEW SECONDS ARE ALL THE HULK NEEDS AND--
IT'S CLOBBERIN' TIME!*
KA-THOOMM
*"IT'S CLOBBERIN' TIME!" © AND™ BENJAMIN J. GRIMM. ALL RIGHTS RESERVED. PATENT PENDING.
NO! THE REGULATORY CIRCUITS IN MY SUIT ARE BEING FUSED BY FEEDBACK! THEIR POLARITY IS REVERSING!
LOOK--I GOT NO IDEA WHAT THIS TECH REALLY DOES, LET ALONE HOW IT WORKS...
...ALL I KNOW IS THE WIZARD SHOOTS OUT OF THERE LIKE A BOTTLE ROCKET!
NOOOOOOOO
SURE, HE PROBABLY HAS AN ESCAPE PLAN BEFORE HE HITS AIRLESS SPACE--BUT IF HE DOESN'T...
DAMN. HOW COME I DON'T GET TO RESCUE BEAUTIFUL BABES ANYMORE?

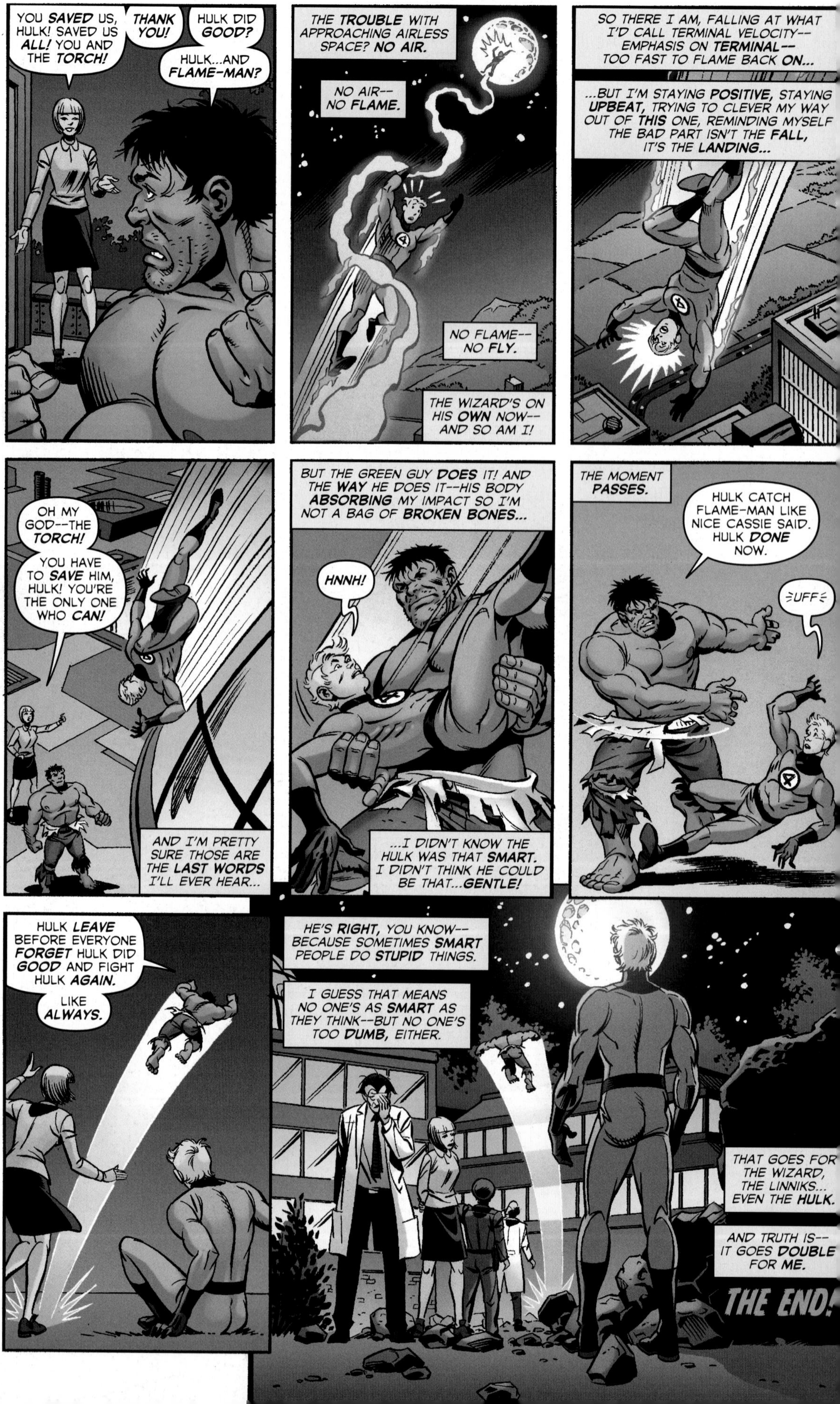
YOU SAVED US, HULK! SAVED US ALL! YOU AND THE TORCH!
THANK YOU!
HULK DID GOOD?
HULK...AND FLAME-MAN?
THE TROUBLE WITH APPROACHING AIRLESS SPACE? NO AIR.
NO AIR-- NO FLAME.
NO FLAME-- NO FLY.
THE WIZARD'S ON HIS OWN NOW-- AND SO AM I!
SO THERE I AM, FALLING AT WHAT I'D CALL TERMINAL VELOCITY-- EMPHASIS ON TERMINAL-- TOO FAST TO FLAME BACK ON...
...BUT I'M STAYING POSITIVE, STAYING UPBEAT, TRYING TO CLEVER MY WAY OUT OF THIS ONE, REMINDING MYSELF THE BAD PART ISN'T THE FALL, IT'S THE LANDING...
OH MY GOD--THE TORCH!
YOU HAVE TO SAVE HIM, HULK! YOU'RE THE ONLY ONE WHO CAN!
AND I'M PRETTY SURE THOSE ARE THE LAST WORDS I'LL EVER HEAR...
BUT THE GREEN GUY DOES IT! AND THE WAY HE DOES IT--HIS BODY ABSORBING MY IMPACT SO I'M NOT A BAG OF BROKEN BONES...
HNNH!
...I DIDN'T KNOW THE HULK WAS THAT SMART. I DIDN'T THINK HE COULD BE THAT...GENTLE!
THE MOMENT PASSES.
HULK CATCH FLAME-MAN LIKE NICE CASSIE SAID. HULK DONE NOW.
UFF
HULK LEAVE BEFORE EVERYONE FORGET HULK DID GOOD AND FIGHT HULK AGAIN.
LIKE ALWAYS.
HE'S RIGHT, YOU KNOW-- BECAUSE SOMETIMES SMART PEOPLE DO STUPID THINGS.
I GUESS THAT MEANS NO ONE'S AS SMART AS THEY THINK--BUT NO ONE'S TOO DUMB, EITHER.
THAT GOES FOR THE WIZARD, THE LINNIKS... EVEN THE HULK.
AND TRUTH IS-- IT GOES DOUBLE FOR ME.
THE END!

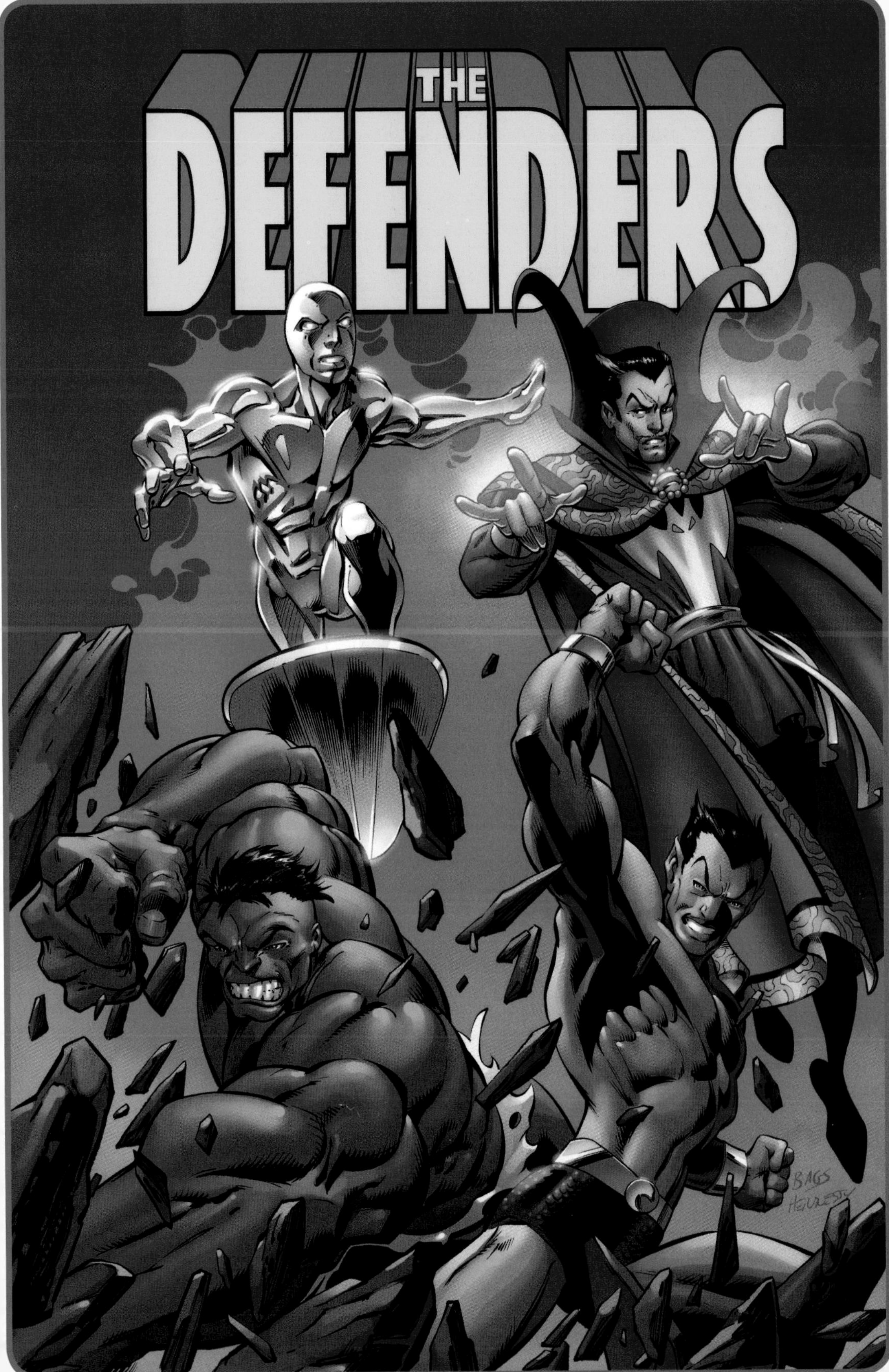
THE
DEFENDERS
BAGS
HEURESTY

FROM THE MARVEL VAULT...KIND OF

THIS MAY BE ONE OF THE GREATEST DEFENDERS STORIES EVER TOLD. OR IT MAY BE A TOTAL TRAIN WRECK. OR, JUST POSSIBLY, BOTH.

[OR, YOU KNOW, SOMEWHERE IN BETWEEN, BUT WHO SELLS COMICS WITH WISHY-WASHY STATEMENTS LIKE "SOMEWHERE IN-BETWEEN"?]

I KINDA LIKE IT, ANYWAY. AND AS IT SAYS IN THE CREDITS, THERE'S A STORY BEHIND THE STORY.
HERE'S WHAT HAPPENED:

BACK WHEN ERIK LARSEN AND I WERE DOING DEFENDERS, EDITOR TOM BREVOORT HAD A FILL-IN PREPARED, JUST IN CASE. ERIK WAS FIGHTING PNEUMONIA, I WAS OVERWORKED—IT SEEMED LIKE A GOOD IDEA TO BE PREPARED, IN CASE THE SCHEDULE WENT HAYWIRE. MARK BAGLEY HAD SOME TIME IN HIS SCHEDULE, SO TOM HAD FABIAN NICIEZA WRITE UP A PLOT—APPARENTLY VERY QUICKLY, FROM WHAT FABIAN REMEMBERS—AND THEN MARK DREW IT UP, AND IT GOT PUT IN A DRAWER. AND AS I RECALL, ERIK AND I SKATED THE DEADLINES PRETTY CLOSE, HERE AND THERE ("HERE AND THERE"? HOW ABOUT "ALMOST CONSTANTLY"?), BUT WE NEVER QUITE WENT OVER THE EDGE, AND FABIAN AND MARK'S STORY WAS NEVER USED.

UNTIL NOW.

AS PART OF THIS WHOLE "FROM THE MARVEL VAULT" PROGRAM, THE FINE FOLKS AT THE HOUSE OF IDEAS RESURRECTED THIS STORY AND FINISHED IT UP. BUT THERE WERE A FEW PROBLEMS ALONG THE WAY.

FIRST OFF, FABIAN COULDN'T SCRIPT IT, BECAUSE HE'S CURRENTLY COMMITTED ELSEWHERE, AND UNAVAILABLE.

SO ASSISTANT EDITOR RACHEL PINNELAS ASKED ME IF I'D SCRIPT IT, SINCE I WAS THE REGULAR WRITER BACK THEN. AND IT SOUNDED LIKE FUN TO ME. I LIKE WRITING THE DEFENDERS AND I HAD A BLAST ON THAT RUN WITH ERIK, SO WHY NOT REVISIT IT? IT'S MARK BAGLEY ART, AND WITH FABIAN PLOTTING IT, I'M SURE THE STORY IS SOLID. "SURE, I'D BE GLAD TO," I TOLD RACHEL. "JUST SEND ME THE ART AND A COPY OF THE PLOT."

"AH, WELL, THAT'S THE THING," STARTED RACHEL.

THEY COULD SEND ME THE ART. BUT THEY DON'T HAVE THE PLOT.

"NO PROBLEM," I SAY. I'LL JUST ASK FABIAN.

NO, IT IS A PROBLEM. HE DOESN'T HAVE ONE EITHER. LOST IN A HARD-DRIVE CRASH, YEARS AGO.

AND TO MAKE MATTERS WORSE, FABIAN DOESN'T EVEN REMEMBER WHAT THE STORY WAS. HE REMEMBERS THAT HE WROTE IT—PROBABLY GOT THE JOB ON FRIDAY AND HAD A PLOT IN BY MONDAY OR TUESDAY—BUT HE DOESN'T HAVE A CLUE WHAT THE DETAILS OF THE STORY ARE. EVEN THE ART DOESN'T JOG HIS MEMORY BEYOND, "YEAH, MARK SURE DID A NICE JOB, DIDN'T HE?"

MARK DOESN'T REMEMBER MUCH MORE. IT WAS YEARS AGO.

SO I LOOK OVER THE ART, AND MARK BAGLEY DID INDEED DO A VERY NICE JOB. AND HE'S A GOOD ENOUGH STORYTELLER THAT I CAN PIECE TOGETHER AN OUTLINE OF WHAT THE STORY MUST BE, AT LEAST IN THE BASICS. BUT THE BITS WHERE EXPLANATIONS HAPPEN, WHERE THE TEXTURE AND DETAIL GO THAT MAKE IT MORE THAN JUST A SIMPLE STRUCTURE?

HAVEN'T A CLUE.

SO I HAVE TO COME UP WITH A STORY TO FIT THE ART. A NEW STORY. ONE THAT MIGHT BEAR SOME RESEMBLANCE TO WHAT FABIAN INTENDED, AT LEAST AT THE BIG STRUCTURAL MOMENTS, BUT OTHER THAN THAT, IT'S WIDE OPEN. KIND OF LIKE PLAYING MAD LIBS WITH ARTWORK.

AND AS I KEEP LOOKING THROUGH THE ART, I GET AN IDEA. A PRETTY DEMENTED IDEA, REALLY, BASED ON ONE CRYPTIC PANEL LATE IN THE BOOK (THE ONE WHERE THE SCRIPT IS "HTNN--!", IF YOU WERE WONDERING). BUT IT'S AN IDEA THAT, DEMENTED AS IT IS, WON'T GO AWAY. AND ACTUALLY, I'M THINKING, IT COULD BE KINDA FUN...

I TELL FABIAN THE IDEA, MOSTLY AS A JOKE. BUT HE LAUGHS, AND SAYS THAT IT SOUNDS LIKE A HOOT, AND IT MIGHT EVEN BE BETTER THAN WHATEVER HIS ORIGINAL STORY WAS.

AND I TELL RACHEL, WHO'S EDITING IT, AND SHE CRACKS UP, AND SAYS "DO IT, DO IT."

SO I DO IT. AND HERE IT IS.

IT'S NOT WHAT FABIAN PLOTTED, NOT BY ANY MEANS. BUT IT'S DEFINITELY A DEFENDERS STORY, AND IT FITS THE TONE OF WHAT ERIK AND I WERE DOING BACK THEN. THERE'S BANTER, DISAGREEMENT, THE CURSE OF YANDROTH. HEROES STEP UP, AND THE WORLD IS SAVED. AND I GOT TO STICK A VERY OLD JOKE ABOUT A HOT-DOG VENDOR INTO IT.

I HAD A GREAT TIME SCRIPTING IT. ANDREW HENNESSY, CHRIS SOTOMAYOR AND CHRIS ELIOPOULOS FINISHED IT UP BEAUTIFULLY. ONE OF THE GREATEST DEFENDERS STORIES EVER? A COMPLETE TRAIN WRECK? BOTH? SOMEWHERE IN BETWEEN?

I DUNNO. BUT I HOPE YOU ENJOY IT.

— KURT BUSIEK, JUNE 2011

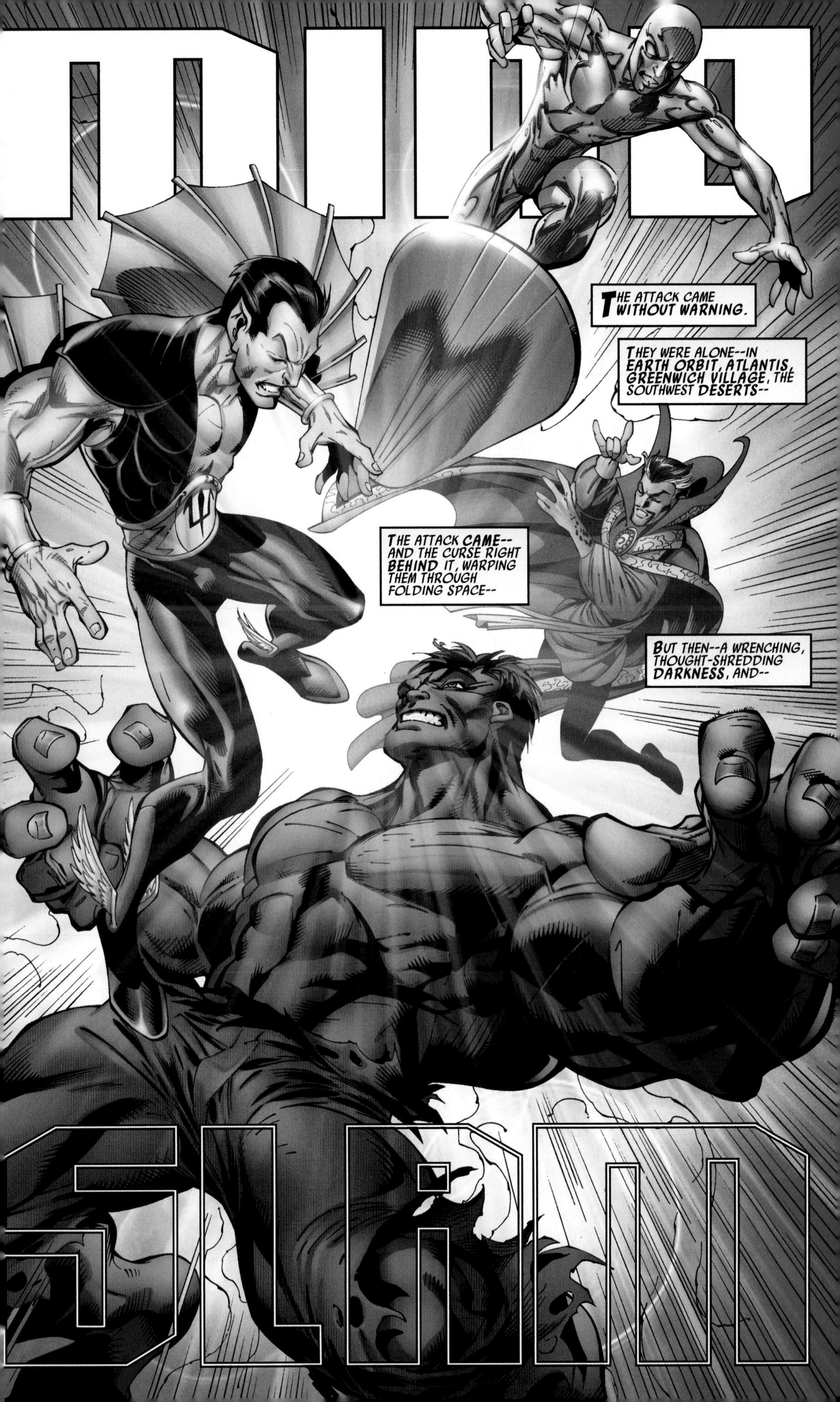
THE ATTACK CAME WITHOUT WARNING.
THEY WERE ALONE--IN EARTH ORBIT, ATLANTIS, GREENWICH VILLAGE, THE SOUTHWEST DESERTS--
THE ATTACK CAME--AND THE CURSE RIGHT BEHIND IT, WARPING THEM THROUGH FOLDING SPACE--
BUT THEN--A WRENCHING, THOUGHT-SHREDDING DARKNESS, AND--

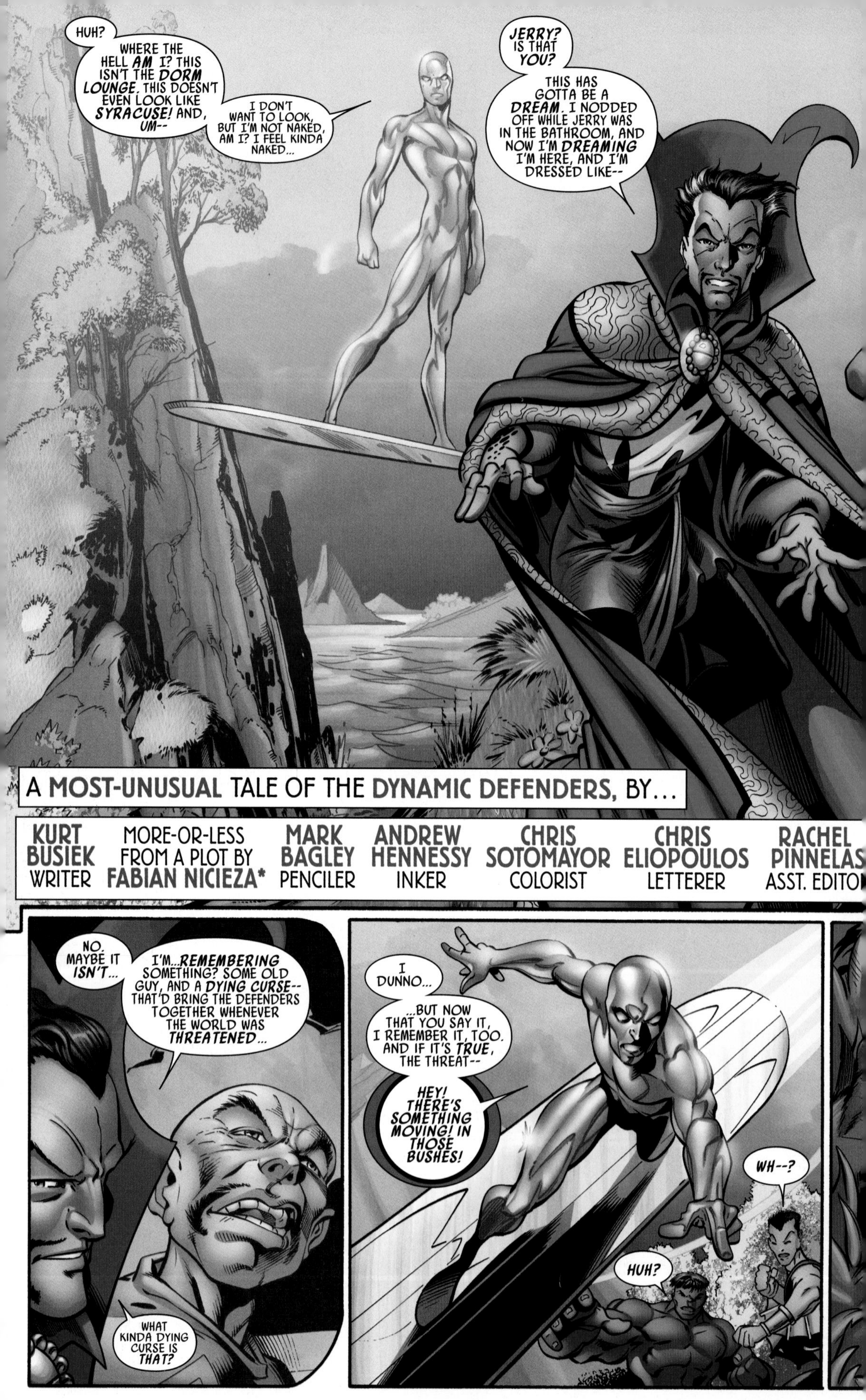
HUH?
WHERE THE HELL AM I? THIS ISN'T THE DORM LOUNGE. THIS DOESN'T EVEN LOOK LIKE SYRACUSE! AND, UM--
I DON'T WANT TO LOOK, BUT I'M NOT NAKED, AM I? I FEEL KINDA NAKED...
JERRY? IS THAT YOU?
THIS HAS GOTTA BE A DREAM. I NODDED OFF WHILE JERRY WAS IN THE BATHROOM, AND NOW I'M DREAMING I'M HERE, AND I'M DRESSED LIKE--
A MOST-UNUSUAL TALE OF THE DYNAMIC DEFENDERS, BY...
KURT BUSIEK WRITER
MORE-OR-LESS FROM A PLOT BY FABIAN NICIEZA*
MARK BAGLEY PENCILER
ANDREW HENNESSY INKER
CHRIS SOTOMAYOR COLORIST
CHRIS ELIOPOULOS LETTERER
RACHEL PINNELAS ASST. EDITO
NO. MAYBE IT ISN'T...
I'M...REMEMBERING SOMETHING? SOME OLD GUY, AND A DYING CURSE--THAT'D BRING THE DEFENDERS TOGETHER WHENEVER THE WORLD WAS THREATENED...
WHAT KINDA DYING CURSE IS THAT?
I DUNNO...
...BUT NOW THAT YOU SAY IT, I REMEMBER IT, TOO. AND IF IT'S TRUE, THE THREAT--
HEY! THERE'S SOMETHING MOVING! IN THOSE BUSHES!
WH--?
HUH?

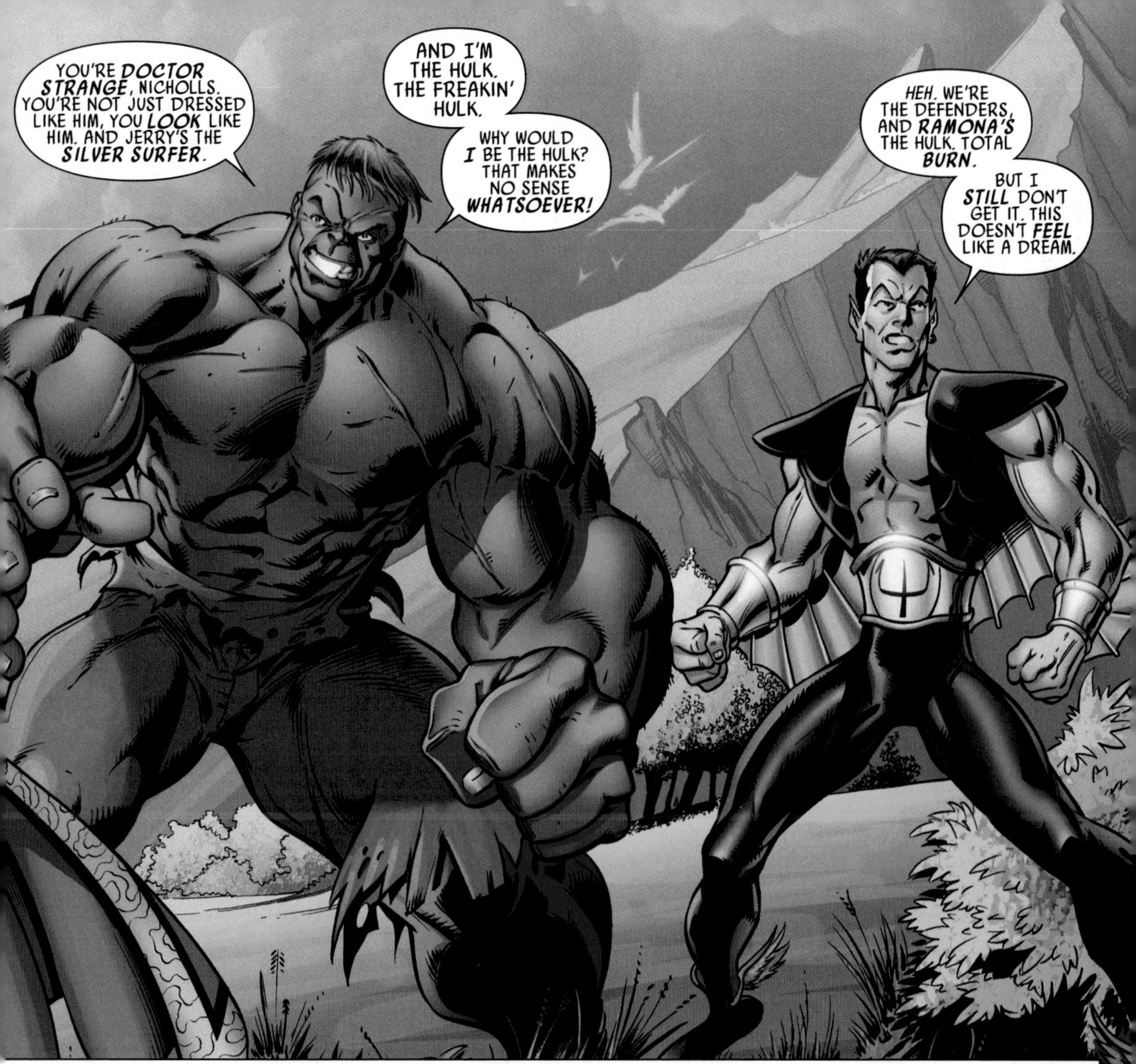

YOU'RE DOCTOR STRANGE, NICHOLLS. YOU'RE NOT JUST DRESSED LIKE HIM, YOU LOOK LIKE HIM. AND JERRY'S THE SILVER SURFER.
AND I'M THE HULK. THE FREAKIN' HULK.
WHY WOULD I BE THE HULK? THAT MAKES NO SENSE WHATSOEVER!
HEH. WE'RE THE DEFENDERS, AND RAMONA'S THE HULK. TOTAL BURN.
BUT I STILL DON'T GET IT. THIS DOESN'T FEEL LIKE A DREAM.

TOM BREVOORT
ECUTIVE EDITOR

AXEL ALONSO
EDITOR IN CHIEF

JOE QUESADA
CHIEF CREATIVE OFFICER

DAN BUCKLEY
PUBLISHER

ALAN FINE
EXECUTIVE PRODUCER

*SEE OUR TEXT PAGE FOR DETAILS!

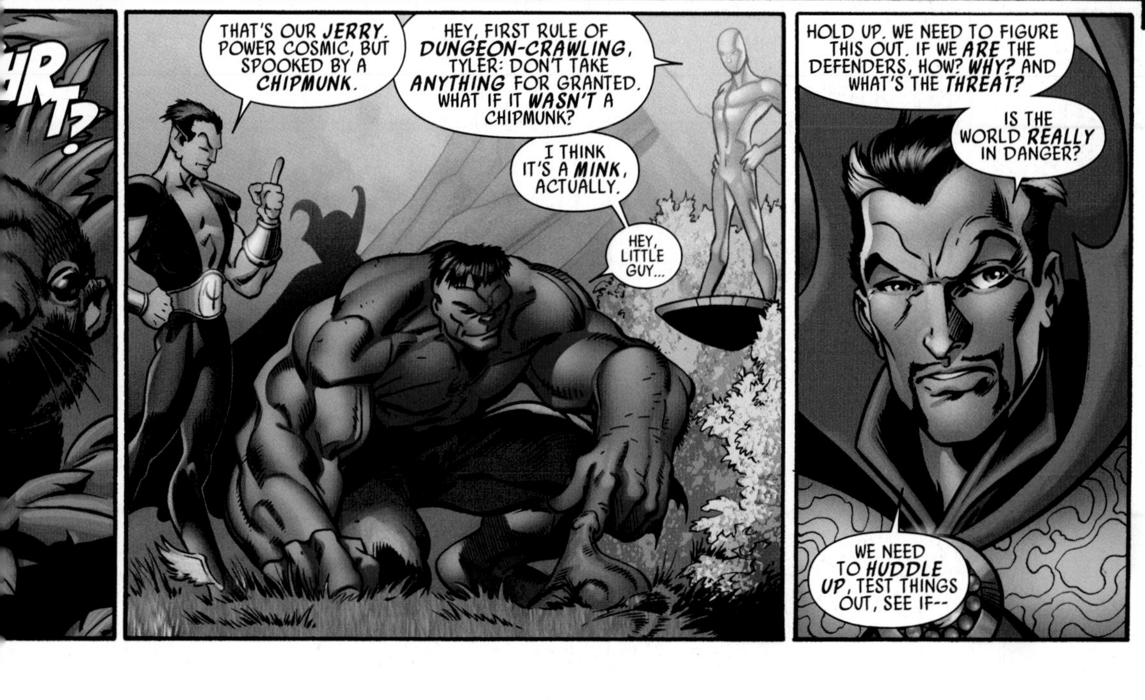

THAT'S OUR JERRY. POWER COSMIC, BUT SPOOKED BY A CHIPMUNK.
HEY, FIRST RULE OF DUNGEON-CRAWLING, TYLER: DON'T TAKE ANYTHING FOR GRANTED. WHAT IF IT WASN'T A CHIPMUNK?
I THINK IT'S A MINK, ACTUALLY.
HEY, LITTLE GUY...
HOLD UP. WE NEED TO FIGURE THIS OUT. IF WE ARE THE DEFENDERS, HOW? WHY? AND WHAT'S THE THREAT?
IS THE WORLD REALLY IN DANGER?
WE NEED TO HUDDLE UP, TEST THINGS OUT, SEE IF--

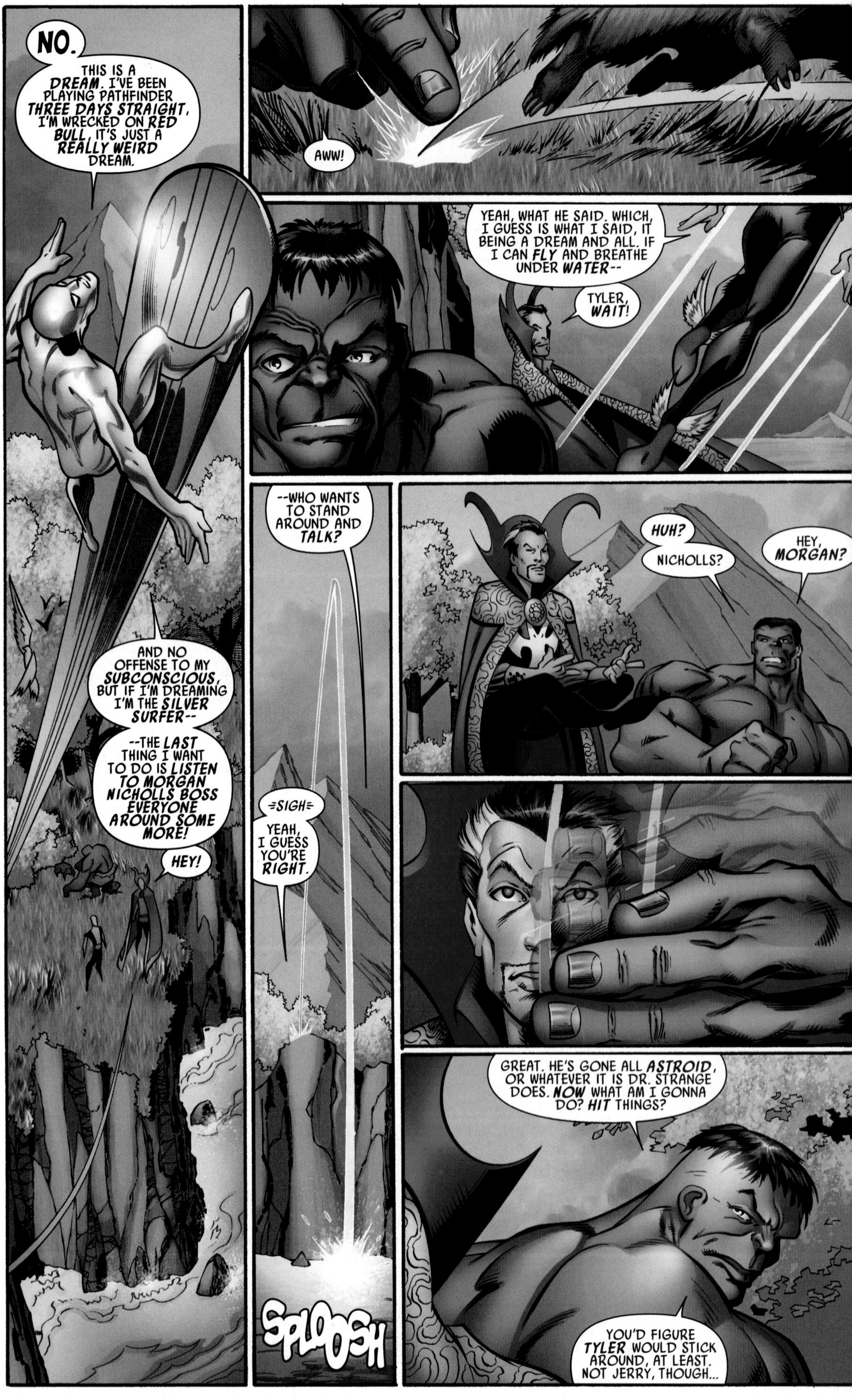

NO.
THIS IS A DREAM. I'VE BEEN PLAYING PATHFINDER THREE DAYS STRAIGHT, I'M WRECKED ON RED BULL, IT'S JUST A REALLY WEIRD DREAM.
AWW!
YEAH, WHAT HE SAID. WHICH, I GUESS IS WHAT I SAID, IT BEING A DREAM AND ALL. IF I CAN FLY AND BREATHE UNDER WATER--
TYLER, WAIT!
AND NO OFFENSE TO MY SUBCONSCIOUS, BUT IF I'M DREAMING I'M THE SILVER SURFER--
--THE LAST THING I WANT TO DO IS LISTEN TO MORGAN NICHOLLS BOSS EVERYONE AROUND SOME MORE!
HEY!
--WHO WANTS TO STAND AROUND AND TALK?
=SIGH=
YEAH, I GUESS YOU'RE RIGHT.
SPLOOSH
HUH?
NICHOLLS?
HEY, MORGAN?
GREAT. HE'S GONE ALL ASTROID, OR WHATEVER IT IS DR. STRANGE DOES. NOW WHAT AM I GONNA DO? HIT THINGS?
YOU'D FIGURE TYLER WOULD STICK AROUND, AT LEAST. NOT JERRY, THOUGH...

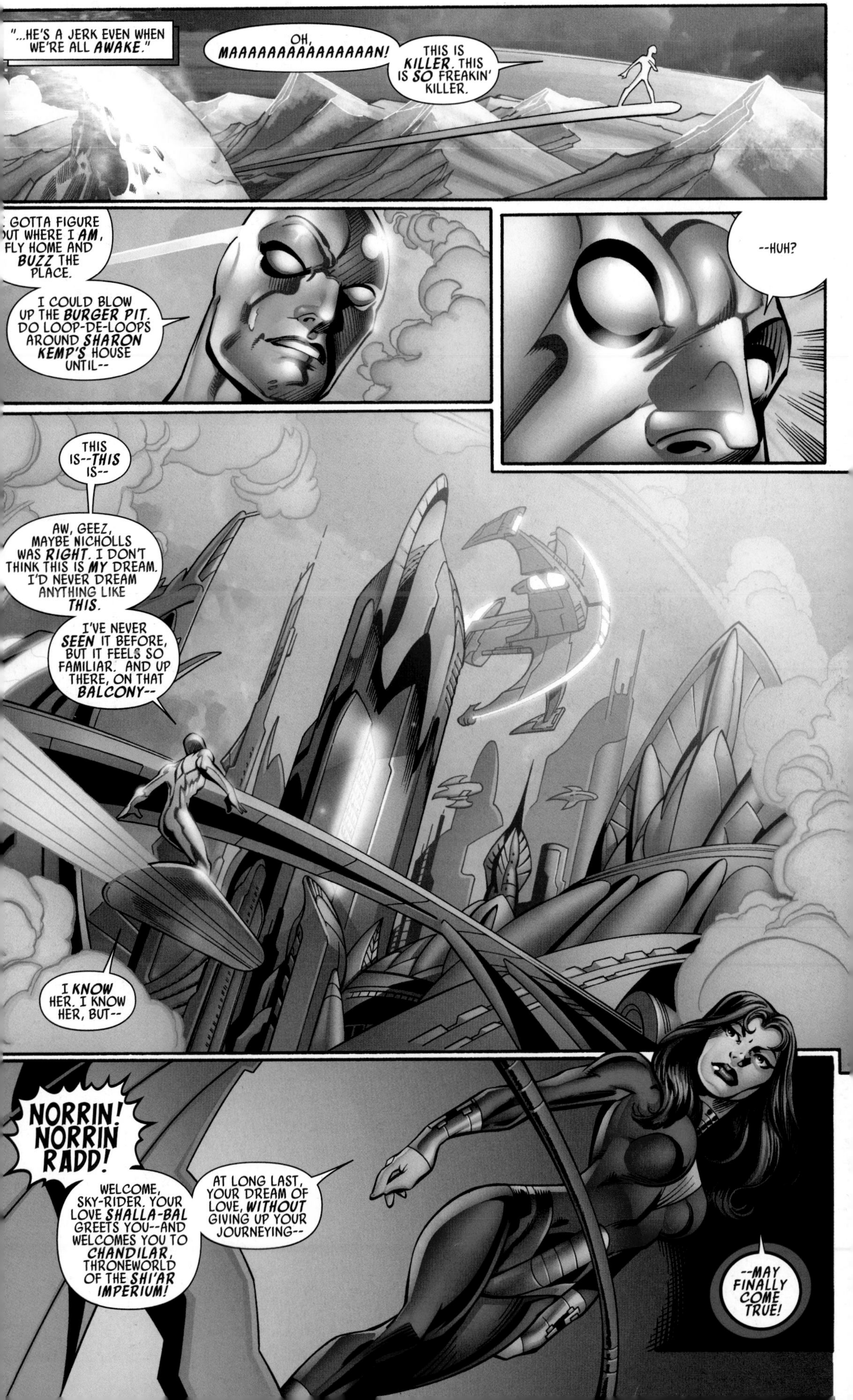
"...HE'S A JERK EVEN WHEN WE'RE ALL AWAKE."
OH, MAAAAAAAAAAAAAAAN!
THIS IS KILLER. THIS IS SO FREAKIN' KILLER.
GOTTA FIGURE OUT WHERE I AM, FLY HOME AND BUZZ THE PLACE.
I COULD BLOW UP THE BURGER PIT. DO LOOP-DE-LOOPS AROUND SHARON KEMP'S HOUSE UNTIL--
--HUH?
THIS IS--THIS IS--
AW, GEEZ, MAYBE NICHOLLS WAS RIGHT. I DON'T THINK THIS IS MY DREAM. I'D NEVER DREAM ANYTHING LIKE THIS.
I'VE NEVER SEEN IT BEFORE, BUT IT FEELS SO FAMILIAR. AND UP THERE, ON THAT BALCONY--
I KNOW HER. I KNOW HER, BUT--
NORRIN! NORRIN RADD!
WELCOME, SKY-RIDER. YOUR LOVE SHALLA-BAL GREETS YOU--AND WELCOMES YOU TO CHANDILAR, THRONEWORLD OF THE SHI'AR IMPERIUM!
AT LONG LAST, YOUR DREAM OF LOVE, WITHOUT GIVING UP YOUR JOURNEYING--
--MAY FINALLY COME TRUE!

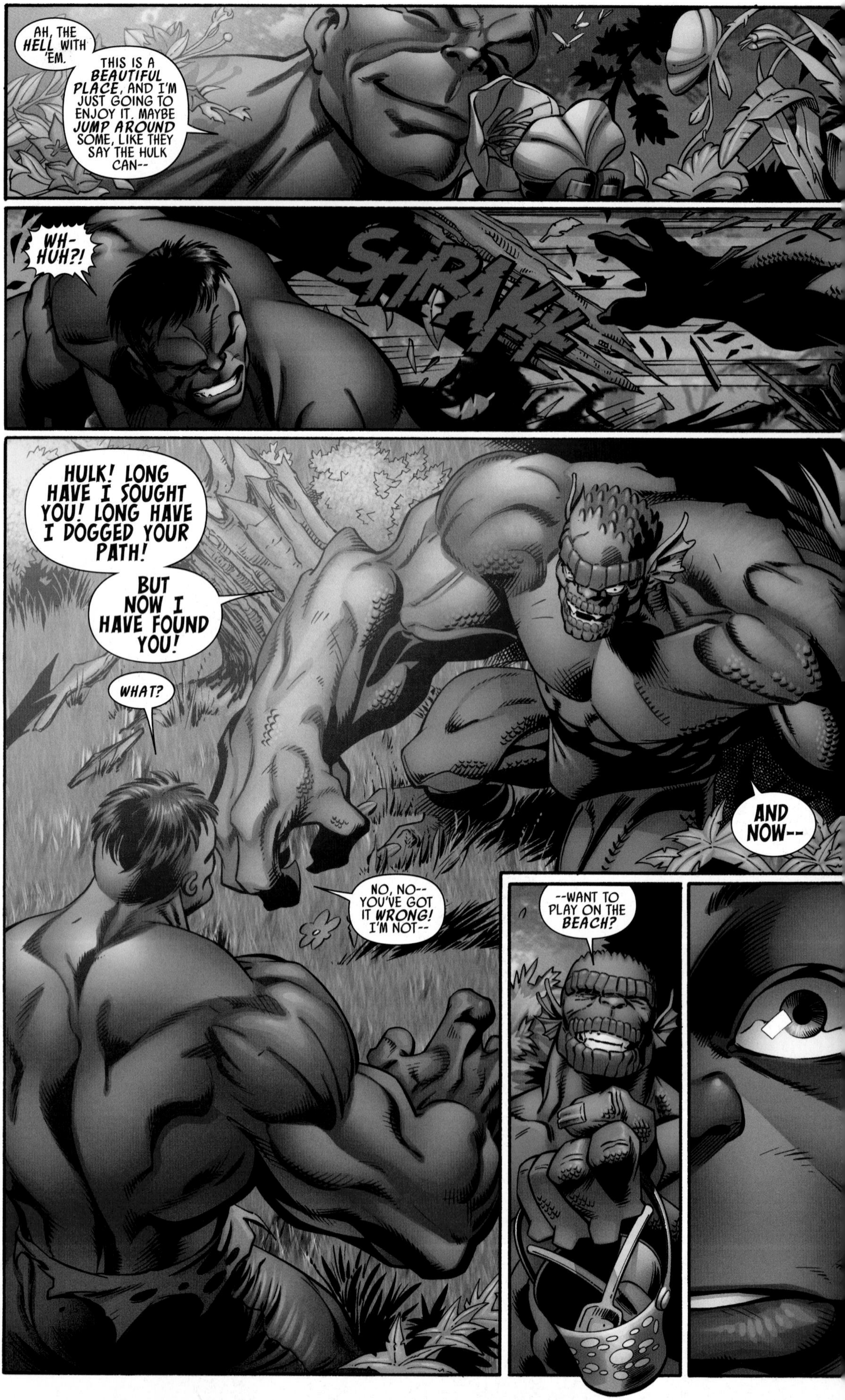
AH, THE HELL WITH 'EM.
THIS IS A BEAUTIFUL PLACE, AND I'M JUST GOING TO ENJOY IT. MAYBE JUMP AROUND SOME, LIKE THEY SAY THE HULK CAN--
WH-HUH?!
SHRAKK
HULK! LONG HAVE I SOUGHT YOU! LONG HAVE I DOGGED YOUR PATH!
BUT NOW I HAVE FOUND YOU!
WHAT?
AND NOW--
NO, NO-- YOU'VE GOT IT WRONG! I'M NOT--
--WANT TO PLAY ON THE BEACH?

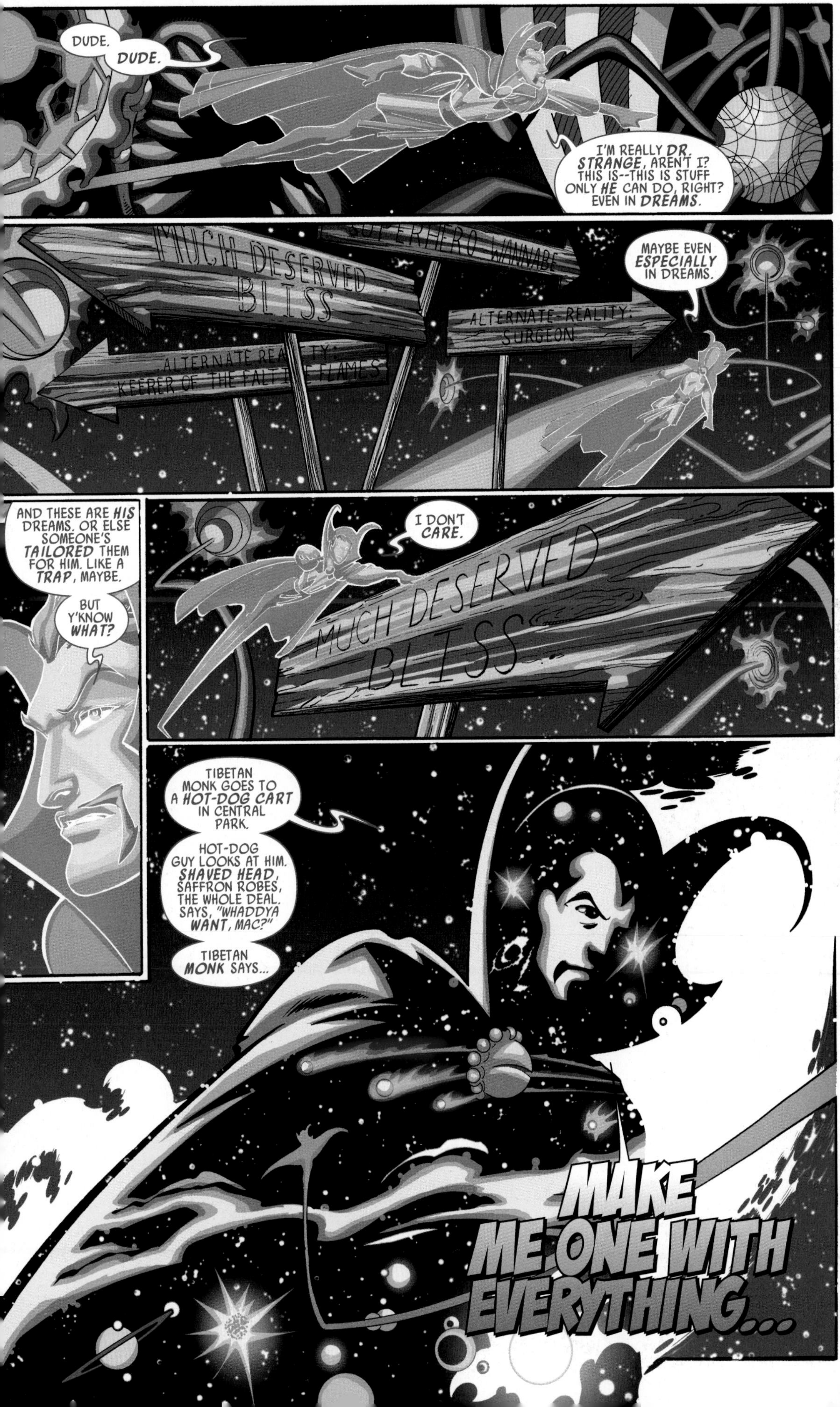
DUDE. DUDE.
I'M REALLY DR. STRANGE, AREN'T I? THIS IS--THIS IS STUFF ONLY HE CAN DO, RIGHT? EVEN IN DREAMS.
MUCH DESERVED BLISS
SUPERHERO WANNABE
ALTERNATE-REALITY: SURGEON
MAYBE EVEN ESPECIALLY IN DREAMS.
AND THESE ARE HIS DREAMS. OR ELSE SOMEONE'S TAILORED THEM FOR HIM. LIKE A TRAP, MAYBE.
BUT Y'KNOW WHAT?
I DON'T CARE.
MUCH DESERVED BLISS
TIBETAN MONK GOES TO A HOT-DOG CART IN CENTRAL PARK.
HOT-DOG GUY LOOKS AT HIM. SHAVED HEAD, SAFFRON ROBES, THE WHOLE DEAL. SAYS, "WHADDYA WANT, MAC?"
TIBETAN MONK SAYS...
MAKE ME ONE WITH EVERYTHING...

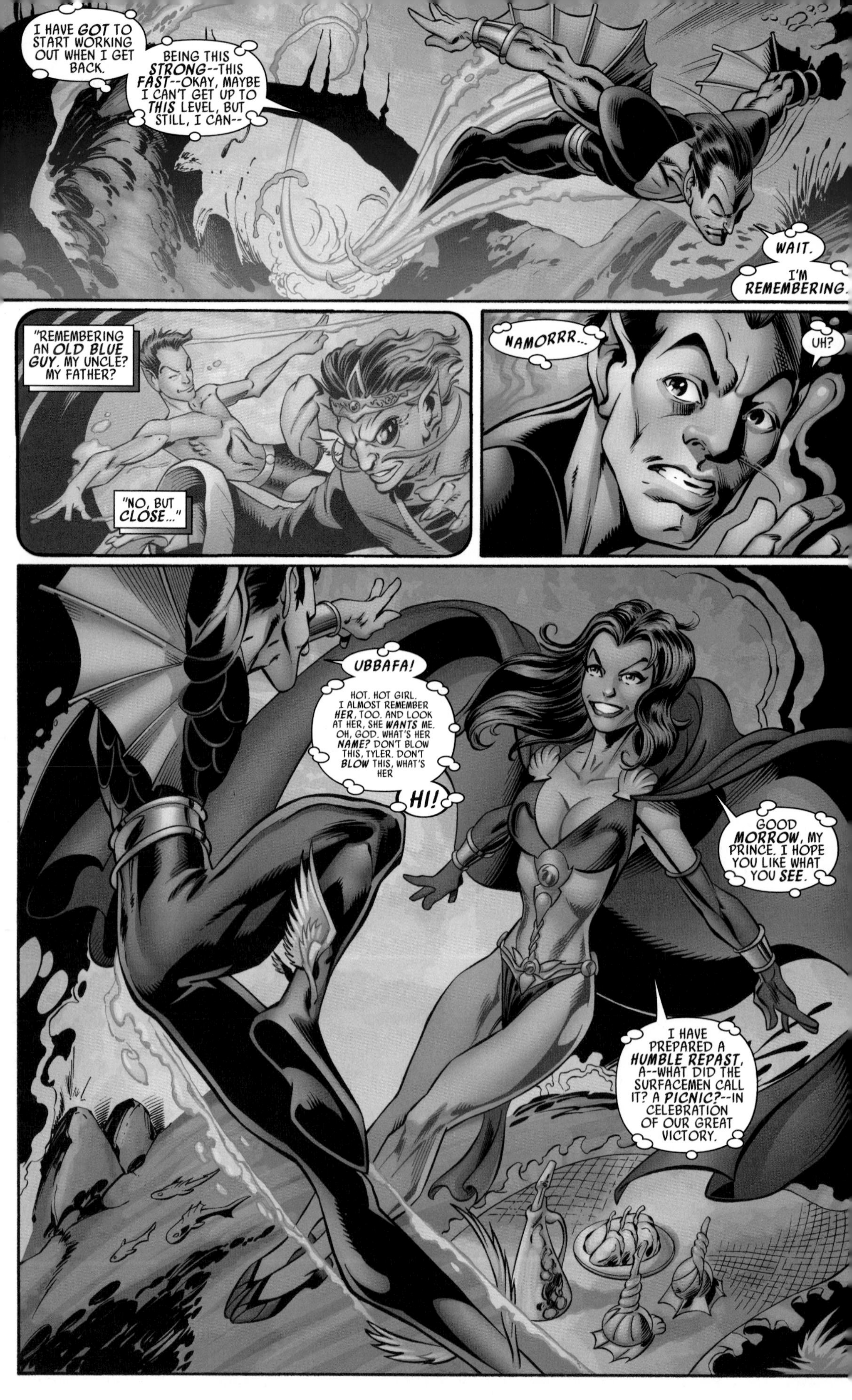

I HAVE GOT TO START WORKING OUT WHEN I GET BACK.
BEING THIS STRONG--THIS FAST--OKAY, MAYBE I CAN'T GET UP TO THIS LEVEL, BUT STILL, I CAN--
WAIT.
I'M REMEMBERING.
"REMEMBERING AN OLD BLUE GUY. MY UNCLE? MY FATHER?
"NO, BUT CLOSE..."
NAMORRR...
UH?
UBBAFA!
HOT. HOT GIRL. I ALMOST REMEMBER HER, TOO. AND LOOK AT HER, SHE WANTS ME. OH, GOD. WHAT'S HER NAME? DON'T BLOW THIS, TYLER. DON'T BLOW THIS, WHAT'S HER
HI!
GOOD MORROW, MY PRINCE. I HOPE YOU LIKE WHAT YOU SEE.
I HAVE PREPARED A HUMBLE REPAST, A--WHAT DID THE SURFACEMEN CALL IT? A PICNIC?--IN CELEBRATION OF OUR GREAT VICTORY.

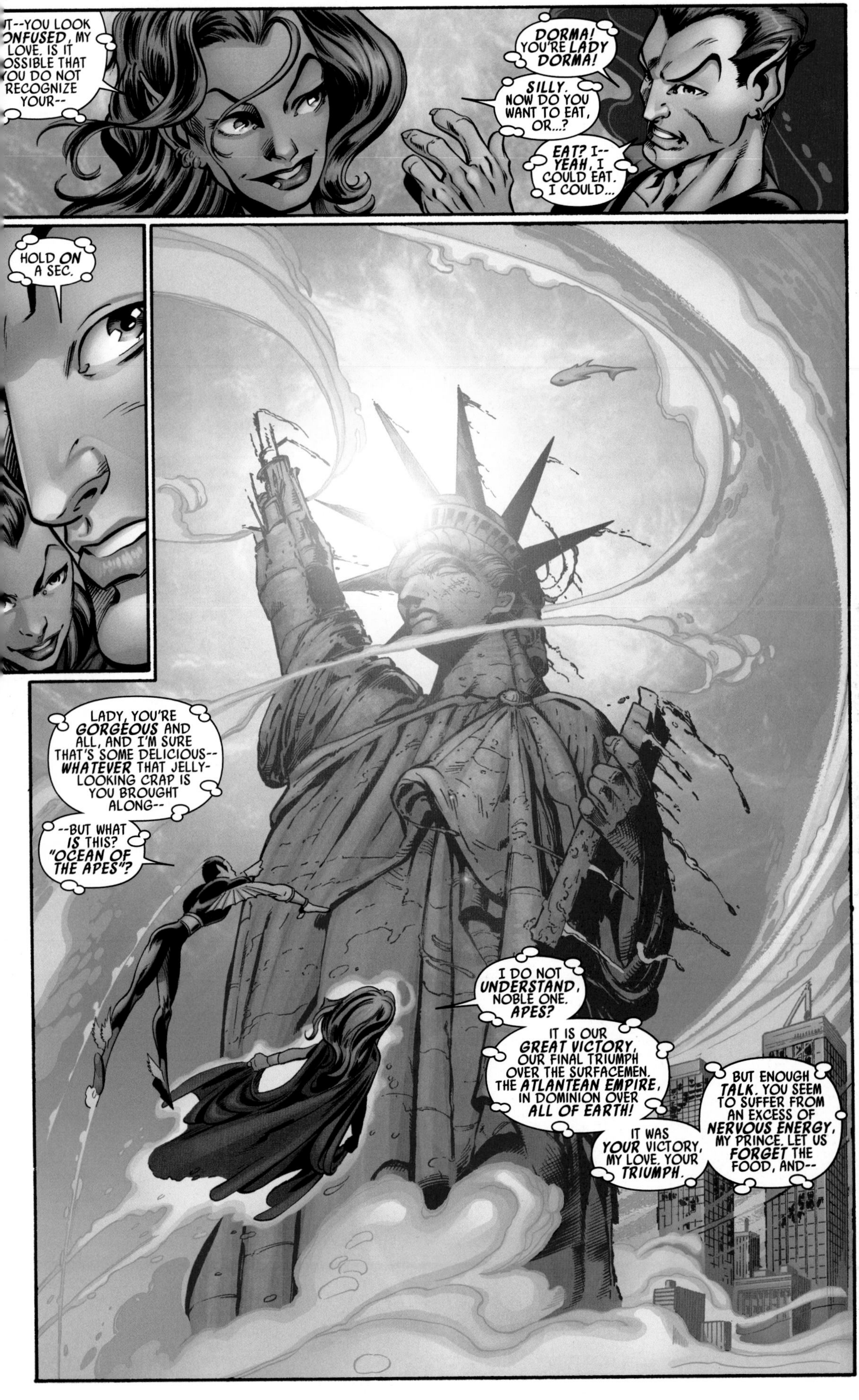

T--YOU LOOK ONFUSED, MY LOVE. IS IT OSSIBLE THAT YOU DO NOT RECOGNIZE YOUR--
DORMA! YOU'RE LADY DORMA!
SILLY. NOW DO YOU WANT TO EAT, OR...?
EAT? I-- YEAH, I COULD EAT. I COULD...
HOLD ON A SEC.
LADY, YOU'RE GORGEOUS AND ALL, AND I'M SURE THAT'S SOME DELICIOUS-- WHATEVER THAT JELLY-LOOKING CRAP IS YOU BROUGHT ALONG--
--BUT WHAT IS THIS? "OCEAN OF THE APES"?
I DO NOT UNDERSTAND, NOBLE ONE. APES?
IT IS OUR GREAT VICTORY, OUR FINAL TRIUMPH OVER THE SURFACEMEN. THE ATLANTEAN EMPIRE, IN DOMINION OVER ALL OF EARTH!
IT WAS YOUR VICTORY, MY LOVE. YOUR TRIUMPH.
BUT ENOUGH TALK. YOU SEEM TO SUFFER FROM AN EXCESS OF NERVOUS ENERGY, MY PRINCE. LET US FORGET THE FOOD, AND--

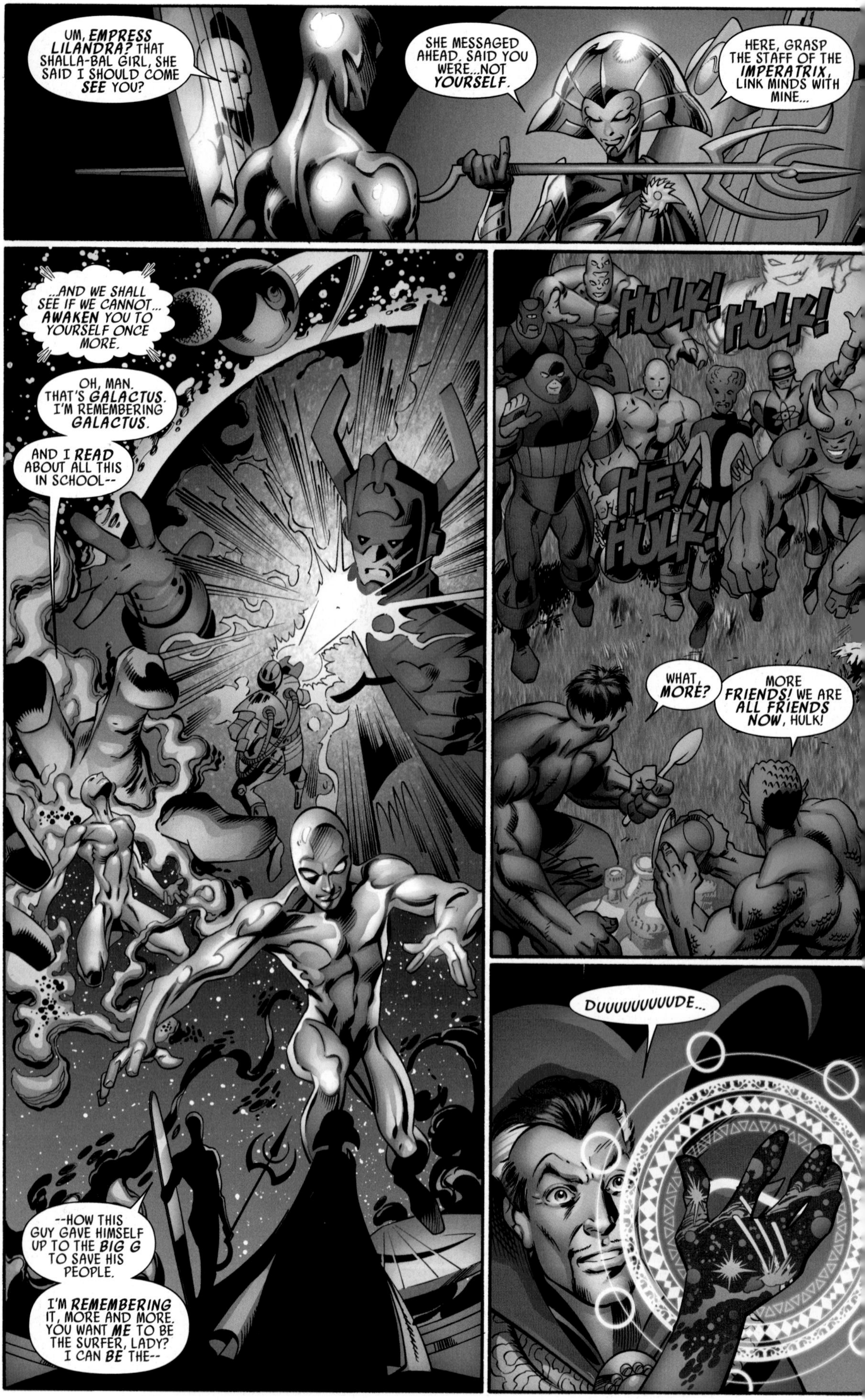

UM, EMPRESS LILANDRA? THAT SHALLA-BAL GIRL, SHE SAID I SHOULD COME SEE YOU?
SHE MESSAGED AHEAD. SAID YOU WERE...NOT YOURSELF.
HERE, GRASP THE STAFF OF THE IMPERATRIX, LINK MINDS WITH MINE...
...AND WE SHALL SEE IF WE CANNOT... AWAKEN YOU TO YOURSELF ONCE MORE.
OH, MAN. THAT'S GALACTUS. I'M REMEMBERING GALACTUS.
AND I READ ABOUT ALL THIS IN SCHOOL--
--HOW THIS GUY GAVE HIMSELF UP TO THE BIG G TO SAVE HIS PEOPLE.
I'M REMEMBERING IT, MORE AND MORE. YOU WANT ME TO BE THE SURFER, LADY? I CAN BE THE--
HULK! HULK!
HEY, HULK!
WHAT, MORE?
MORE FRIENDS! WE ARE ALL FRIENDS NOW, HULK!
DUUUUUUUUUDE...

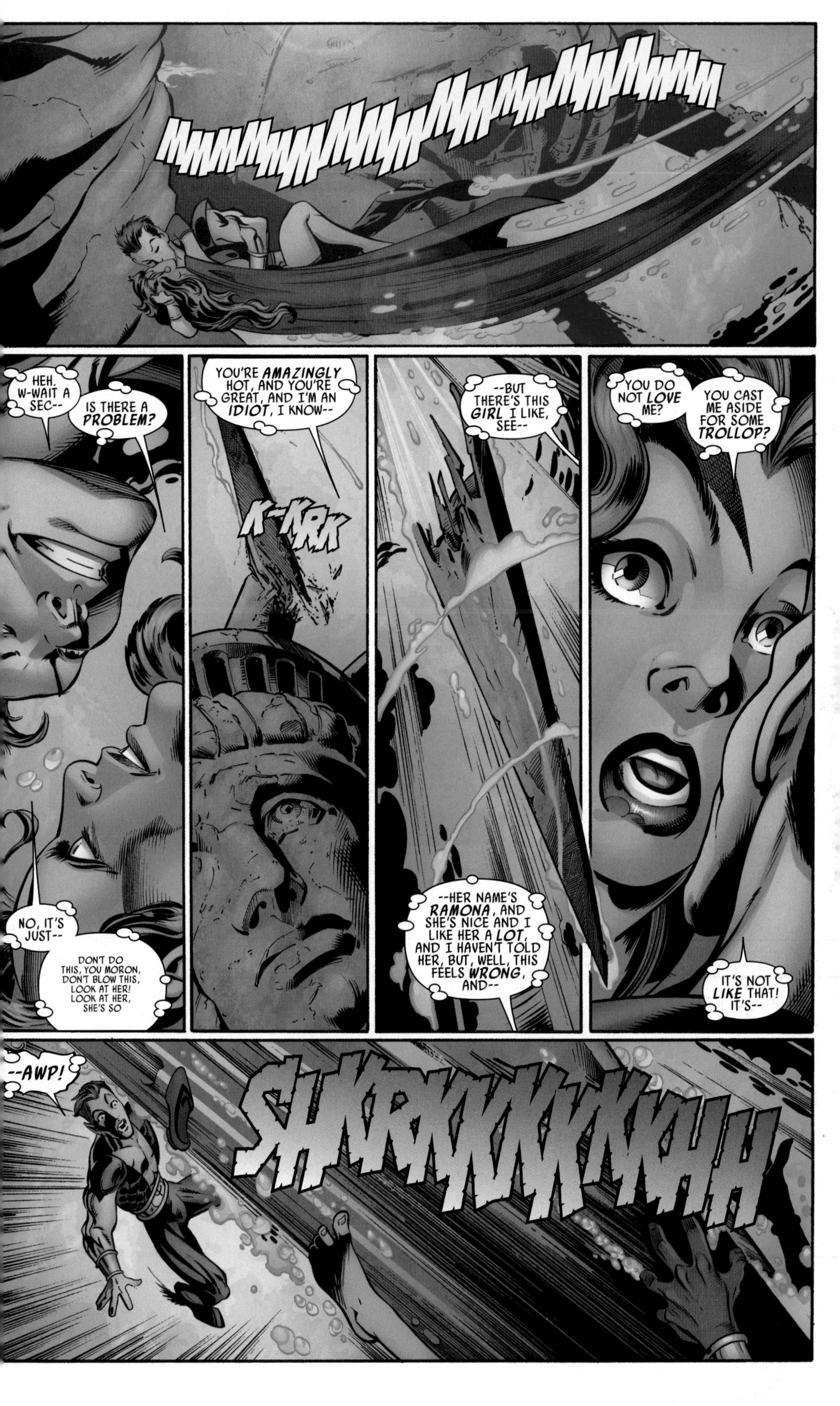
MMMMMMMMMMMMMMMMMMMMMMMMMMMMMM
HEH. W-WAIT A SEC--
IS THERE A PROBLEM?
NO, IT'S JUST--
DON'T DO THIS, YOU MORON, DON'T BLOW THIS, LOOK AT HER! LOOK AT HER, SHE'S SO
YOU'RE AMAZINGLY HOT, AND YOU'RE GREAT, AND I'M AN IDIOT, I KNOW--
K-KRK
--BUT THERE'S THIS GIRL I LIKE, SEE--
--HER NAME'S RAMONA, AND SHE'S NICE AND I LIKE HER A LOT, AND I HAVEN'T TOLD HER, BUT, WELL, THIS FEELS WRONG, AND--
YOU DO NOT LOVE ME?
YOU CAST ME ASIDE FOR SOME TROLLOP?
IT'S NOT LIKE THAT! IT'S--
--AWP!
SHKRKKKKKKKKKKKKKAH

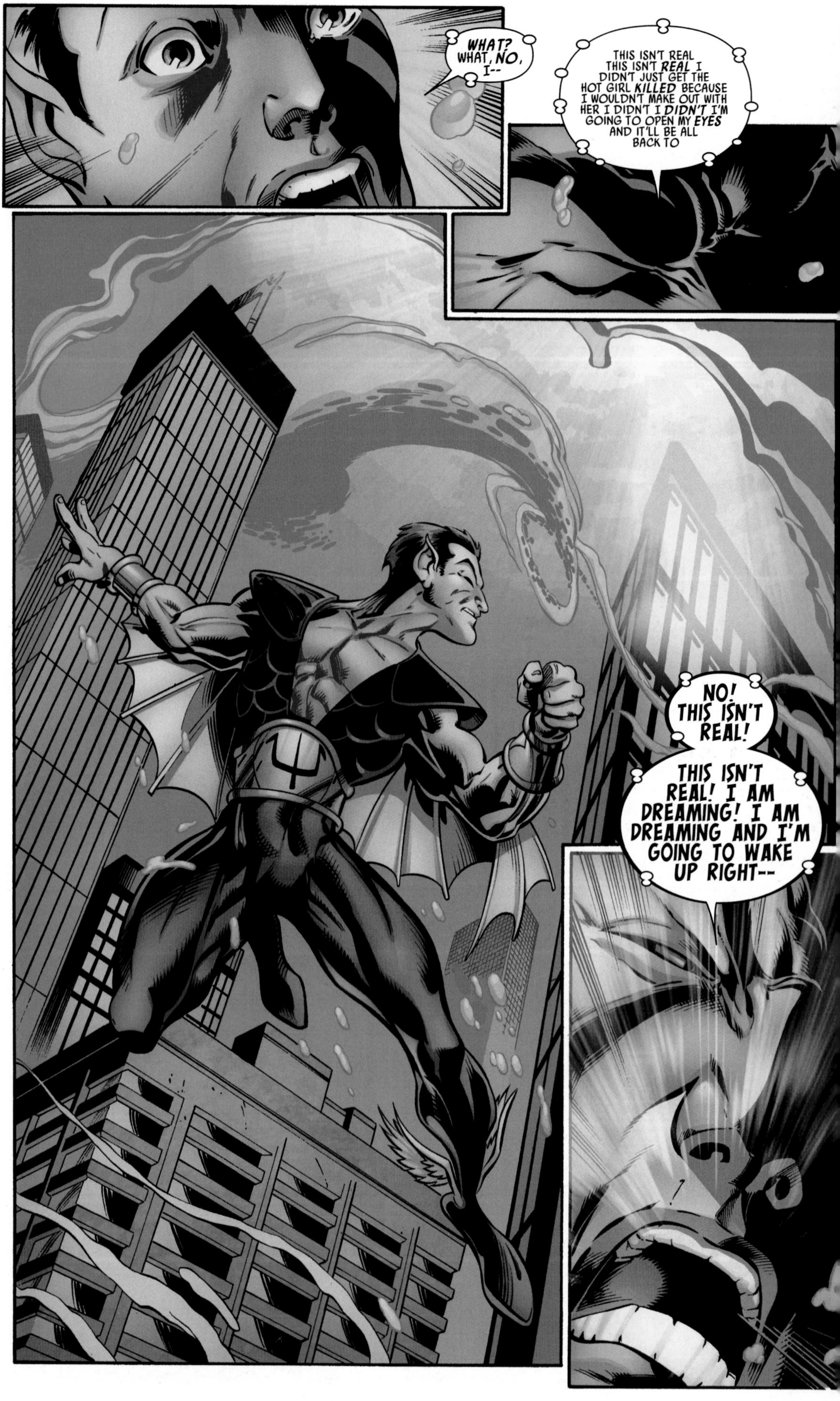
WHAT? WHAT, NO, I--
THIS ISN'T REAL THIS ISN'T REAL I DIDN'T JUST GET THE HOT GIRL KILLED BECAUSE I WOULDN'T MAKE OUT WITH HER I DIDN'T I DIDN'T I'M GOING TO OPEN MY EYES AND IT'LL BE ALL BACK TO
NO! THIS ISN'T REAL!
THIS ISN'T REAL! I AM DREAMING! I AM DREAMING AND I'M GOING TO WAKE UP RIGHT--

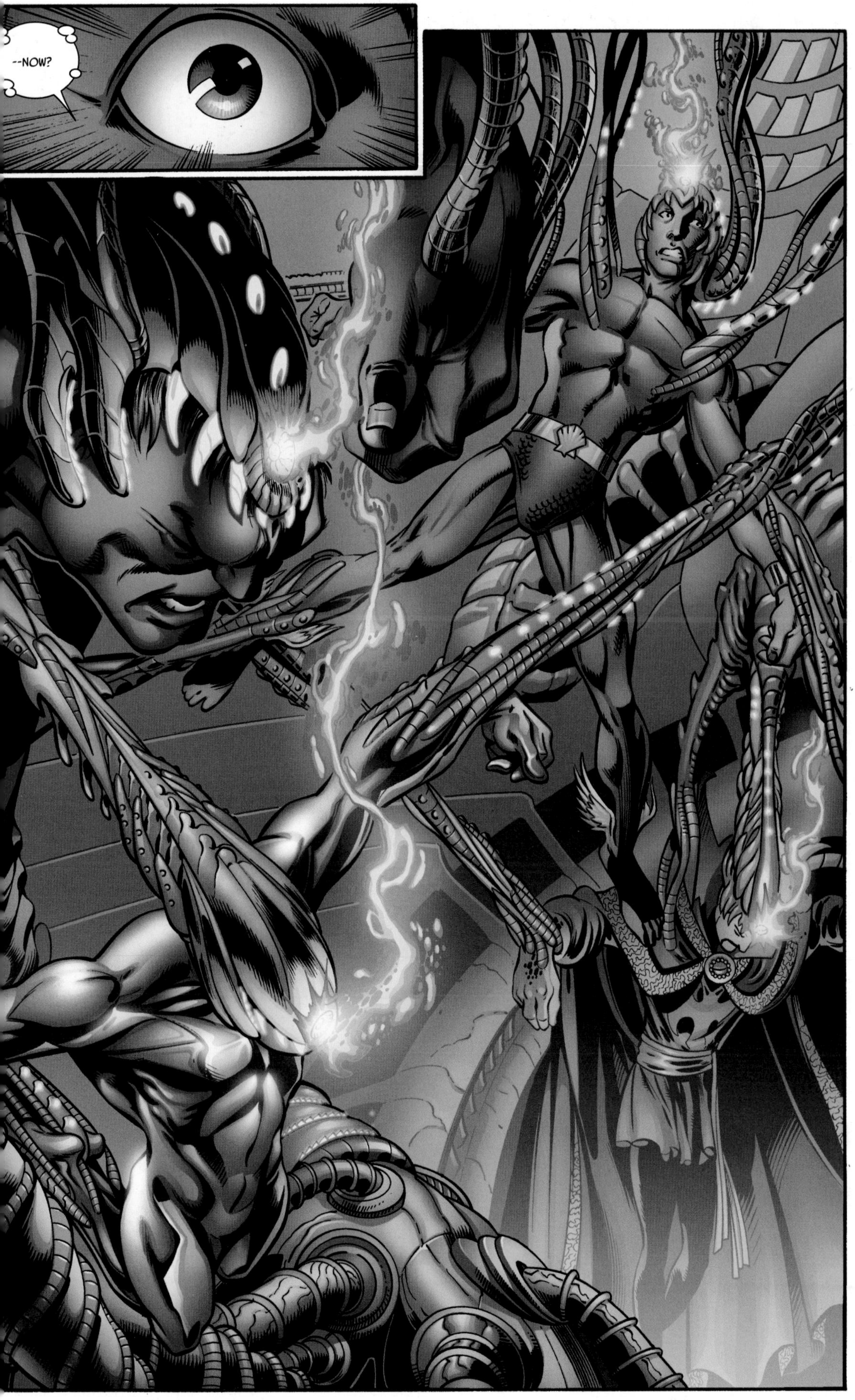
--NOW?

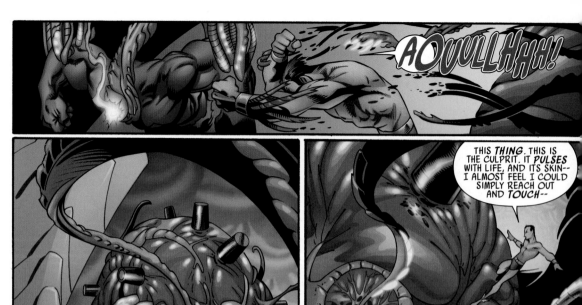

AOUULLHHH!

POSEIDON'S TRIDENT! WHAT IS THIS PLACE?

WHY AM I HERE?

AND--THESE THOUGHTS, CHURNING IN MY BRAIN, OF LOST LOVES, KINDER TIMES, AND--AND "RANDOM ENCOUNTER TABLES"?--

THIS THING. THIS IS THE CULPRIT. IT PULSES WITH LIFE, AND ITS SKIN-- I ALMOST FEEL I COULD SIMPLY REACH OUT AND TOUCH--

HTNN--!

NO! OUT, VILE CREATURE! OUT OF MY MIND!

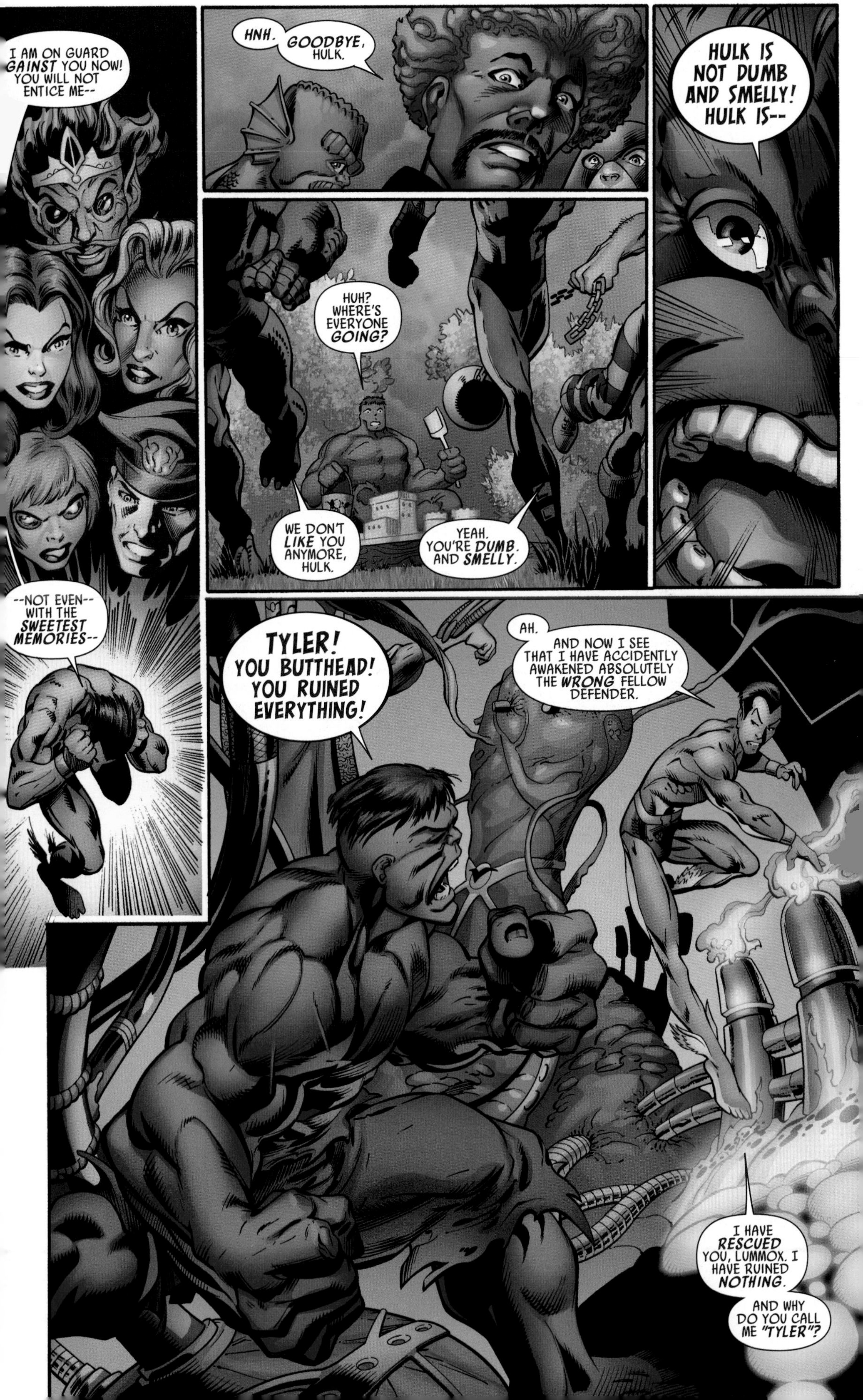
I AM ON GUARD GAINST YOU NOW! YOU WILL NOT ENTICE ME--
HNH.
GOODBYE, HULK.
HULK IS NOT DUMB AND SMELLY! HULK IS--
HUH? WHERE'S EVERYONE GOING?
WE DON'T LIKE YOU ANYMORE, HULK.
YEAH. YOU'RE DUMB. AND SMELLY.
--NOT EVEN-- WITH THE SWEETEST MEMORIES--
TYLER! YOU BUTTHEAD! YOU RUINED EVERYTHING!
AH.
AND NOW I SEE THAT I HAVE ACCIDENTLY AWAKENED ABSOLUTELY THE WRONG FELLOW DEFENDER.
I HAVE RESCUED YOU, LUMMOX. I HAVE RUINED NOTHING.
AND WHY DO YOU CALL ME "TYLER"?

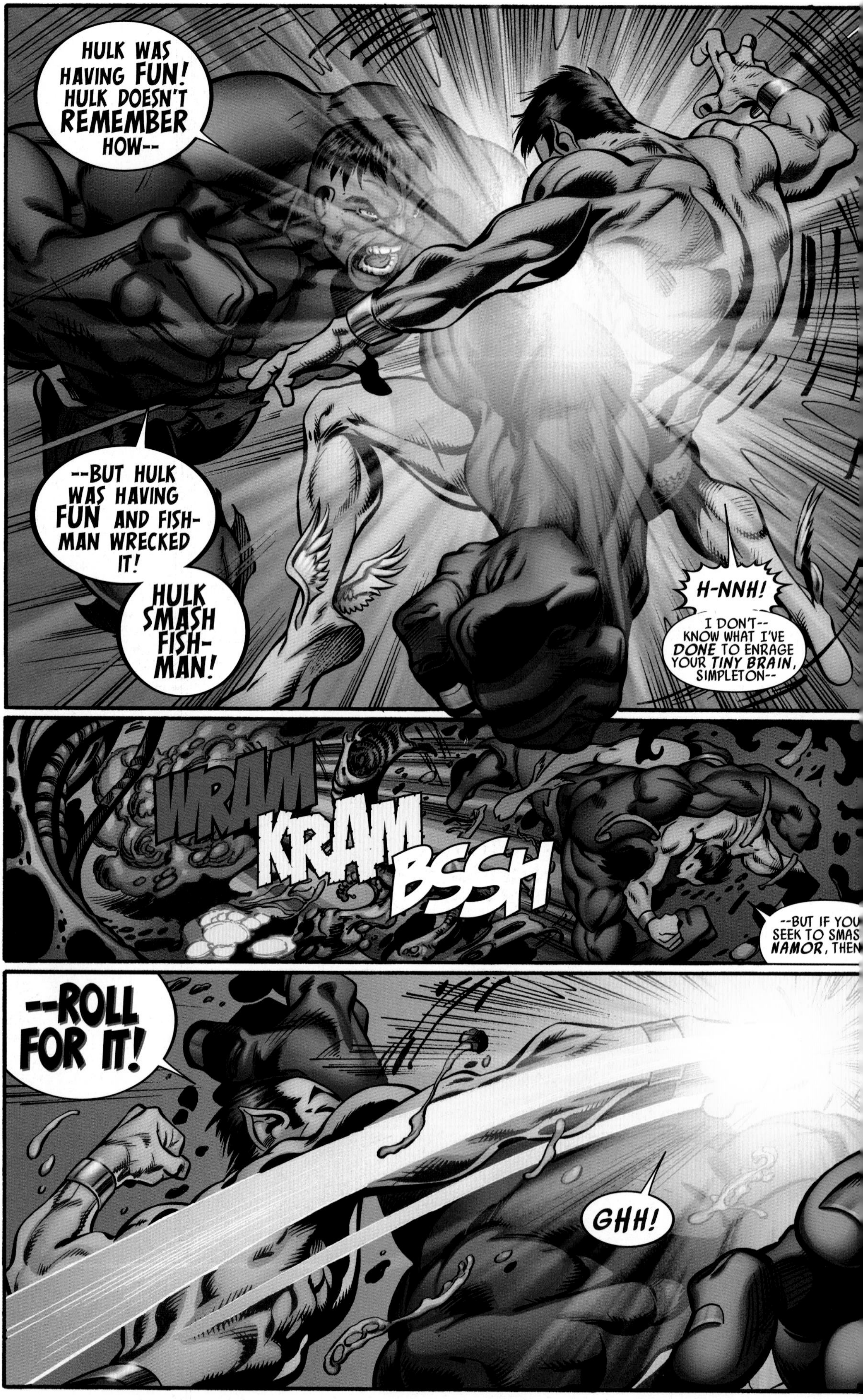
HULK WAS HAVING FUN! HULK DOESN'T REMEMBER HOW--
--BUT HULK WAS HAVING FUN AND FISH-MAN WRECKED IT!
HULK SMASH FISH-MAN!
H-NNH!
I DON'T-- KNOW WHAT I'VE DONE TO ENRAGE YOUR TINY BRAIN, SIMPLETON--
WRAM
KRAM
BSSH
--BUT IF YOU SEEK TO SMAS NAMOR, THEN
--ROLL FOR IT!
GHH!

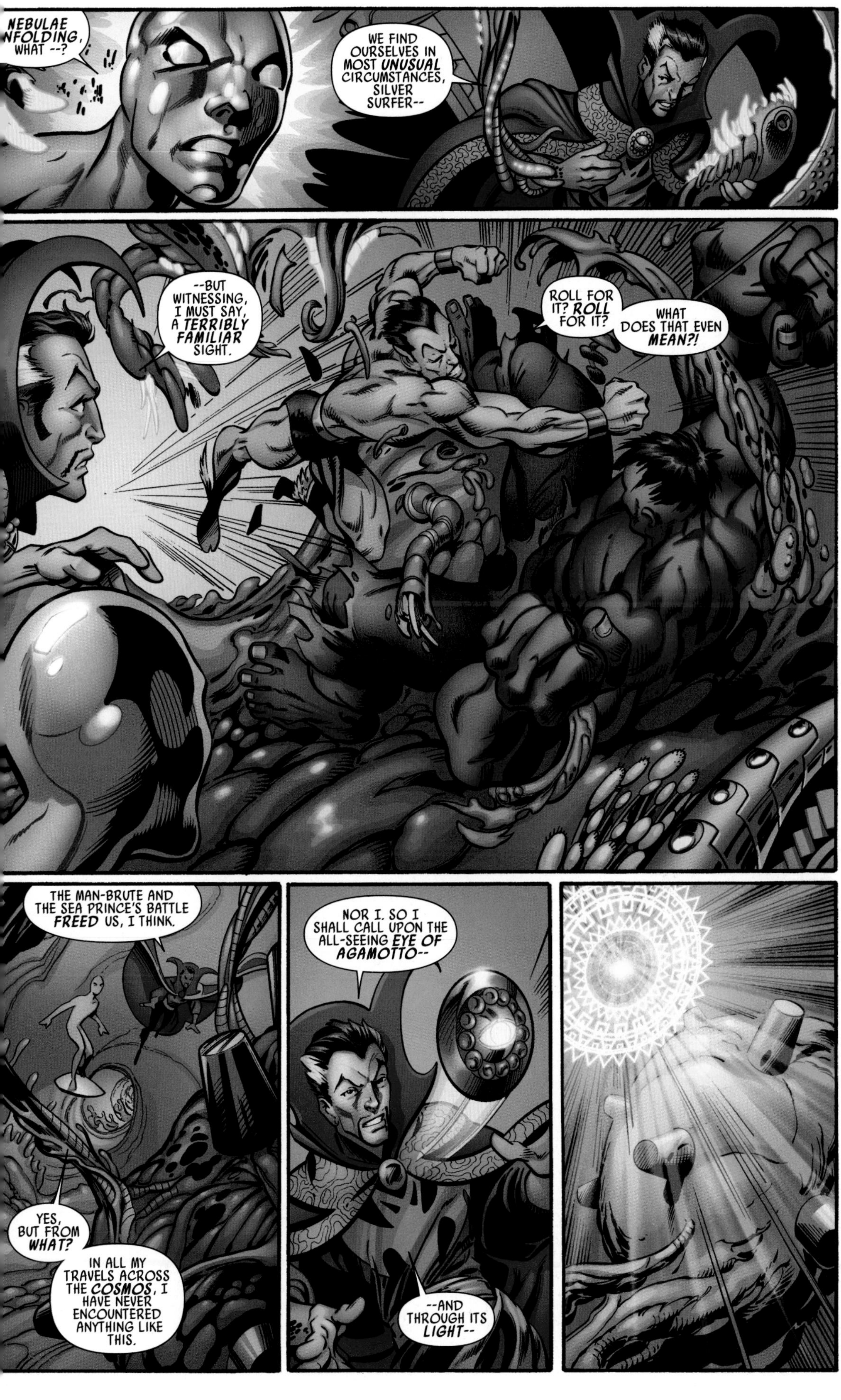
NEBULAE
NFOLDING,
WHAT --?
WE FIND OURSELVES IN MOST UNUSUAL CIRCUMSTANCES, SILVER SURFER--
--BUT WITNESSING, I MUST SAY, A TERRIBLY FAMILIAR SIGHT.
ROLL FOR IT? ROLL FOR IT?
WHAT DOES THAT EVEN MEAN?!
THE MAN-BRUTE AND THE SEA PRINCE'S BATTLE FREED US, I THINK.
YES, BUT FROM WHAT?
IN ALL MY TRAVELS ACROSS THE COSMOS, I HAVE NEVER ENCOUNTERED ANYTHING LIKE THIS.
NOR I. SO I SHALL CALL UPON THE ALL-SEEING EYE OF AGAMOTTO--
--AND THROUGH ITS LIGHT--

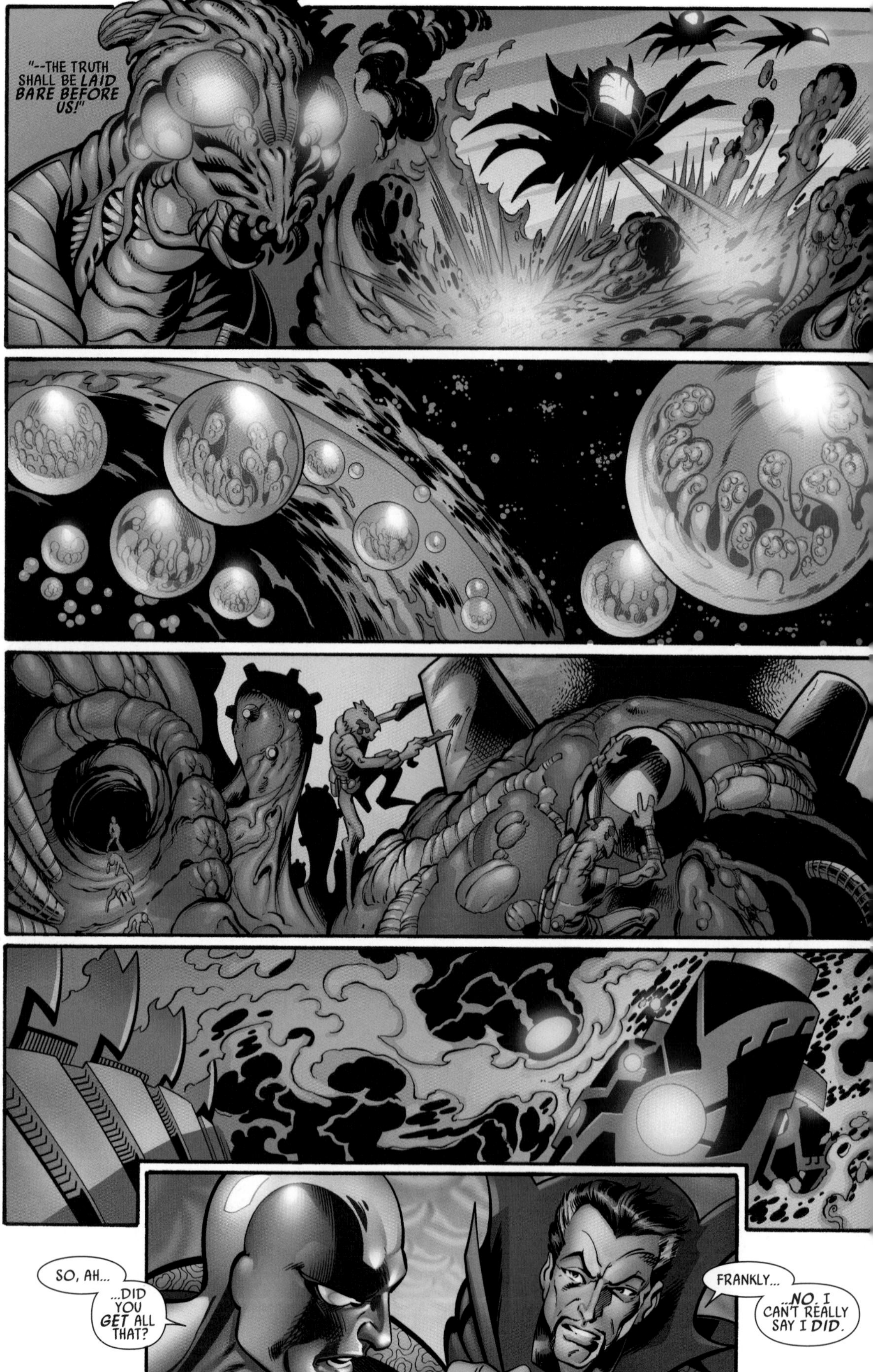
"--THE TRUTH SHALL BE LAID BARE BEFORE US!"
SO, AH...
...DID YOU GET ALL THAT?
FRANKLY...
...NO. I CAN'T REALLY SAY I DID.

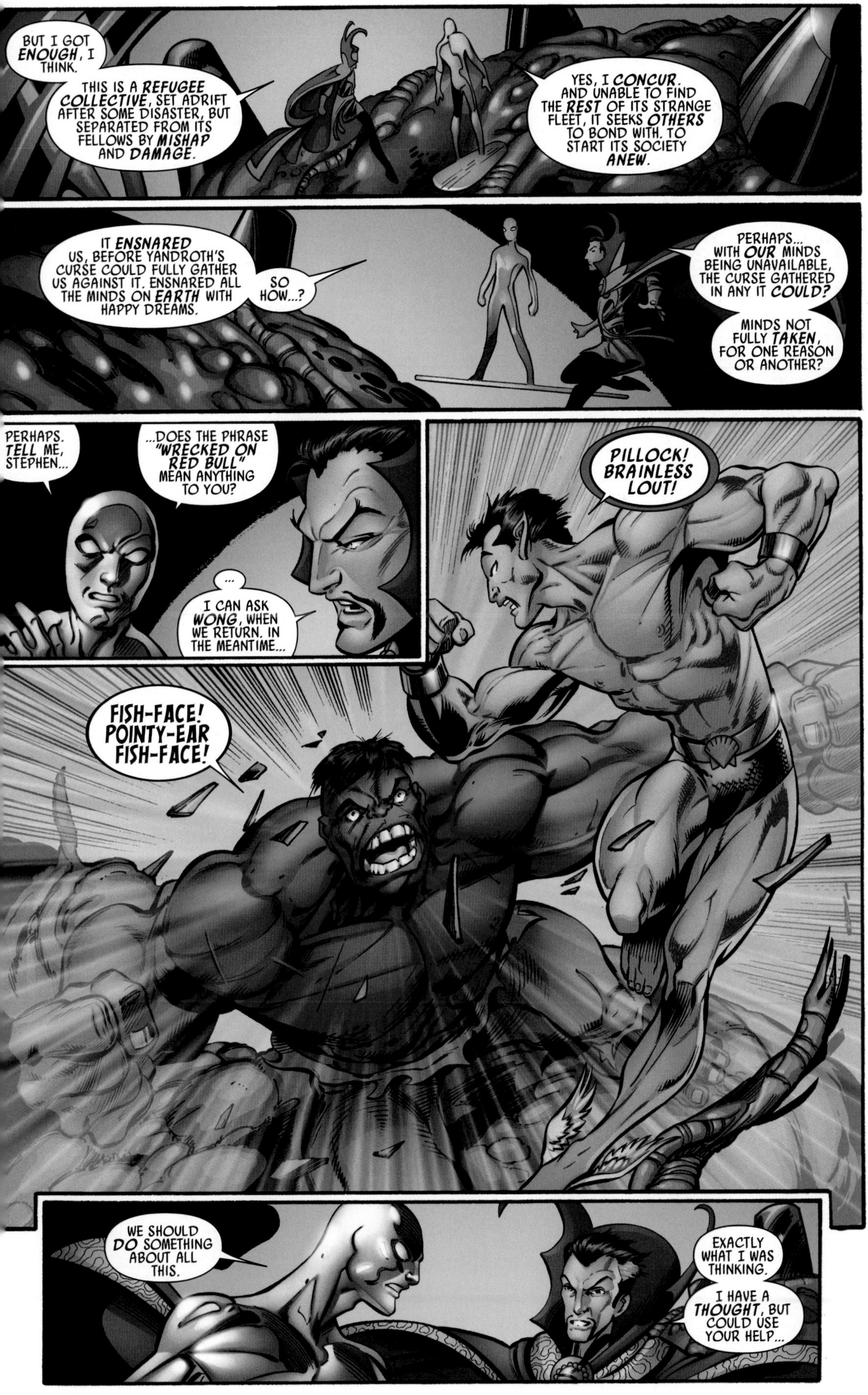

BUT I GOT ENOUGH, I THINK.
THIS IS A REFUGEE COLLECTIVE, SET ADRIFT AFTER SOME DISASTER, BUT SEPARATED FROM ITS FELLOWS BY MISHAP AND DAMAGE.
YES, I CONCUR. AND UNABLE TO FIND THE REST OF ITS STRANGE FLEET, IT SEEKS OTHERS TO BOND WITH. TO START ITS SOCIETY ANEW.
IT ENSNARED US, BEFORE YANDROTH'S CURSE COULD FULLY GATHER US AGAINST IT. ENSNARED ALL THE MINDS ON EARTH WITH HAPPY DREAMS.
SO HOW...?
PERHAPS... WITH OUR MINDS BEING UNAVAILABLE, THE CURSE GATHERED IN ANY IT COULD?
MINDS NOT FULLY TAKEN, FOR ONE REASON OR ANOTHER?
PERHAPS. TELL ME, STEPHEN...
...DOES THE PHRASE "WRECKED ON RED BULL" MEAN ANYTHING TO YOU?
...
I CAN ASK WONG, WHEN WE RETURN. IN THE MEANTIME...
PILLOCK! BRAINLESS LOUT!
FISH-FACE! POINTY-EAR FISH-FACE!
WE SHOULD DO SOMETHING ABOUT ALL THIS.
EXACTLY WHAT I WAS THINKING.
I HAVE A THOUGHT, BUT COULD USE YOUR HELP...

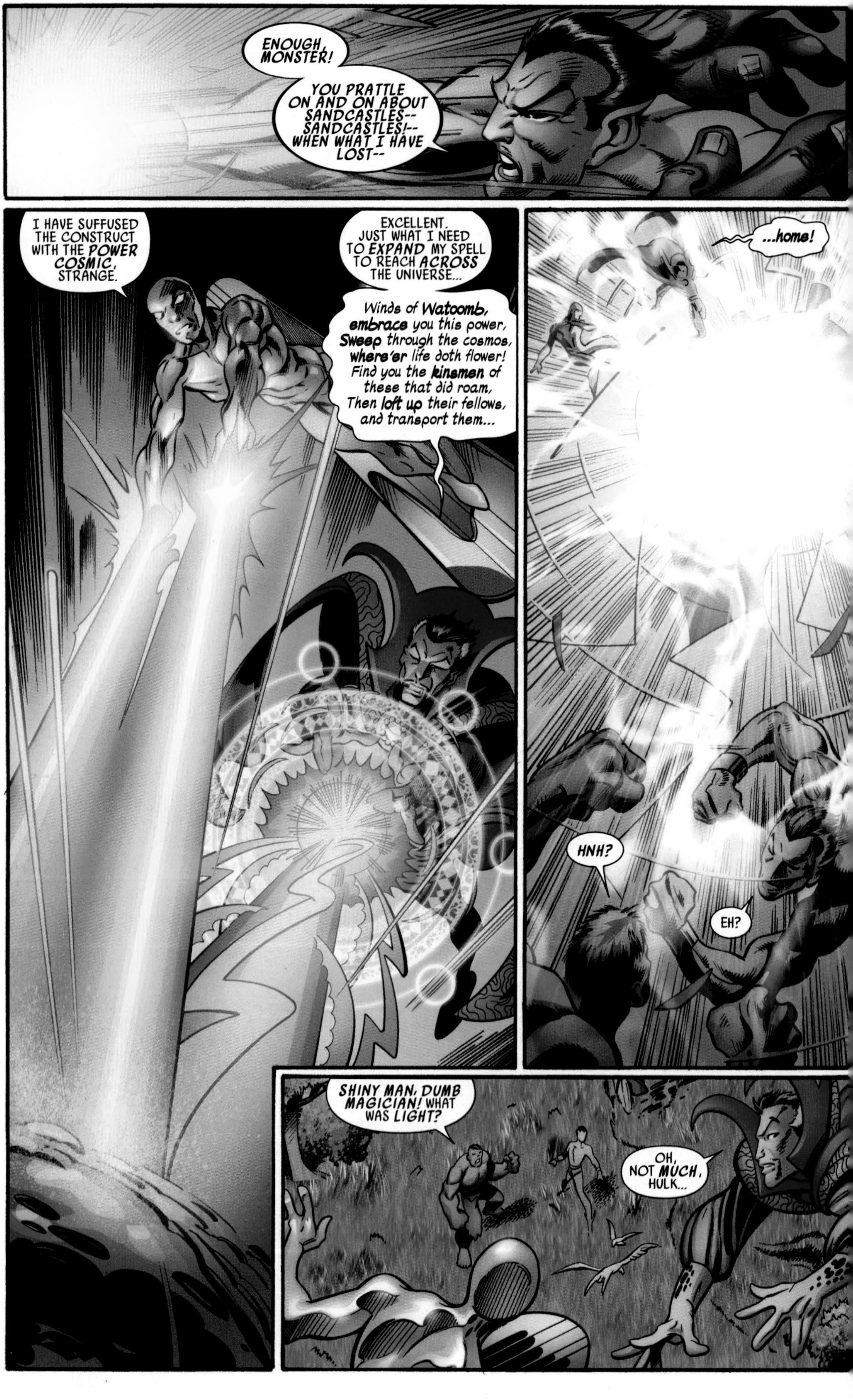
ENOUGH, MONSTER!
YOU PRATTLE ON AND ON ABOUT SANDCASTLES-- SANDCASTLES!-- WHEN WHAT I HAVE LOST--
I HAVE SUFFUSED THE CONSTRUCT WITH THE POWER COSMIC, STRANGE.
EXCELLENT. JUST WHAT I NEED TO EXPAND MY SPELL TO REACH ACROSS THE UNIVERSE...
Winds of Watoomb, embrace you this power, Sweep through the cosmos, where'er life doth flower! Find you the kinsmen of these that did roam, Then loft up their fellows, and transport them...
...home!
HNH?
EH?
SHINY MAN, DUMB MAGICIAN! WHAT WAS LIGHT?
OH, NOT MUCH, HULK...

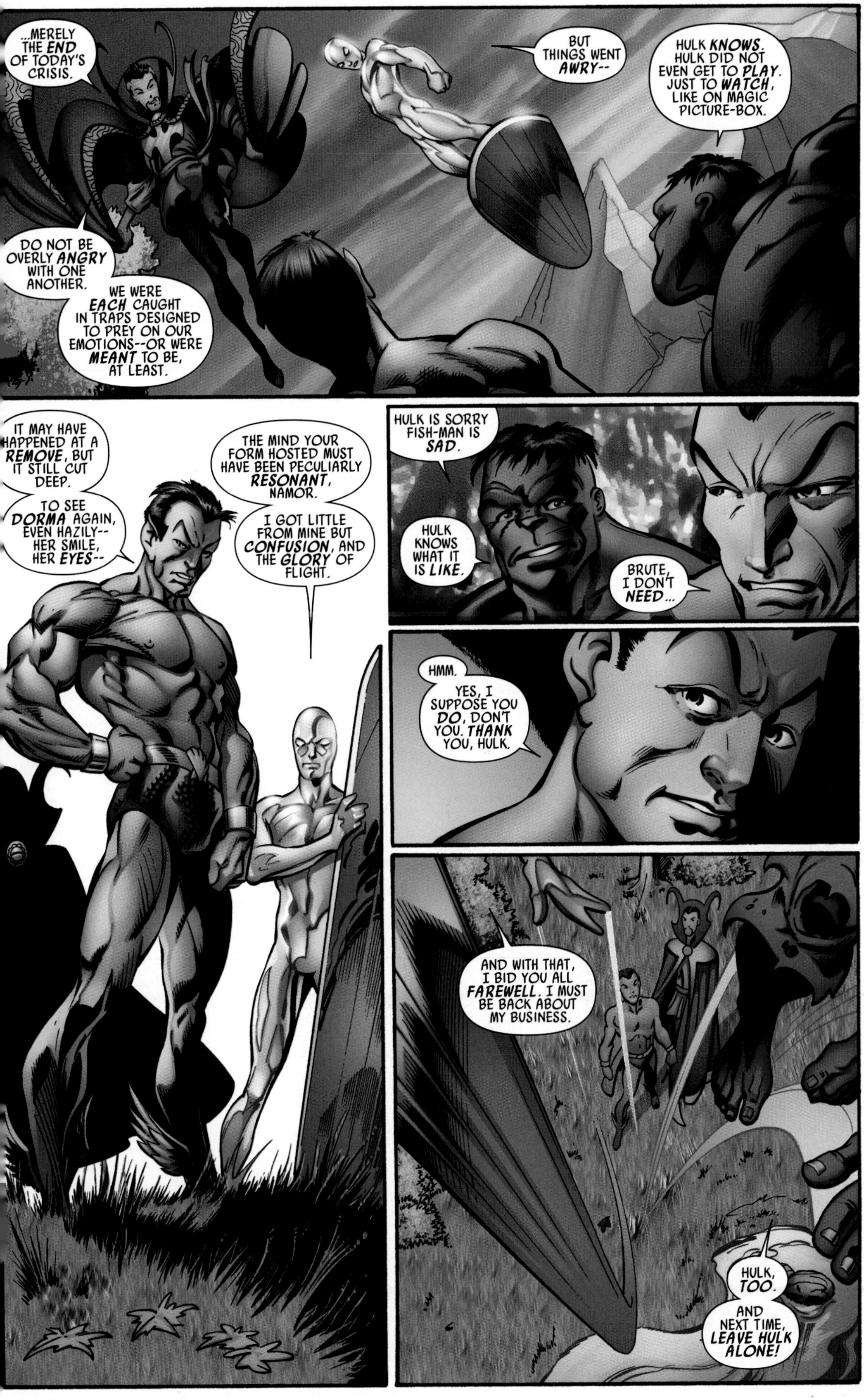

...MERELY THE END OF TODAY'S CRISIS.
BUT THINGS WENT AWRY--
HULK KNOWS. HULK DID NOT EVEN GET TO PLAY. JUST TO WATCH, LIKE ON MAGIC PICTURE-BOX.
DO NOT BE OVERLY ANGRY WITH ONE ANOTHER.
WE WERE EACH CAUGHT IN TRAPS DESIGNED TO PREY ON OUR EMOTIONS--OR WERE MEANT TO BE, AT LEAST.
IT MAY HAVE HAPPENED AT A REMOVE, BUT IT STILL CUT DEEP.
TO SEE DORMA AGAIN, EVEN HAZILY-- HER SMILE, HER EYES--
THE MIND YOUR FORM HOSTED MUST HAVE BEEN PECULIARLY RESONANT, NAMOR.
I GOT LITTLE FROM MINE BUT CONFUSION, AND THE GLORY OF FLIGHT.
HULK IS SORRY FISH-MAN IS SAD.
HULK KNOWS WHAT IT IS LIKE.
BRUTE, I DON'T NEED...
HMM.
YES, I SUPPOSE YOU DO, DON'T YOU. THANK YOU, HULK.
AND WITH THAT, I BID YOU ALL FAREWELL. I MUST BE BACK ABOUT MY BUSINESS.
HULK, TOO.
AND NEXT TIME, LEAVE HULK ALONE!

YOU SEEM *PENSIVE*, NAMOR.

IF IT HELPS, I DO NOT BELIEVE THAT ALIEN COLLECTIVE MEANT TO *HURT* ANYONE--

--JUST TO GRANT OUR *DREAMS*, EVEN AS ILLUSION, AND MAKE US GLAD TO BE *MADE ONE* WITH THEM.

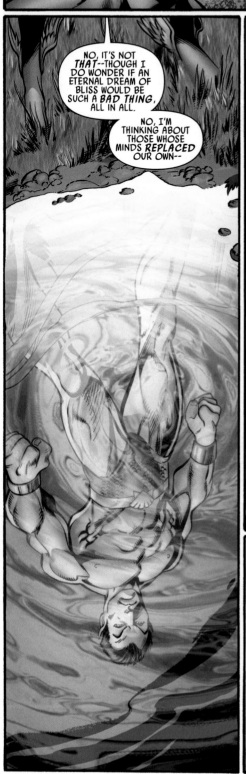

NO, IT'S NOT *THAT*--THOUGH I DO WONDER IF AN ETERNAL DREAM OF BLISS WOULD BE SUCH A *BAD THING*, ALL IN ALL.

NO, I'M THINKING ABOUT THOSE WHOSE MINDS *REPLACED* OUR OWN--

A *LUCKY STROKE*, THAT. MINE WAS *USELESS*--NO GREATER SURRENDER TO THE TRAP COULD BE *IMAGINED*.

BUT YOURS WAS MADE OF *STERNER STUFF*, EH?

YES, SO IT SEEMS.

THEN *I'LL* BE OFF AS WELL. I'LL SEE YOU *NEXT TIME*, NAMOR--THOUGH YOU'LL FORGIVE ME, I THINK, IF I HOPE THAT WILL BE A *LONG WAY* OFF.

LUCKY. WE WERE *INDEED* LUCKY, THIS NIGHT.

AND *RAMONA FISCHER*-- WHEREVER YOU ARE, *WHOEVER* YOU ARE--

I HAVE FELT THE DEPTH OF YOUR YOUNG MAN'S *REGARD* FOR YOU. I DO NOT KNOW WHETHER YOU WILL *RECIPROCATE*, ONCE YOU KNOW OF IT.

BUT I HOPE THAT YOU WILL *TREASURE* IT. FOR TONIGHT...

...IT WAS ENOUGH TO *SAVE A WORLD*.

THE END

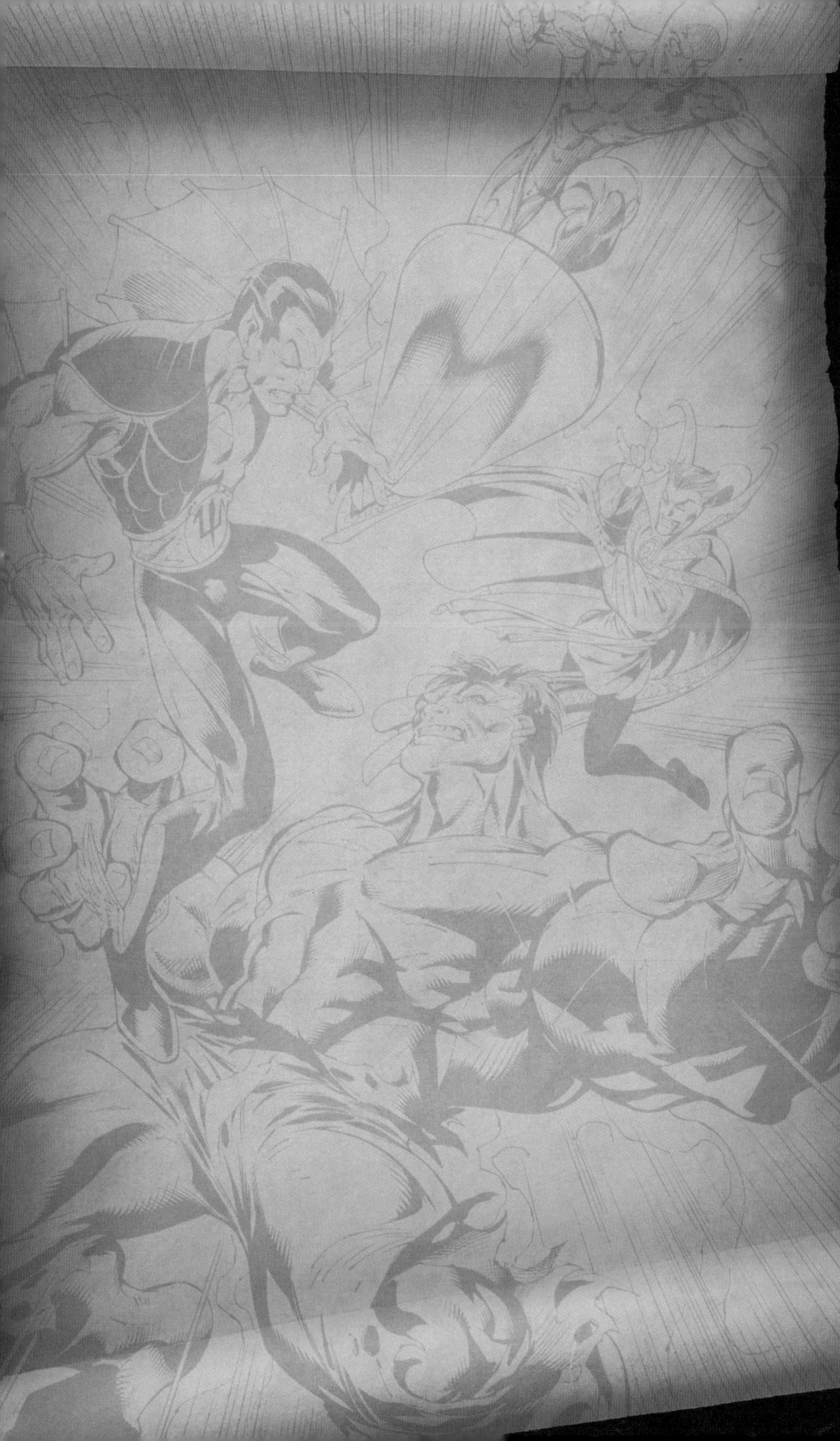

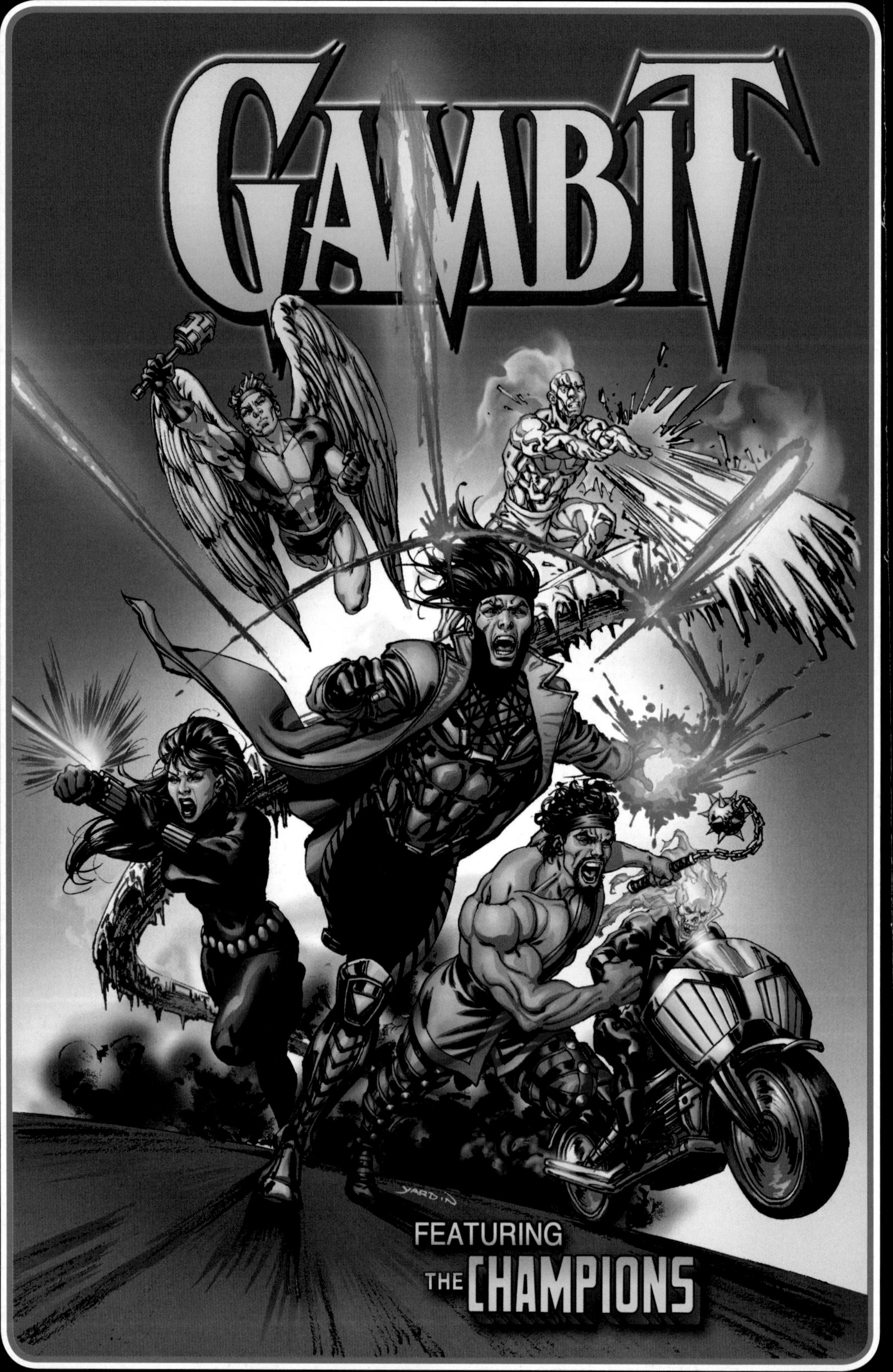
GAMBIT
YARDIN
FEATURING
THE CHAMPIONS

FROM THE MARVEL VAULT!

George Tuska did everything. And we mean everything. His career spanned from 1930s into the 21st century. He wrote, penciled and inked comics from mystery to romance to westerns and, yes, super heroes. He was there for Timely and Atlas before there was Marvel, worked on both sides of the Big Two, and there were few major characters he left untouched. When the art boards for his never-before-seen last issue were unearthed in our archives, we knew there was something precious here, and too cool to leave unpublished. One problem, no one knew where the script might be!

Luckily, Marvel coined the term for plot-first comics, and all the story we needed was right there in the pages. Enter Scott Lobdell to give us that perfect addition of banter and detail to match the action, and we had ourselves a genuine lost classic!

So skip this forward already and get to the good stuff, because this comic has got it all: gods, mutants, monsters and M.O.D.O.K.s. A little bit of everything, just like George Tuska.

Scott Lobdell
WRITER

George Tuska
ARTIST

Nick Filardi
COLORIST

Dave Sharpe
LETTERER

Mayela Gutierrez
PRODUCTION

David Yardin
COVER

John Denning
ASSISTANT EDITOR

Ralph Macchio
SENIOR EDITOR

Axel Alonso
EDITOR IN CHIEF

Joe Quesada
CHIEF CREATIVE OFFICER

Dan Buckley
PUBLISHER

Alan Fine
EXECUTIVE PRODUCER

Dedicated to George Tuska
(1916 - 2009)

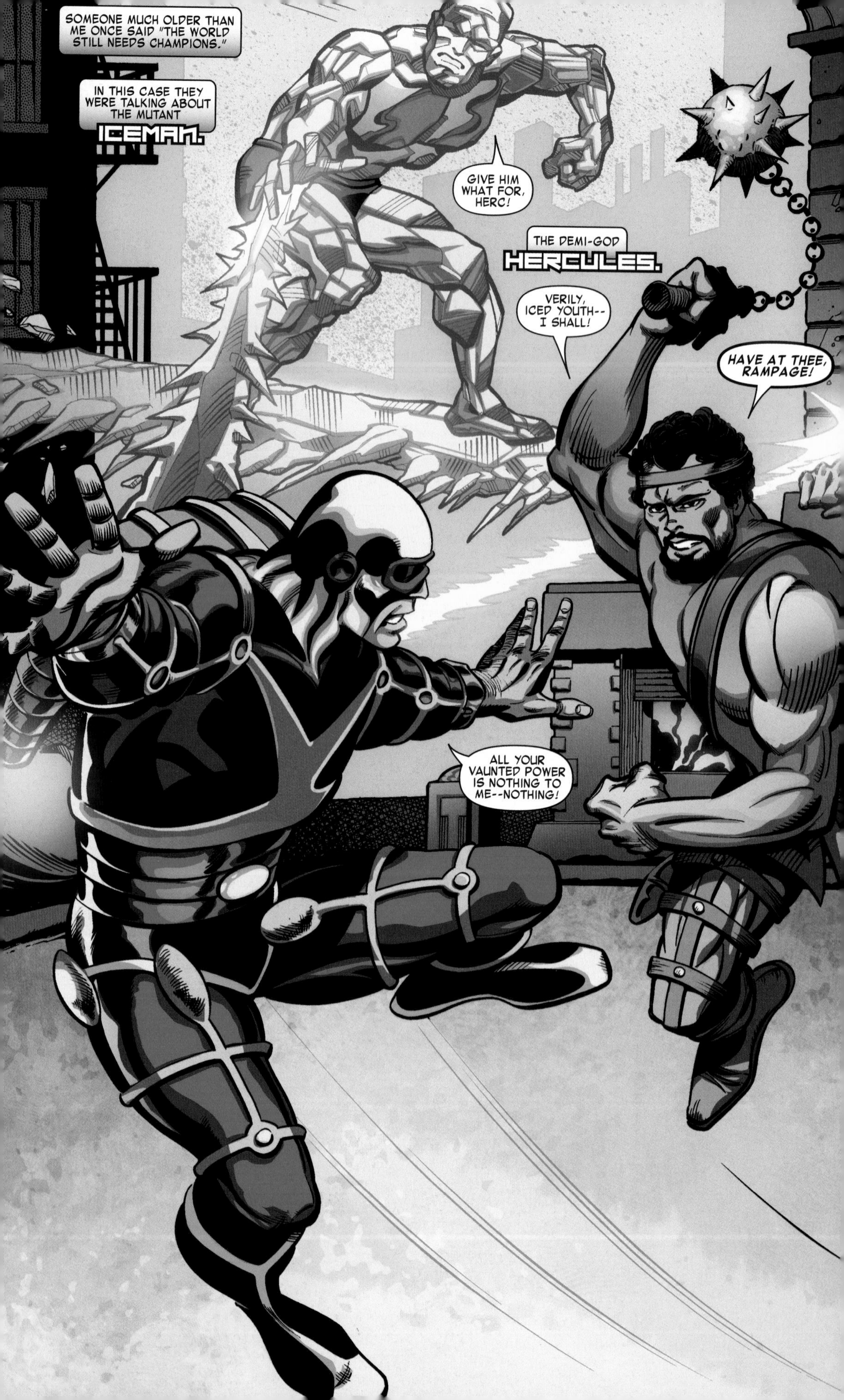
SOMEONE MUCH OLDER THAN ME ONCE SAID "THE WORLD STILL NEEDS CHAMPIONS."
IN THIS CASE THEY WERE TALKING ABOUT THE MUTANT
ICEMAN.
GIVE HIM WHAT FOR, HERC!
THE DEMI-GOD
HERCULES.
VERILY, ICED YOUTH-- I SHALL!
HAVE AT THEE, RAMPAGE!
ALL YOUR VAUNTED POWER IS NOTHING TO ME--NOTHING!

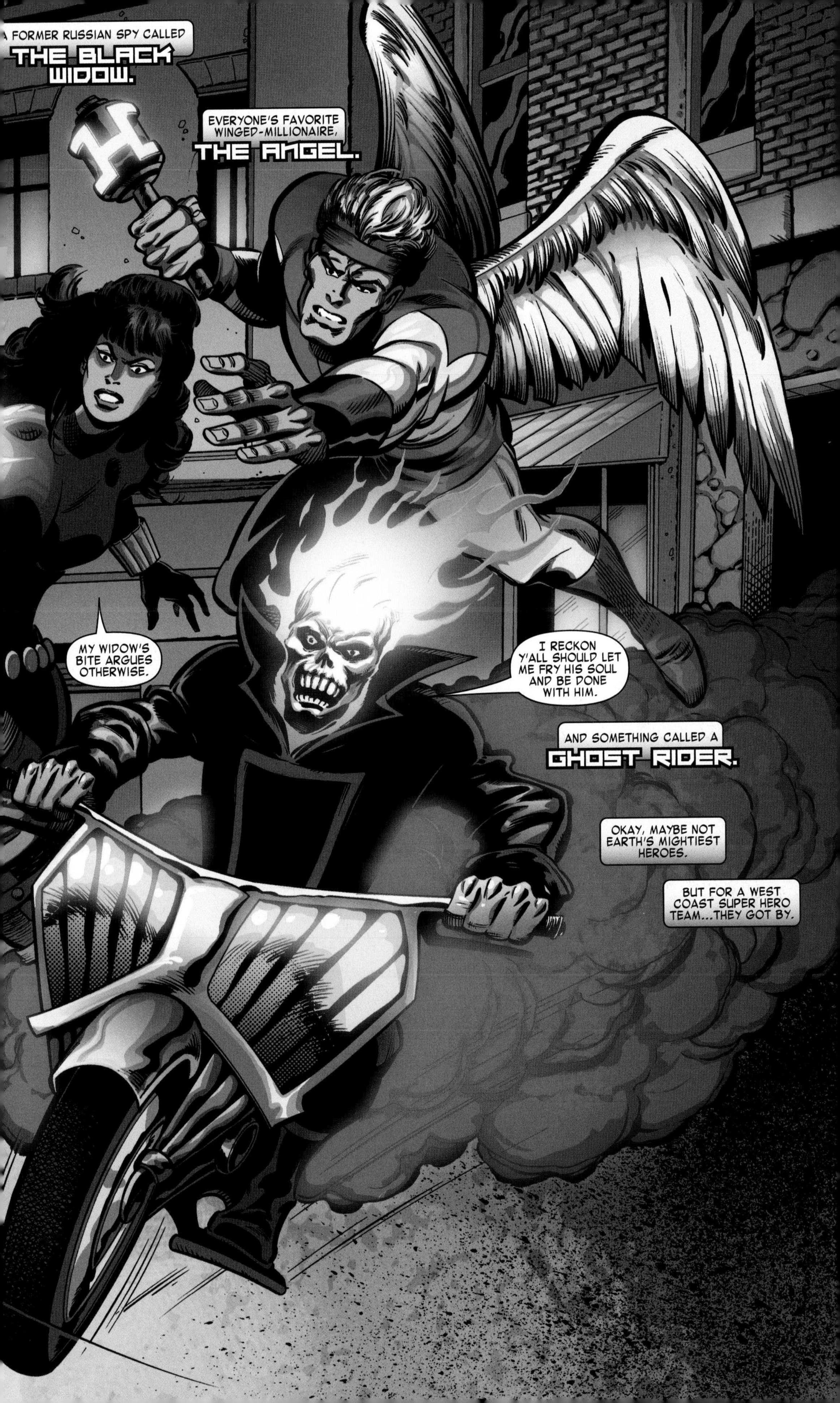

A FORMER RUSSIAN SPY CALLED
THE BLACK WIDOW.
EVERYONE'S FAVORITE WINGED-MILLIONAIRE,
THE ANGEL.
MY WIDOW'S BITE ARGUES OTHERWISE.
I RECKON Y'ALL SHOULD LET ME FRY HIS SOUL AND BE DONE WITH HIM.
AND SOMETHING CALLED A
GHOST RIDER.
OKAY, MAYBE NOT EARTH'S MIGHTIEST HEROES.
BUT FOR A WEST COAST SUPER HERO TEAM...THEY GOT BY.

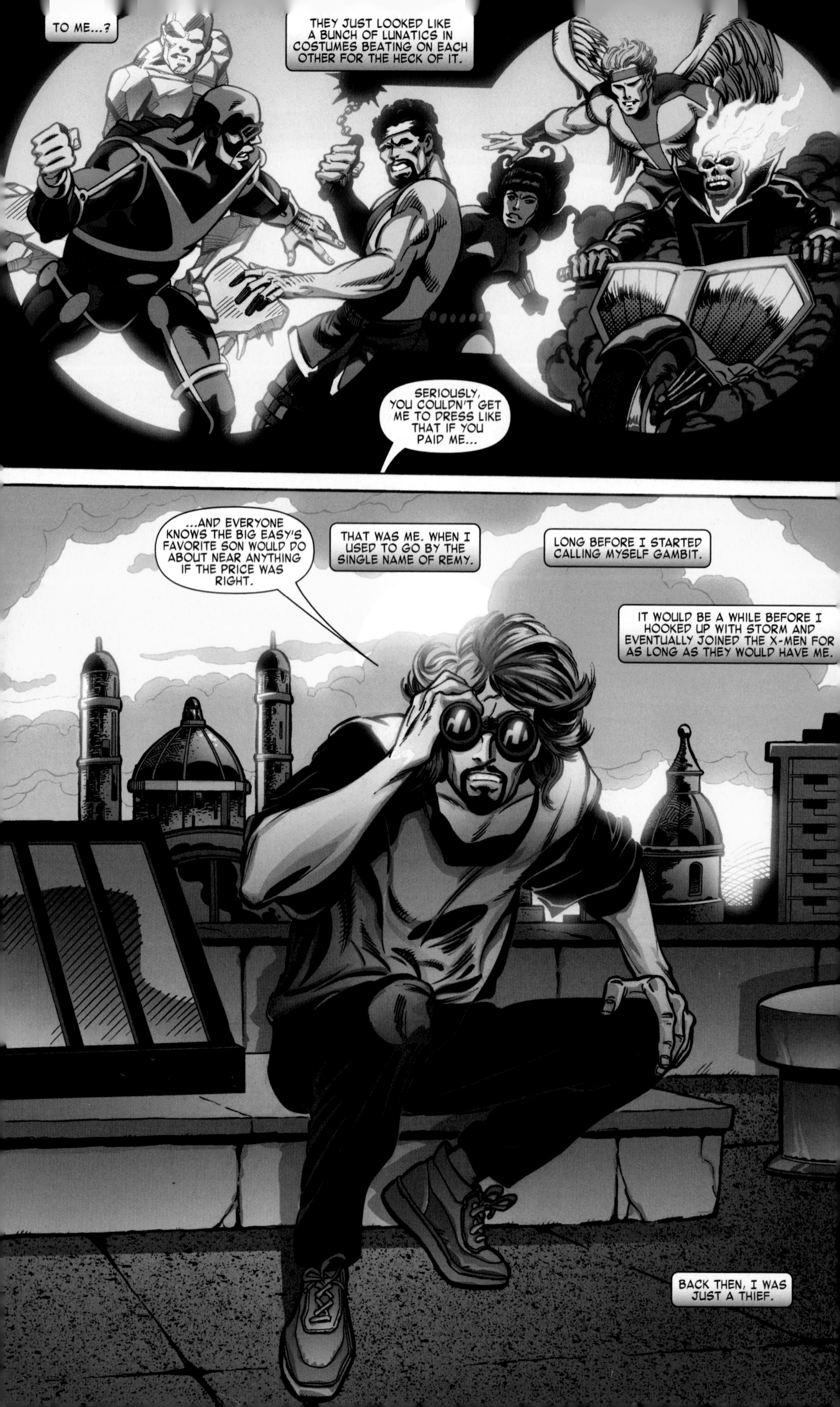
TO ME...?
THEY JUST LOOKED LIKE A BUNCH OF LUNATICS IN COSTUMES BEATING ON EACH OTHER FOR THE HECK OF IT.
SERIOUSLY, YOU COULDN'T GET ME TO DRESS LIKE THAT IF YOU PAID ME...
...AND EVERYONE KNOWS THE BIG EASY'S FAVORITE SON WOULD DO ABOUT NEAR ANYTHING IF THE PRICE WAS RIGHT.
THAT WAS ME. WHEN I USED TO GO BY THE SINGLE NAME OF REMY.
LONG BEFORE I STARTED CALLING MYSELF GAMBIT.
IT WOULD BE A WHILE BEFORE I HOOKED UP WITH STORM AND EVENTUALLY JOINED THE X-MEN FOR AS LONG AS THEY WOULD HAVE ME.
BACK THEN, I WAS JUST A THIEF.

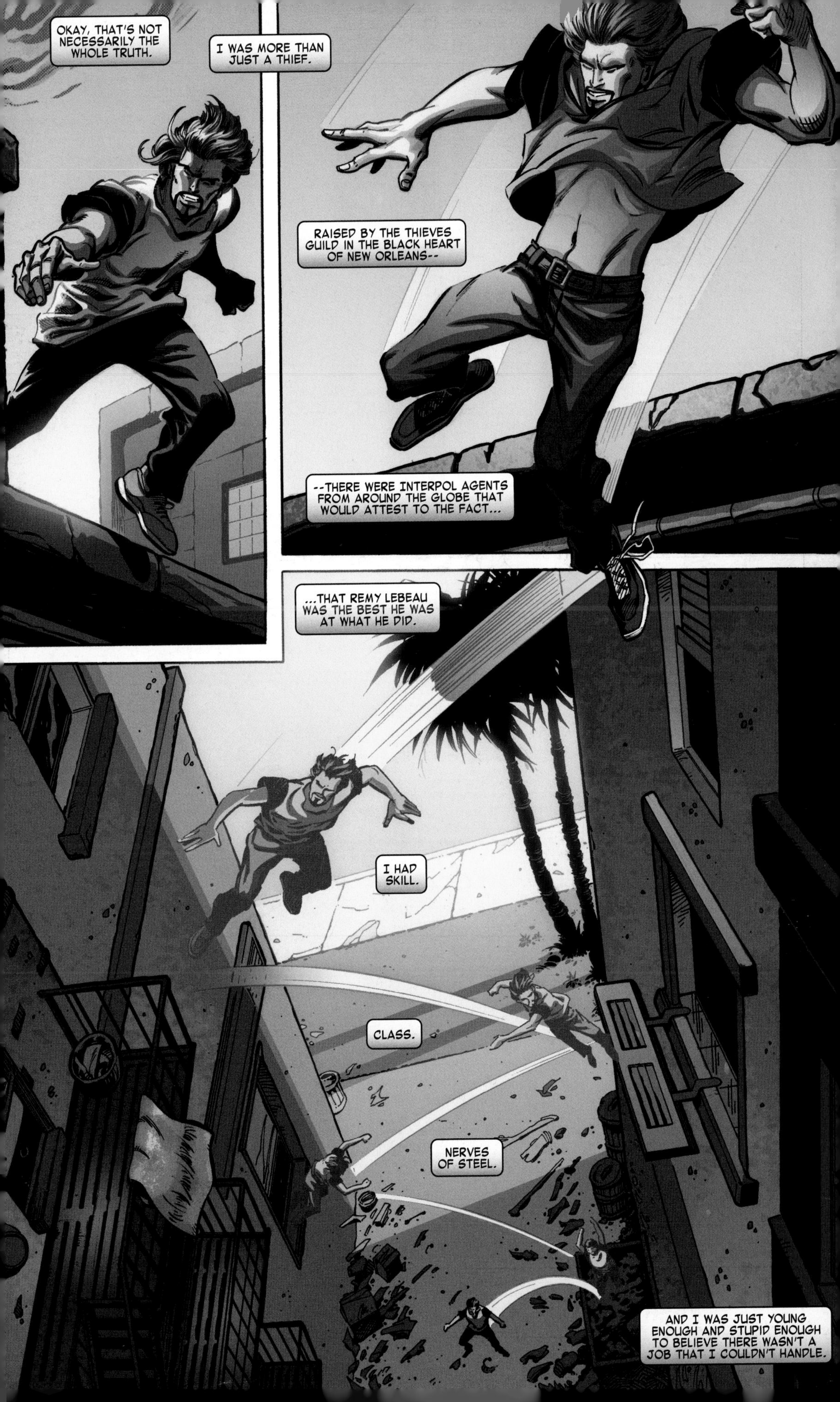
OKAY, THAT'S NOT NECESSARILY THE WHOLE TRUTH.
I WAS MORE THAN JUST A THIEF.
RAISED BY THE THIEVES GUILD IN THE BLACK HEART OF NEW ORLEANS--
--THERE WERE INTERPOL AGENTS FROM AROUND THE GLOBE THAT WOULD ATTEST TO THE FACT...
...THAT REMY LEBEAU WAS THE BEST HE WAS AT WHAT HE DID.
I HAD SKILL.
CLASS.
NERVES OF STEEL.
AND I WAS JUST YOUNG ENOUGH AND STUPID ENOUGH TO BELIEVE THERE WASN'T A JOB THAT I COULDN'T HANDLE.

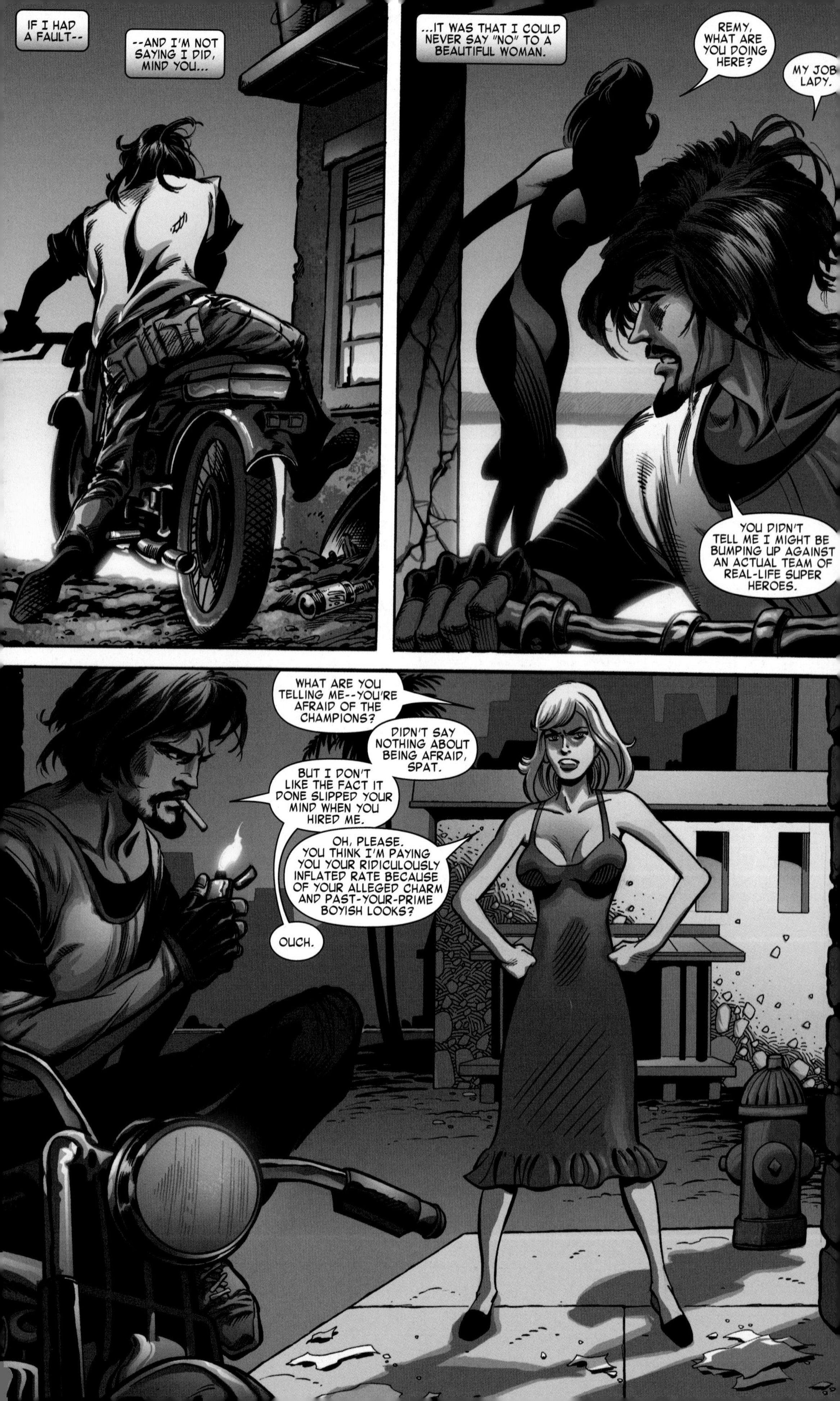
IF I HAD A FAULT--
--AND I'M NOT SAYING I DID, MIND YOU...
...IT WAS THAT I COULD NEVER SAY "NO" TO A BEAUTIFUL WOMAN.
REMY, WHAT ARE YOU DOING HERE?
MY JOB LADY.
YOU DIDN'T TELL ME I MIGHT BE BUMPING UP AGAINST AN ACTUAL TEAM OF REAL-LIFE SUPER HEROES.
WHAT ARE YOU TELLING ME--YOU'RE AFRAID OF THE CHAMPIONS?
DIDN'T SAY NOTHING ABOUT BEING AFRAID, SPAT.
BUT I DON'T LIKE THE FACT IT DONE SLIPPED YOUR MIND WHEN YOU HIRED ME.
OH, PLEASE. YOU THINK I'M PAYING YOU YOUR RIDICULOUSLY INFLATED RATE BECAUSE OF YOUR ALLEGED CHARM AND PAST-YOUR-PRIME BOYISH LOOKS?
OUCH.

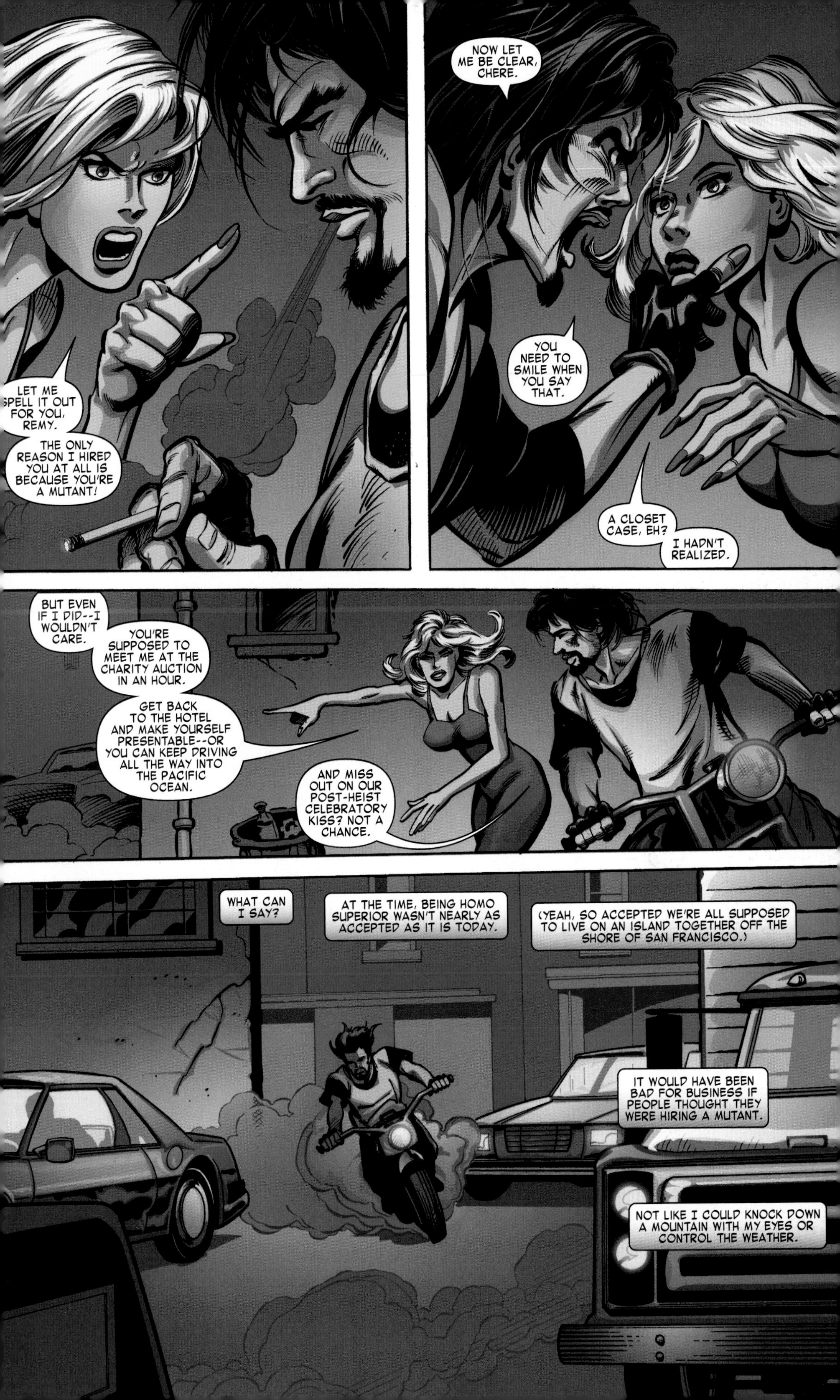
LET ME SPELL IT OUT FOR YOU, REMY.
THE ONLY REASON I HIRED YOU AT ALL IS BECAUSE YOU'RE A MUTANT!
NOW LET ME BE CLEAR, CHERE.
YOU NEED TO SMILE WHEN YOU SAY THAT.
A CLOSET CASE, EH? I HADN'T REALIZED.
BUT EVEN IF I DID--I WOULDN'T CARE.
YOU'RE SUPPOSED TO MEET ME AT THE CHARITY AUCTION IN AN HOUR.
GET BACK TO THE HOTEL AND MAKE YOURSELF PRESENTABLE--OR YOU CAN KEEP DRIVING ALL THE WAY INTO THE PACIFIC OCEAN.
AND MISS OUT ON OUR POST-HEIST CELEBRATORY KISS? NOT A CHANCE.
WHAT CAN I SAY?
AT THE TIME, BEING HOMO SUPERIOR WASN'T NEARLY AS ACCEPTED AS IT IS TODAY.
(YEAH, SO ACCEPTED WE'RE ALL SUPPOSED TO LIVE ON AN ISLAND TOGETHER OFF THE SHORE OF SAN FRANCISCO.)
IT WOULD HAVE BEEN BAD FOR BUSINESS IF PEOPLE THOUGHT THEY WERE HIRING A MUTANT.
NOT LIKE I COULD KNOCK DOWN A MOUNTAIN WITH MY EYES OR CONTROL THE WEATHER.

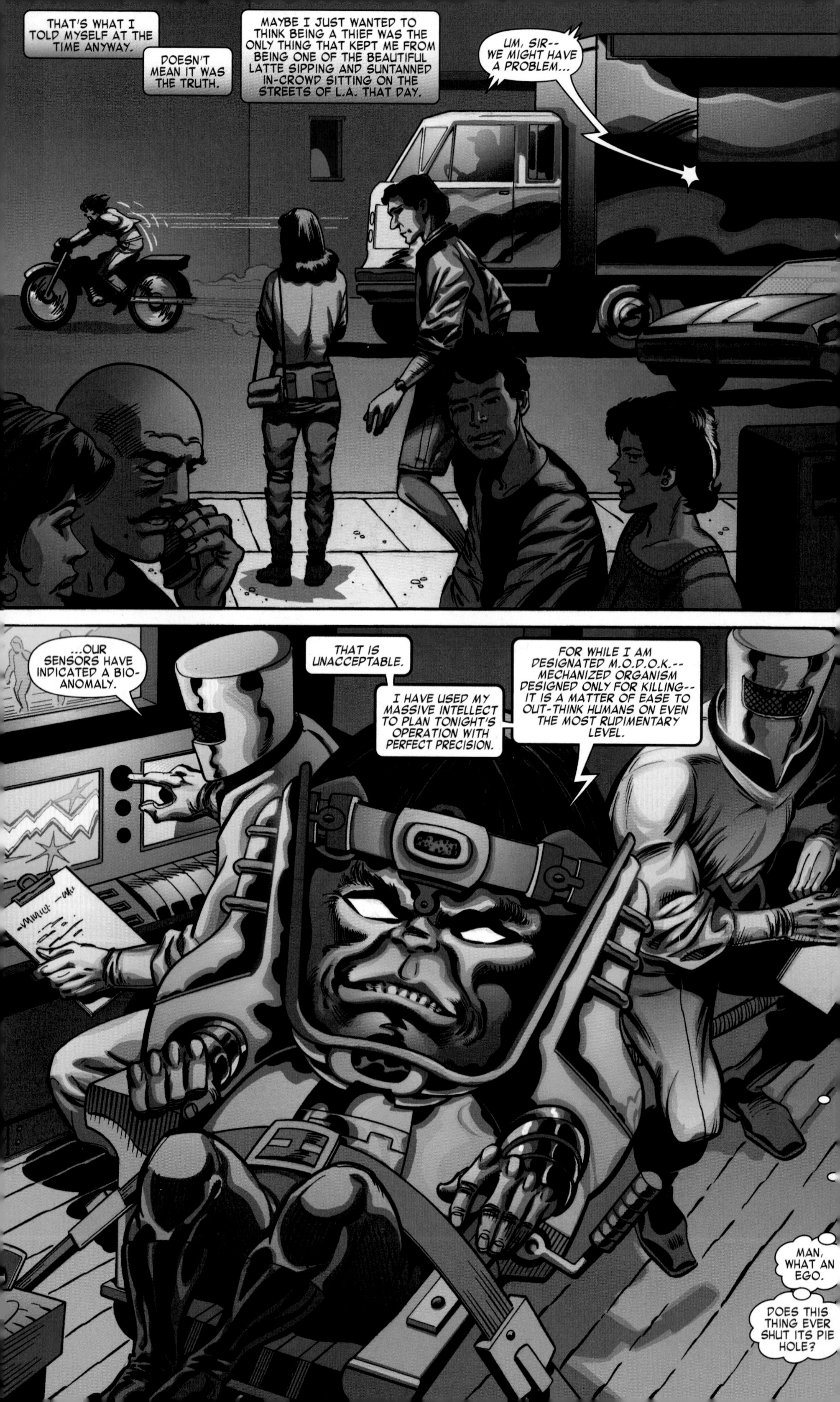
THAT'S WHAT I TOLD MYSELF AT THE TIME ANYWAY.
DOESN'T MEAN IT WAS THE TRUTH.
MAYBE I JUST WANTED TO THINK BEING A THIEF WAS THE ONLY THING THAT KEPT ME FROM BEING ONE OF THE BEAUTIFUL LATTE SIPPING AND SUNTANNED IN-CROWD SITTING ON THE STREETS OF L.A. THAT DAY.
UM, SIR-- WE MIGHT HAVE A PROBLEM...
...OUR SENSORS HAVE INDICATED A BIO-ANOMALY.
THAT IS UNACCEPTABLE.
I HAVE USED MY MASSIVE INTELLECT TO PLAN TONIGHT'S OPERATION WITH PERFECT PRECISION.
FOR WHILE I AM DESIGNATED M.O.D.O.K.-- MECHANIZED ORGANISM DESIGNED ONLY FOR KILLING-- IT IS A MATTER OF EASE TO OUT-THINK HUMANS ON EVEN THE MOST RUDIMENTARY LEVEL.
MAN, WHAT AN EGO.
DOES THIS THING EVER SHUT ITS PIE HOLE?

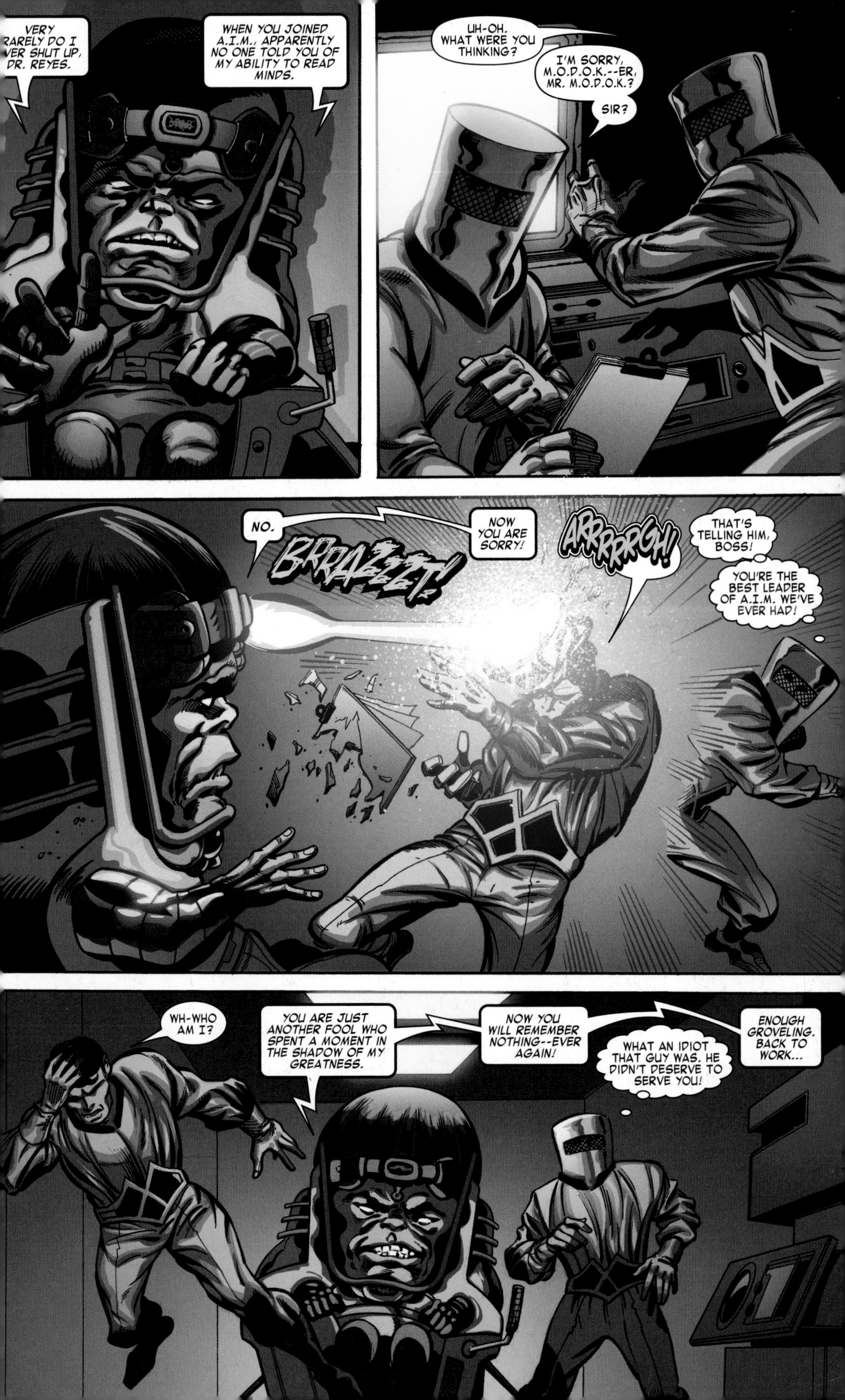
VERY RARELY DO I EVER SHUT UP, DR. REYES.
WHEN YOU JOINED A.I.M., APPARENTLY NO ONE TOLD YOU OF MY ABILITY TO READ MINDS.
UH-OH. WHAT WERE YOU THINKING?
I'M SORRY, M.O.D.O.K.--ER, MR. M.O.D.O.K.?
SIR?
NO.
BRRAZZZT!
NOW YOU ARE SORRY!
ARRRRRGH!
THAT'S TELLING HIM, BOSS!
YOU'RE THE BEST LEADER OF A.I.M. WE'VE EVER HAD!
WH-WHO AM I?
YOU ARE JUST ANOTHER FOOL WHO SPENT A MOMENT IN THE SHADOW OF MY GREATNESS.
NOW YOU WILL REMEMBER NOTHING--EVER AGAIN!
WHAT AN IDIOT THAT GUY WAS. HE DIDN'T DESERVE TO SERVE YOU!
ENOUGH GROVELING. BACK TO WORK...

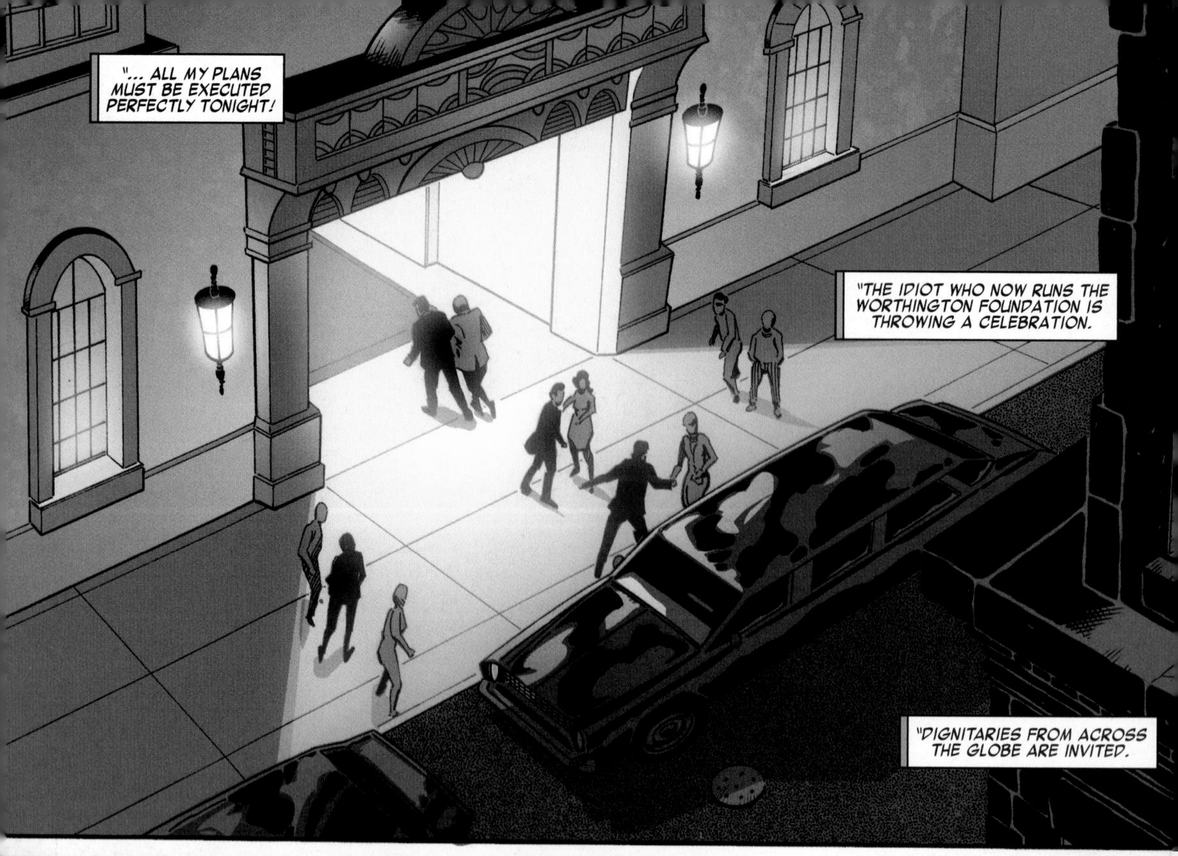
"... ALL MY PLANS MUST BE EXECUTED PERFECTLY TONIGHT!
"THE IDIOT WHO NOW RUNS THE WORTHINGTON FOUNDATION IS THROWING A CELEBRATION.
"DIGNITARIES FROM ACROSS THE GLOBE ARE INVITED.

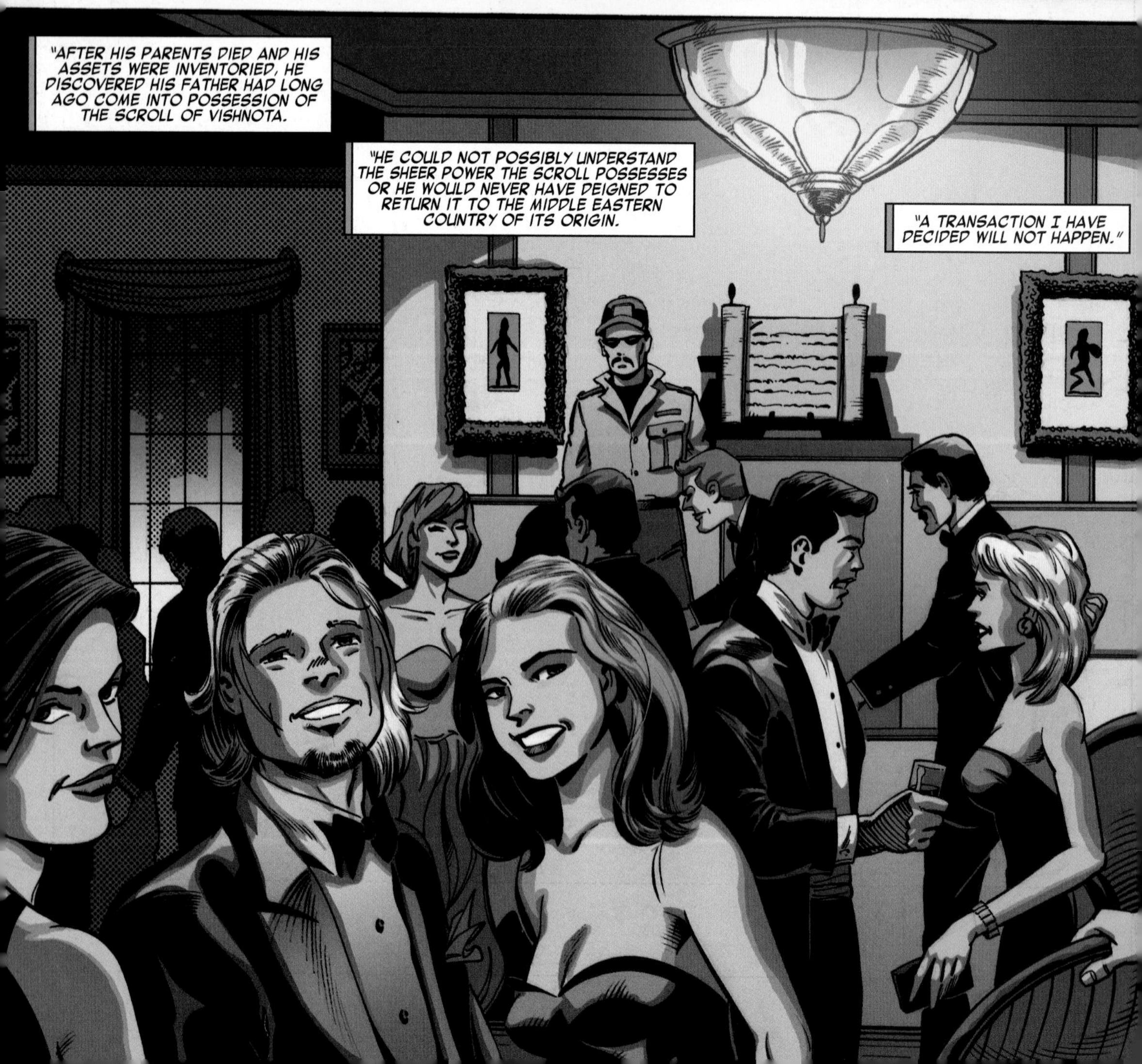
"AFTER HIS PARENTS DIED AND HIS ASSETS WERE INVENTORIED, HE DISCOVERED HIS FATHER HAD LONG AGO COME INTO POSSESSION OF THE SCROLL OF VISHNOTA.
"HE COULD NOT POSSIBLY UNDERSTAND THE SHEER POWER THE SCROLL POSSESSES OR HE WOULD NEVER HAVE DEIGNED TO RETURN IT TO THE MIDDLE EASTERN COUNTRY OF ITS ORIGIN.
"A TRANSACTION I HAVE DECIDED WILL NOT HAPPEN."

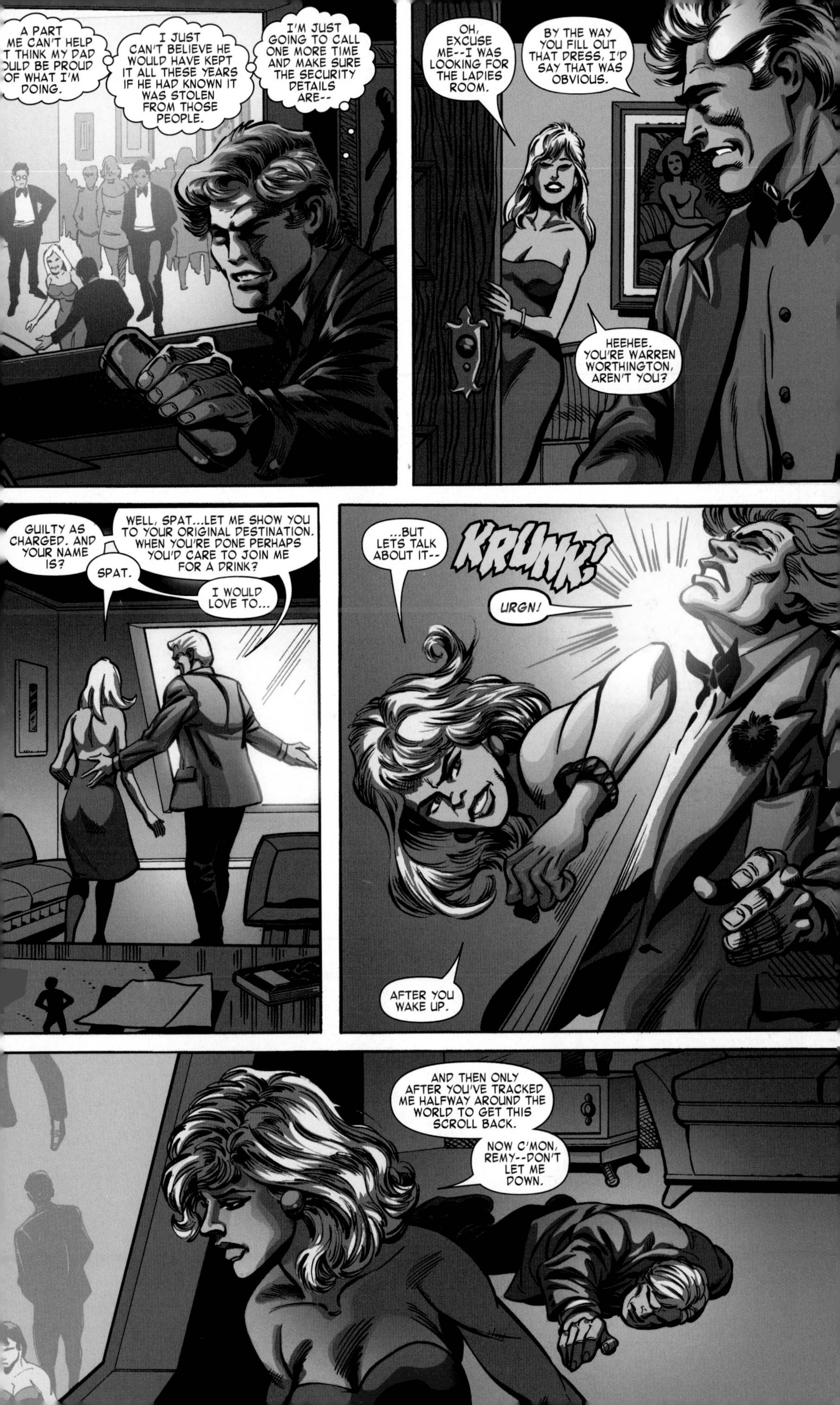

A PART ME CAN'T HELP T THINK MY DAD OULD BE PROUD OF WHAT I'M DOING.
I JUST CAN'T BELIEVE HE WOULD HAVE KEPT IT ALL THESE YEARS IF HE HAD KNOWN IT WAS STOLEN FROM THOSE PEOPLE.
I'M JUST GOING TO CALL ONE MORE TIME AND MAKE SURE THE SECURITY DETAILS ARE--
OH, EXCUSE ME--I WAS LOOKING FOR THE LADIES ROOM.
BY THE WAY YOU FILL OUT THAT DRESS, I'D SAY THAT WAS OBVIOUS.
HEEHEE. YOU'RE WARREN WORTHINGTON, AREN'T YOU?
GUILTY AS CHARGED. AND YOUR NAME IS?
SPAT.
WELL, SPAT...LET ME SHOW YOU TO YOUR ORIGINAL DESTINATION. WHEN YOU'RE DONE PERHAPS YOU'D CARE TO JOIN ME FOR A DRINK?
I WOULD LOVE TO...
...BUT LETS TALK ABOUT IT--
KRUNK!
URGN!
AFTER YOU WAKE UP.
AND THEN ONLY AFTER YOU'VE TRACKED ME HALFWAY AROUND THE WORLD TO GET THIS SCROLL BACK.
NOW C'MON, REMY--DON'T LET ME DOWN.

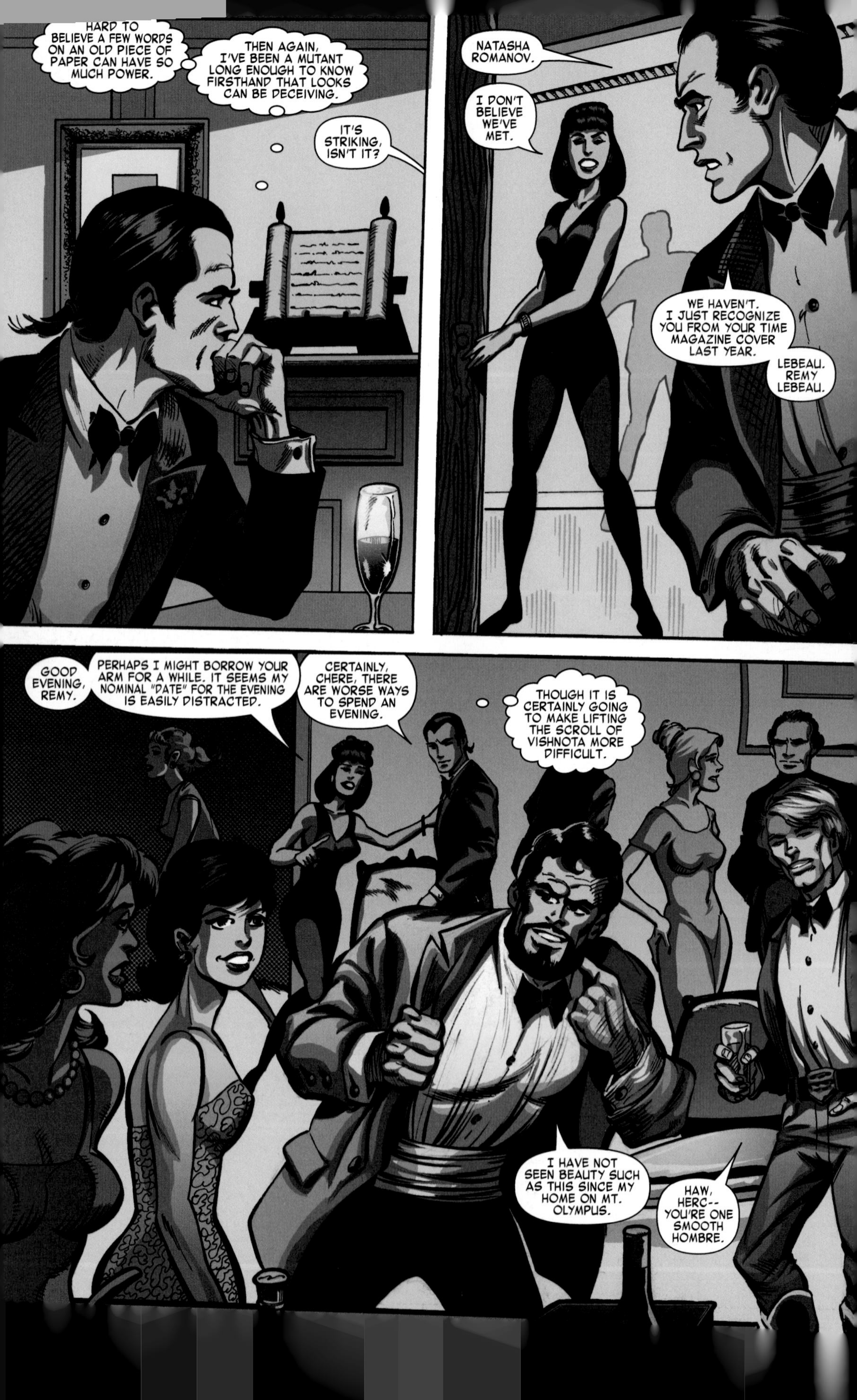
HARD TO BELIEVE A FEW WORDS ON AN OLD PIECE OF PAPER CAN HAVE SO MUCH POWER.
THEN AGAIN, I'VE BEEN A MUTANT LONG ENOUGH TO KNOW FIRSTHAND THAT LOOKS CAN BE DECEIVING.
IT'S STRIKING, ISN'T IT?
NATASHA ROMANOV.
I DON'T BELIEVE WE'VE MET.
WE HAVEN'T. I JUST RECOGNIZE YOU FROM YOUR TIME MAGAZINE COVER LAST YEAR.
LEBEAU. REMY LEBEAU.
GOOD EVENING, REMY.
PERHAPS I MIGHT BORROW YOUR ARM FOR A WHILE. IT SEEMS MY NOMINAL "DATE" FOR THE EVENING IS EASILY DISTRACTED.
CERTAINLY, CHERE, THERE ARE WORSE WAYS TO SPEND AN EVENING.
THOUGH IT IS CERTAINLY GOING TO MAKE LIFTING THE SCROLL OF VISHNOTA MORE DIFFICULT.
I HAVE NOT SEEN BEAUTY SUCH AS THIS SINCE MY HOME ON MT. OLYMPUS.
HAW, HERC-- YOU'RE ONE SMOOTH HOMBRE.

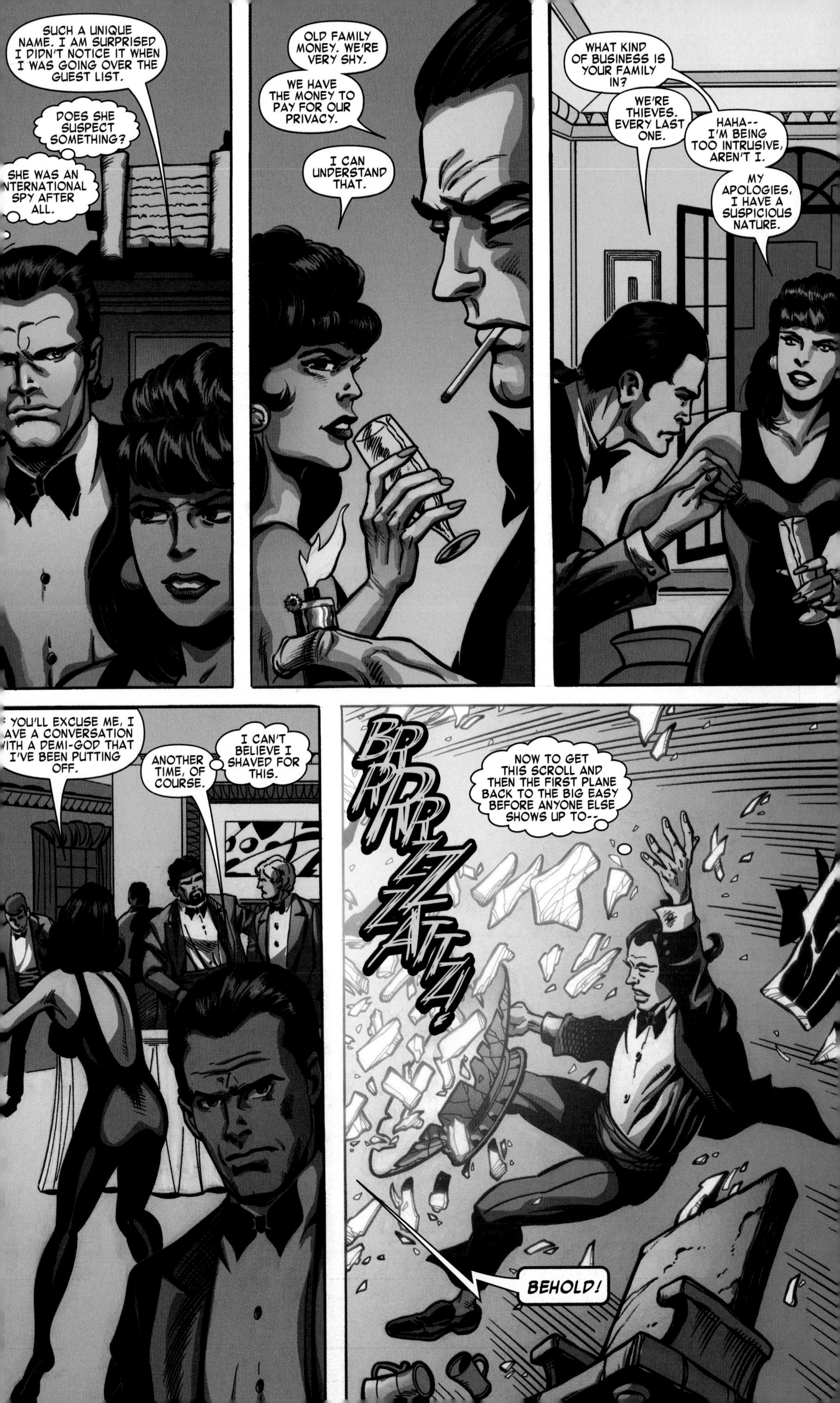
SUCH A UNIQUE NAME. I AM SURPRISED I DIDN'T NOTICE IT WHEN I WAS GOING OVER THE GUEST LIST.
DOES SHE SUSPECT SOMETHING?
SHE WAS AN INTERNATIONAL SPY AFTER ALL.
OLD FAMILY MONEY. WE'RE VERY SHY.
WE HAVE THE MONEY TO PAY FOR OUR PRIVACY.
I CAN UNDERSTAND THAT.
WHAT KIND OF BUSINESS IS YOUR FAMILY IN?
WE'RE THIEVES. EVERY LAST ONE.
HAHA-- I'M BEING TOO INTRUSIVE, AREN'T I.
MY APOLOGIES, I HAVE A SUSPICIOUS NATURE.
YOU'LL EXCUSE ME, I AVE A CONVERSATION WITH A DEMI-GOD THAT I'VE BEEN PUTTING OFF.
ANOTHER TIME, OF COURSE.
I CAN'T BELIEVE I SHAVED FOR THIS.
BRRRRZZZATTZZ!
NOW TO GET THIS SCROLL AND THEN THE FIRST PLANE BACK TO THE BIG EASY BEFORE ANYONE ELSE SHOWS UP TO--
BEHOLD!

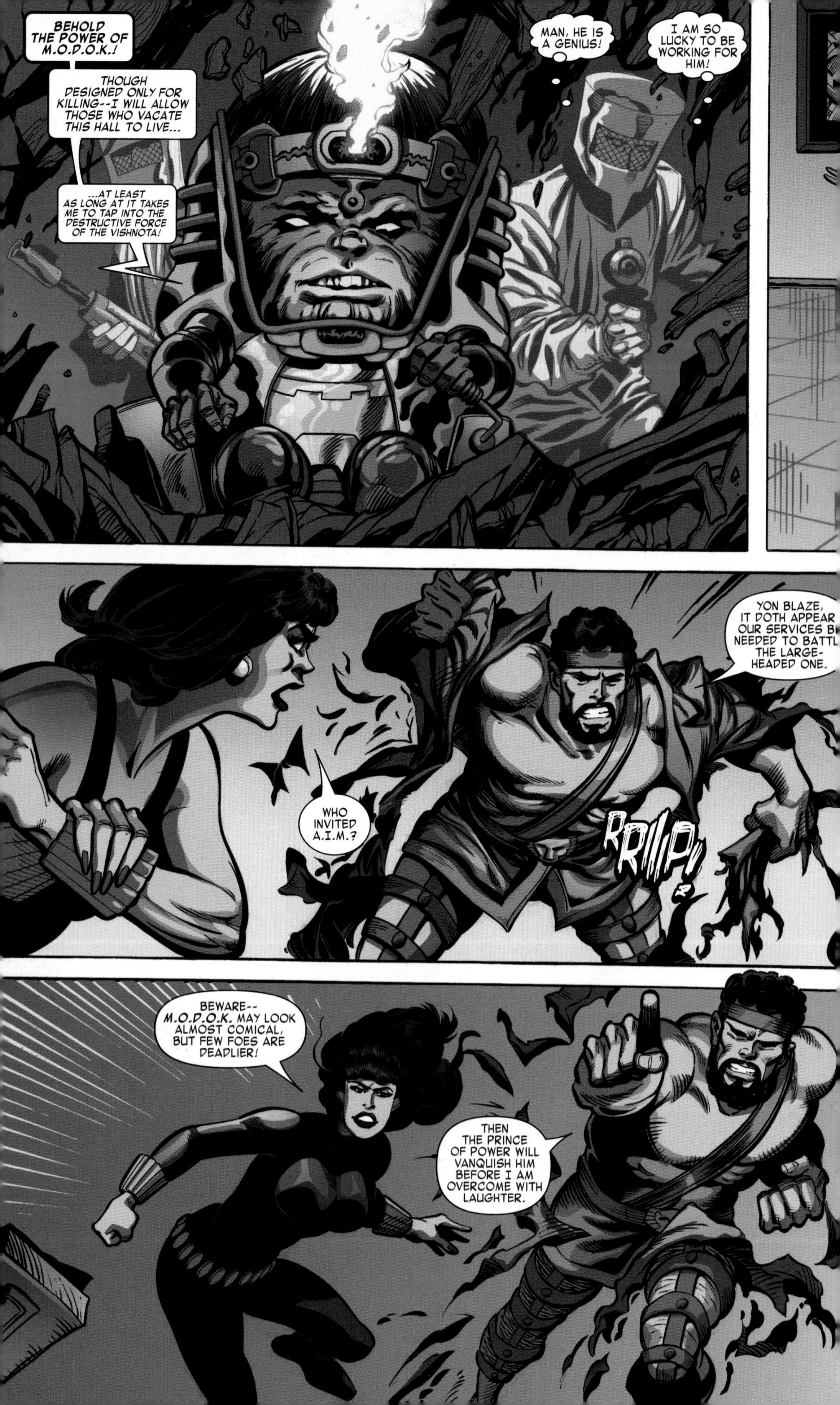
BEHOLD THE POWER OF M.O.D.O.K.!
THOUGH DESIGNED ONLY FOR KILLING--I WILL ALLOW THOSE WHO VACATE THIS HALL TO LIVE...
...AT LEAST AS LONG AT IT TAKES ME TO TAP INTO THE DESTRUCTIVE FORCE OF THE VISHNOTA!
MAN, HE IS A GENIUS!
I AM SO LUCKY TO BE WORKING FOR HIM!
YON BLAZE, IT DOTH APPEAR OUR SERVICES B NEEDED TO BATTL THE LARGE-HEADED ONE.
WHO INVITED A.I.M.?
RRIIP!
BEWARE-- M.O.D.O.K. MAY LOOK ALMOST COMICAL, BUT FEW FOES ARE DEADLIER!
THEN THE PRINCE OF POWER WILL VANQUISH HIM BEFORE I AM OVERCOME WITH LAUGHTER.

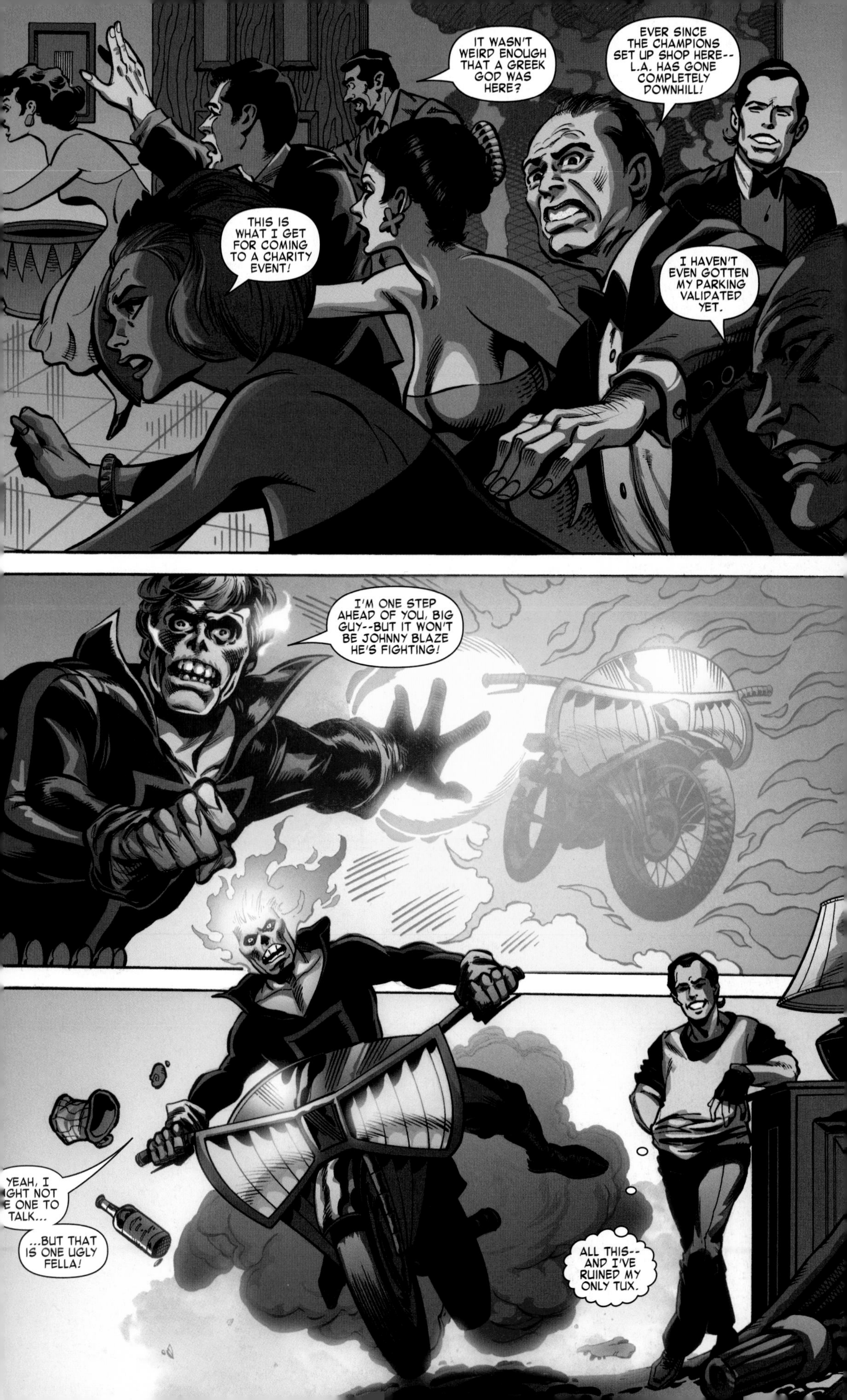

IT WASN'T WEIRD ENOUGH THAT A GREEK GOD WAS HERE?
EVER SINCE THE CHAMPIONS SET UP SHOP HERE-- L.A. HAS GONE COMPLETELY DOWNHILL!
THIS IS WHAT I GET FOR COMING TO A CHARITY EVENT!
I HAVEN'T EVEN GOTTEN MY PARKING VALIDATED YET.
I'M ONE STEP AHEAD OF YOU, BIG GUY--BUT IT WON'T BE JOHNNY BLAZE HE'S FIGHTING!
YEAH, I IGHT NOT E ONE TO TALK...
...BUT THAT IS ONE UGLY FELLA!
ALL THIS-- AND I'VE RUINED MY ONLY TUX.

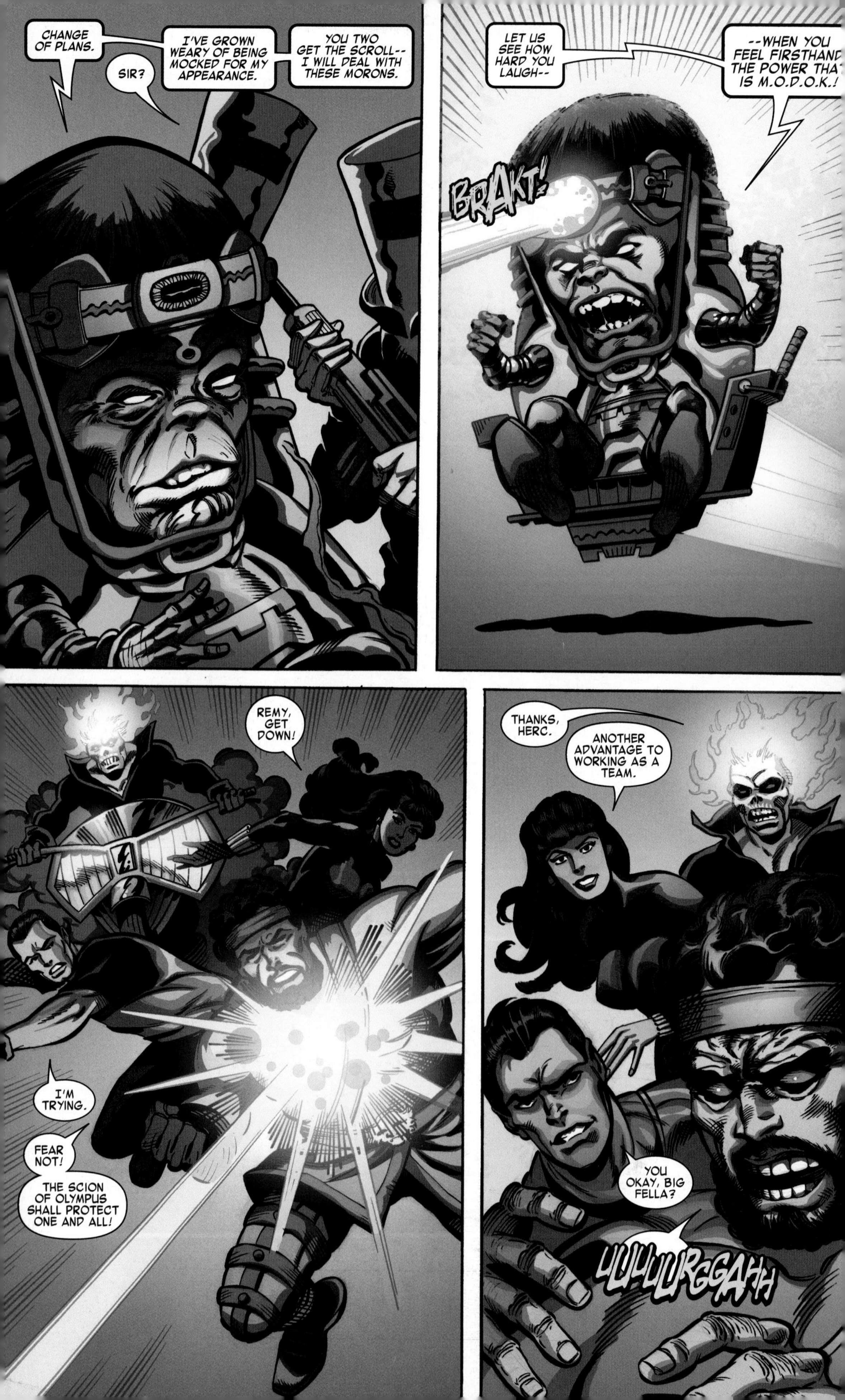
CHANGE OF PLANS.
I'VE GROWN WEARY OF BEING MOCKED FOR MY APPEARANCE.
SIR?
YOU TWO GET THE SCROLL-- I WILL DEAL WITH THESE MORONS.
LET US SEE HOW HARD YOU LAUGH--
--WHEN YOU FEEL FIRSTHAND THE POWER THAT IS M.O.D.O.K.!
BRAKT!
REMY, GET DOWN!
I'M TRYING.
FEAR NOT!
THE SCION OF OLYMPUS SHALL PROTECT ONE AND ALL!
THANKS, HERC.
ANOTHER ADVANTAGE TO WORKING AS A TEAM.
YOU OKAY, BIG FELLA?
UUUUURGGAHH

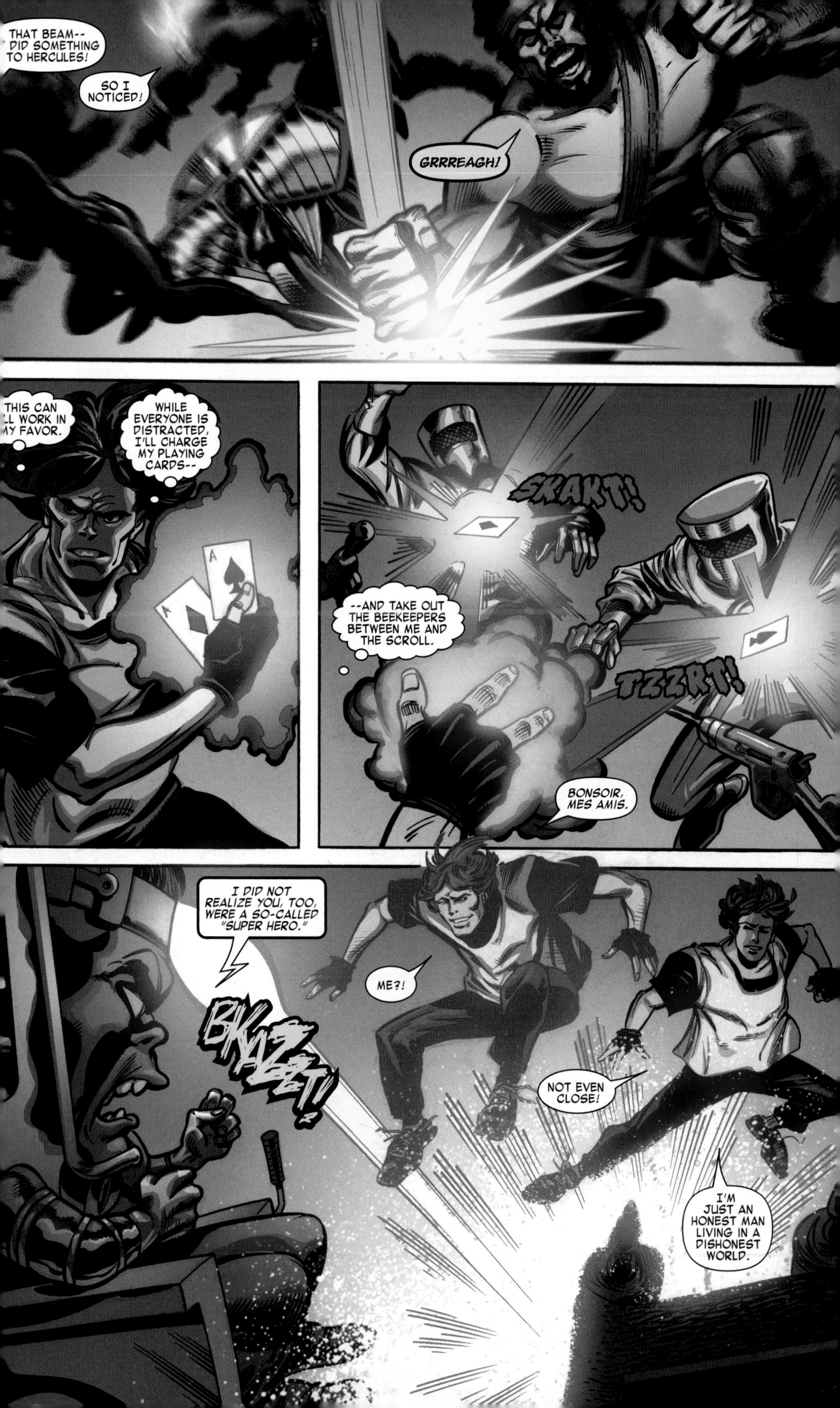
THAT BEAM-- DID SOMETHING TO HERCULES!
SO I NOTICED!
GRRREAGH!
THIS CAN LL WORK IN MY FAVOR.
WHILE EVERYONE IS DISTRACTED, I'LL CHARGE MY PLAYING CARDS--
SKAKT!
--AND TAKE OUT THE BEEKEEPERS BETWEEN ME AND THE SCROLL.
TZZRT!
BONSOIR, MES AMIS.
I DID NOT REALIZE YOU, TOO, WERE A SO-CALLED "SUPER HERO."
ME?!
BKZZT!
NOT EVEN CLOSE!
I'M JUST AN HONEST MAN LIVING IN A DISHONEST WORLD.

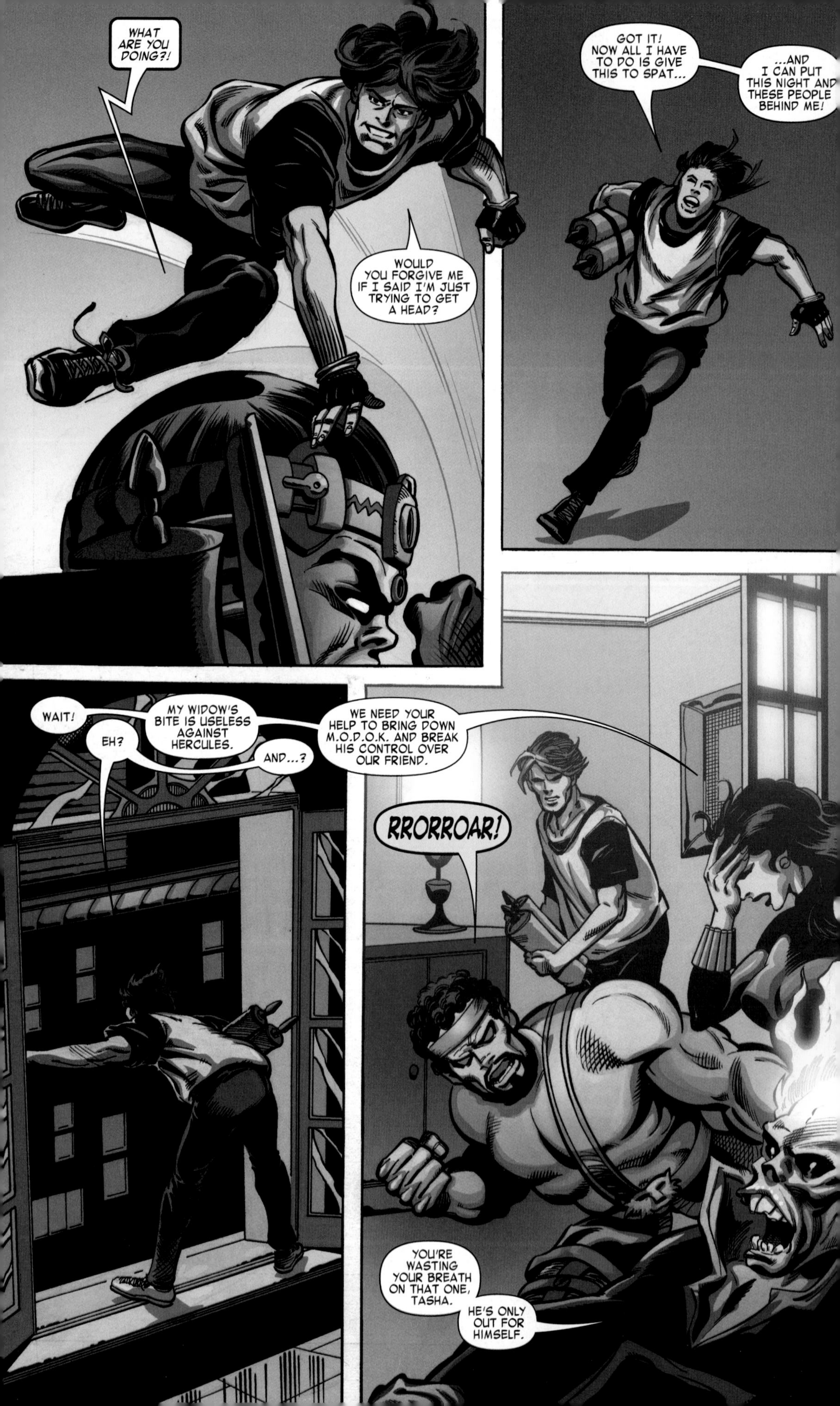
WHAT ARE YOU DOING?!
WOULD YOU FORGIVE ME IF I SAID I'M JUST TRYING TO GET A HEAD?
GOT IT! NOW ALL I HAVE TO DO IS GIVE THIS TO SPAT...
...AND I CAN PUT THIS NIGHT AND THESE PEOPLE BEHIND ME!
WAIT!
MY WIDOW'S BITE IS USELESS AGAINST HERCULES.
EH?
AND...?
WE NEED YOUR HELP TO BRING DOWN M.O.D.O.K. AND BREAK HIS CONTROL OVER OUR FRIEND.
RRORROAR!
YOU'RE WASTING YOUR BREATH ON THAT ONE, TASHA.
HE'S ONLY OUT FOR HIMSELF.

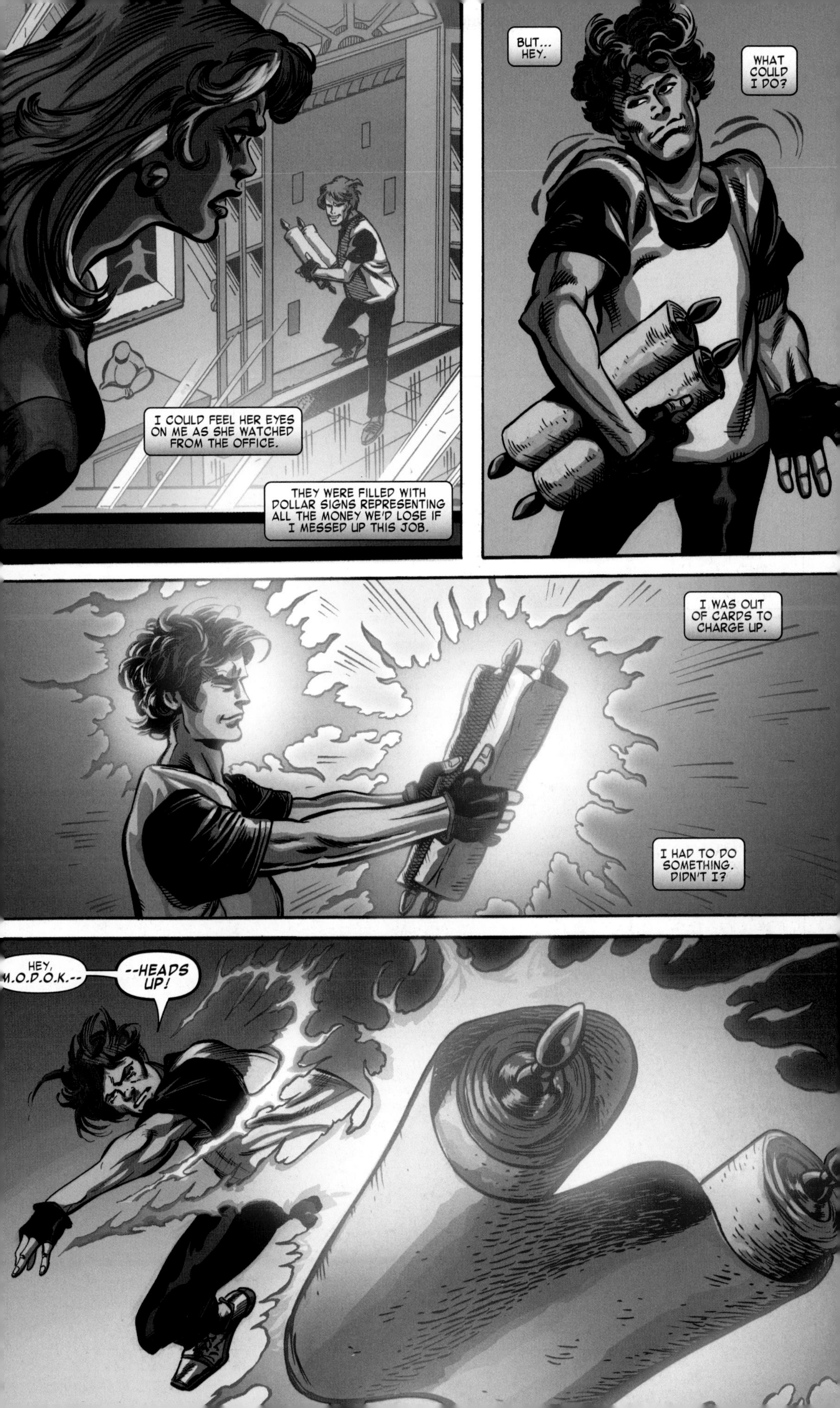
I COULD FEEL HER EYES ON ME AS SHE WATCHED FROM THE OFFICE.
THEY WERE FILLED WITH DOLLAR SIGNS REPRESENTING ALL THE MONEY WE'D LOSE IF I MESSED UP THIS JOB.
BUT... HEY.
WHAT COULD I DO?
I WAS OUT OF CARDS TO CHARGE UP.
I HAD TO DO SOMETHING. DIDN'T I?
HEY, M.O.D.O.K.--
--HEADS UP!

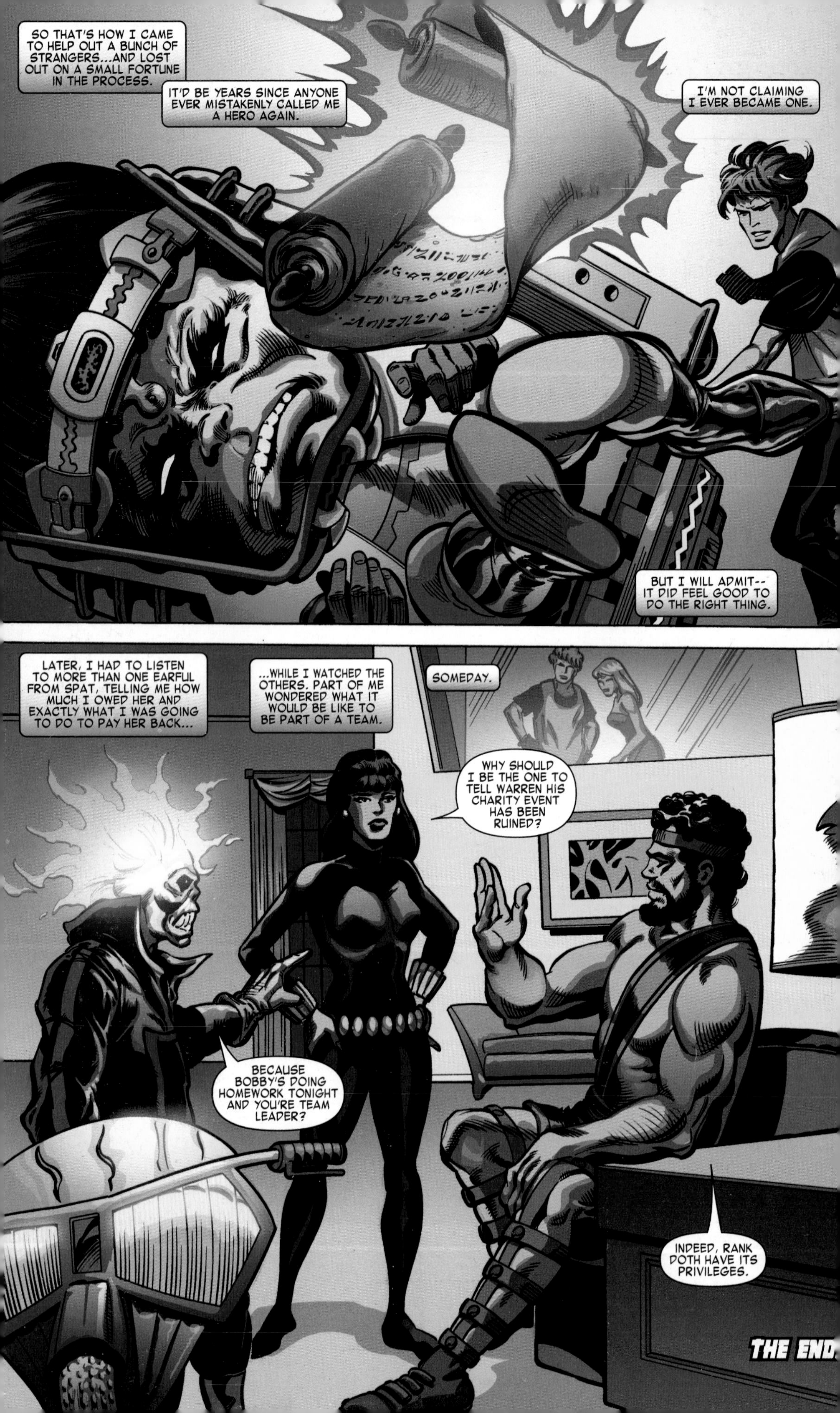
SO THAT'S HOW I CAME TO HELP OUT A BUNCH OF STRANGERS...AND LOST OUT ON A SMALL FORTUNE IN THE PROCESS.
IT'D BE YEARS SINCE ANYONE EVER MISTAKENLY CALLED ME A HERO AGAIN.
I'M NOT CLAIMING I EVER BECAME ONE.
BUT I WILL ADMIT-- IT DID FEEL GOOD TO DO THE RIGHT THING.
LATER, I HAD TO LISTEN TO MORE THAN ONE EARFUL FROM SPAT, TELLING ME HOW MUCH I OWED HER AND EXACTLY WHAT I WAS GOING TO DO TO PAY HER BACK...
...WHILE I WATCHED THE OTHERS. PART OF ME WONDERED WHAT IT WOULD BE LIKE TO BE PART OF A TEAM.
SOMEDAY.
WHY SHOULD I BE THE ONE TO TELL WARREN HIS CHARITY EVENT HAS BEEN RUINED?
BECAUSE BOBBY'S DOING HOMEWORK TONIGHT AND YOU'RE TEAM LEADER?
INDEED, RANK DOTH HAVE ITS PRIVILEGES.
THE END